All that glitters...

Even the stars

All things precious...

Even your life

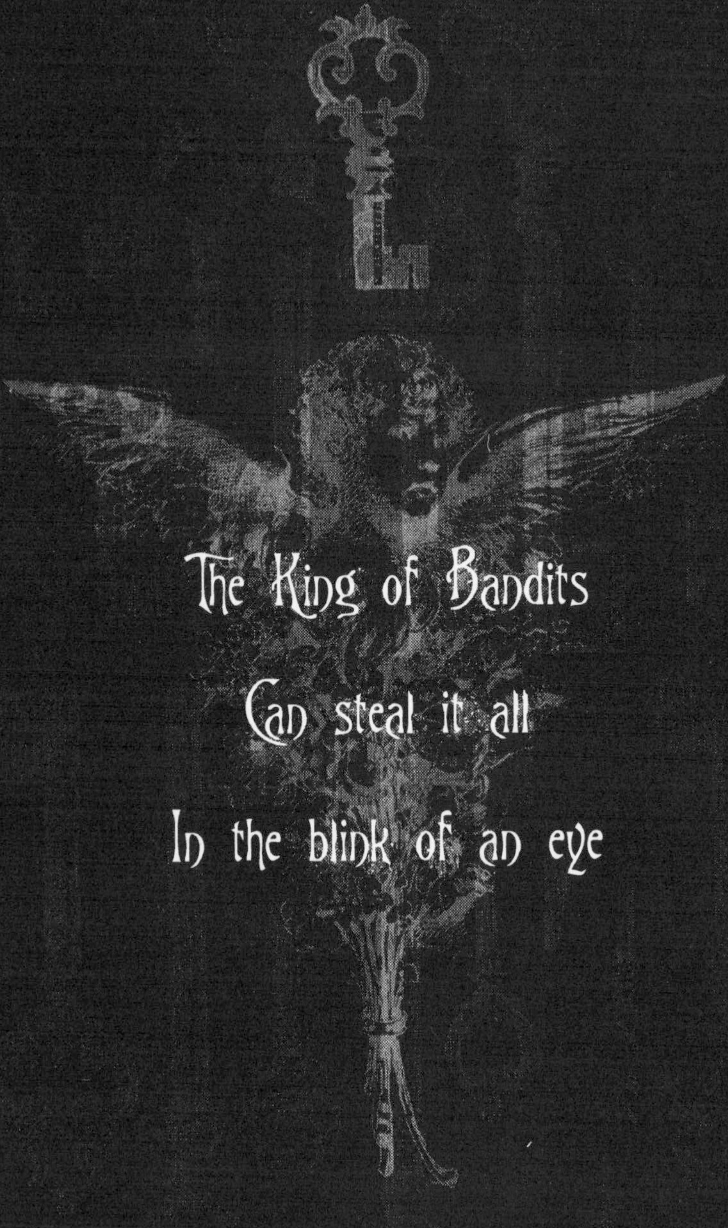
The King of Bandits
Can steal it all
In the blink of an eye

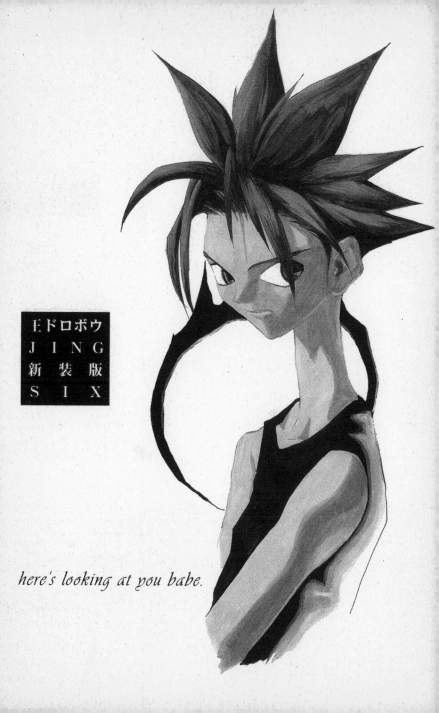

王ドロボウ
JING
新装版
SIX

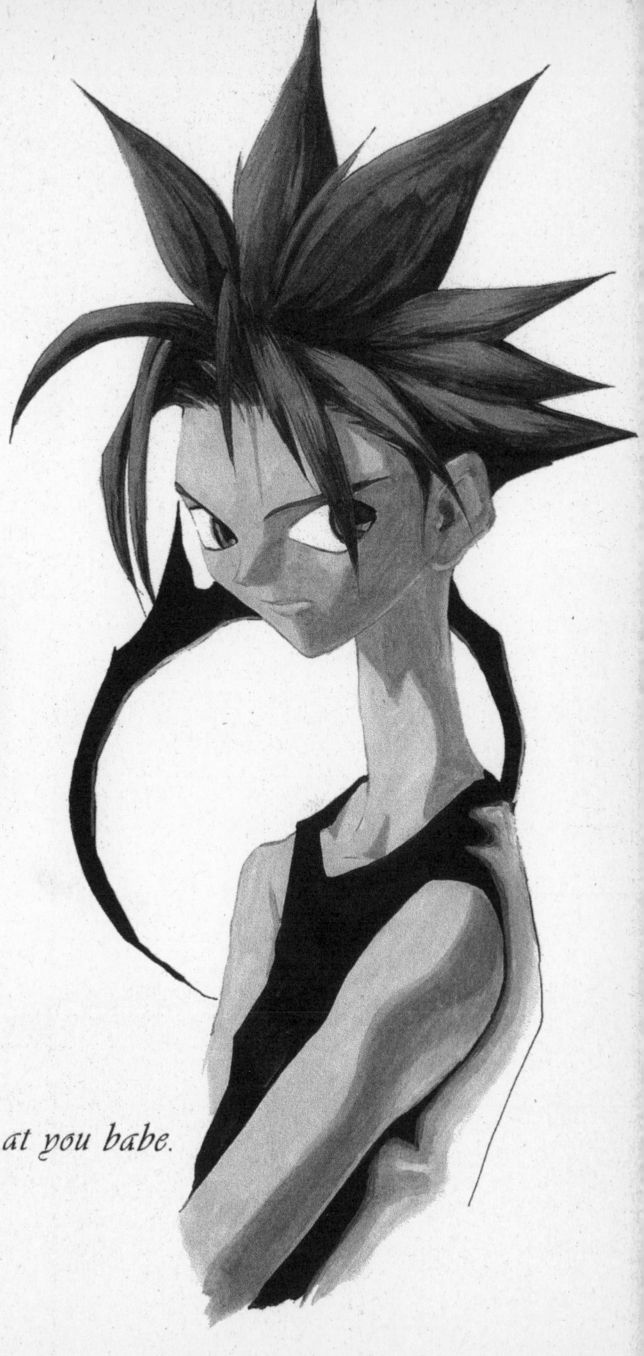

here's looking at you babe.

Is this boy explosive?

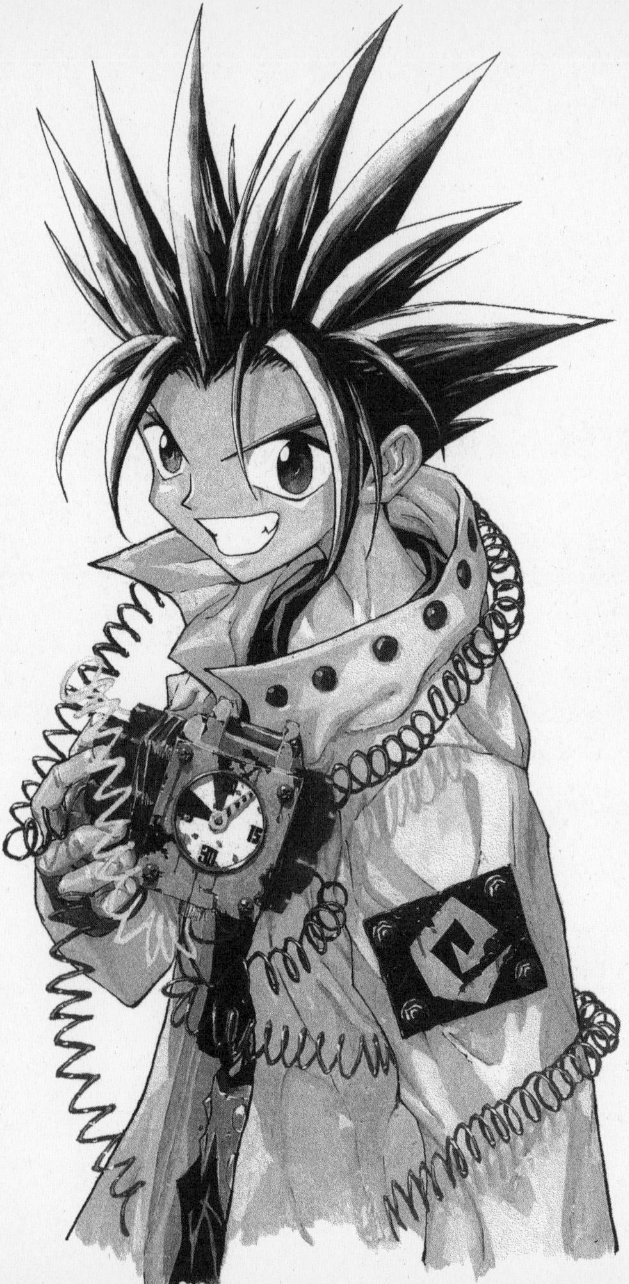

jing & kir in SD style

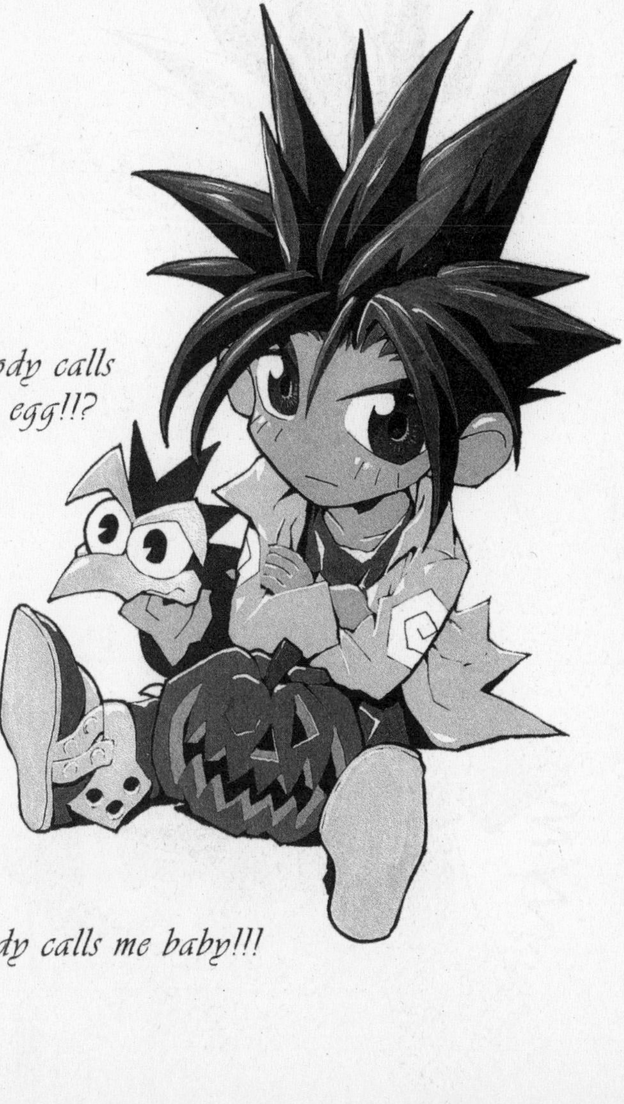

nobody calls
me egg!!?

nobody calls me baby!!!

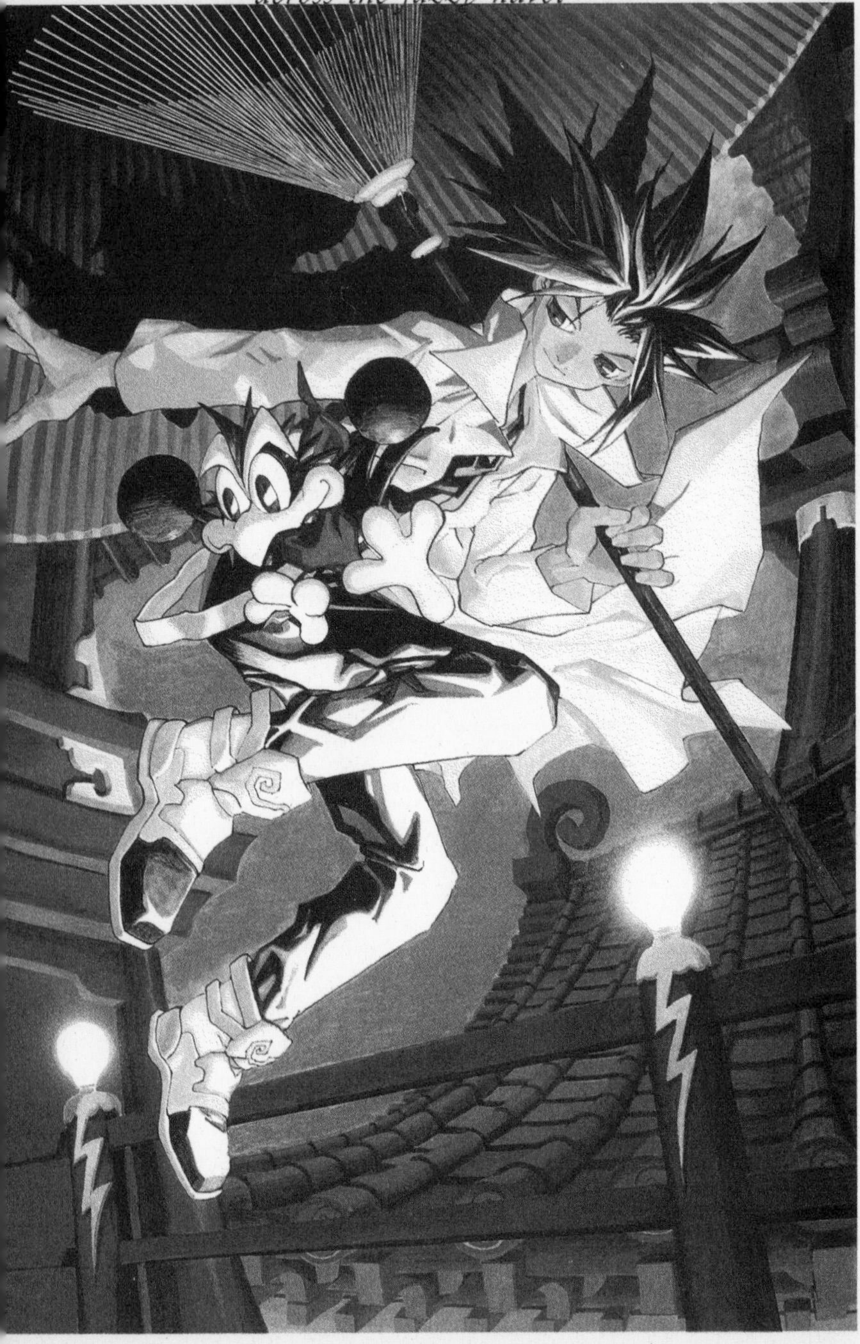

KING OF BANDITS

王ドロボウ JING

VOLUME 6 OF 7

STORY AND ART BY
YUICHI KUMAKURA

TOKYOPOP®

Los Angeles • Tokyo • London

Translator - Kong Chang
English Adaptation - Carol Fox
Copy Editor - Chrissy Schilling
Retouch and Lettering - Vicente Rivera, Jr.
Cover Layout - Gary Shun
Graphic Designer - Mona Lisa De Asis & James Lee

Editor - Paul Morrissey
Digital Imaging Manager - Chris Buford
Pre-Press Manager - Antonio DePietro
Production Managers - Jennifer Miller and Mutsumi Miyazaki
Art Director - Matt Alford
Managing Editor - Jill Freshney
VP of Production - Ron Klamert
President & C.O.O. - John Parker
Publisher & C.E.O. - Stuart Levy

E-mail: info@TOKYOPOP.com
Come visit us online at www.TOKYOPOP.com

A  Manga

TOKYOPOP Inc.
5900 Wilshire Blvd. Suite 2000
Los Angeles, CA 90036

Jing: King of Bandits Vol. 5
©2001 Yuichi Kumakura. All rights reserved. First published in Japan
in 2001 as Odorobo Jing - New Edition by Kodansha, Ltd., Tokyo.
English publication rights arranged through Kodansha, Ltd.

English text copyright ©2004 TOKYOPOP Inc.

ISBN: 1-59182-467-2

First TOKYOPOP printing: May 2004

10 9 8 7 6 5 4 3 2 1

Printed in the USA

Once upon a midnight dreary, a thief named Jing was weak and weary.
Many strange and forgotten lands he did traverse and explore.
His companion was a bird named Kir, his black wings a-flapping.
While Jing nodded, nearly napping, Kir saw booty galore.
"Wake up, Jing," Kir muttered, "all around us is loot galore."
Treasure from ceiling to floor!

Thus, this ebony bird's wiling, sent Jing's sad face into smiling,
For Jing could steal the stars from the sky, thievery he truly did adore.
The albatross sat proudly on Jing's placid bust, his beady eyes did implore,
One more thing Kir did utter, his feathers all a greedy flutter, his voice a roar,
Quoth the albatross, "Let's steal some more!"

JING: King of Bandits

Six

Contents

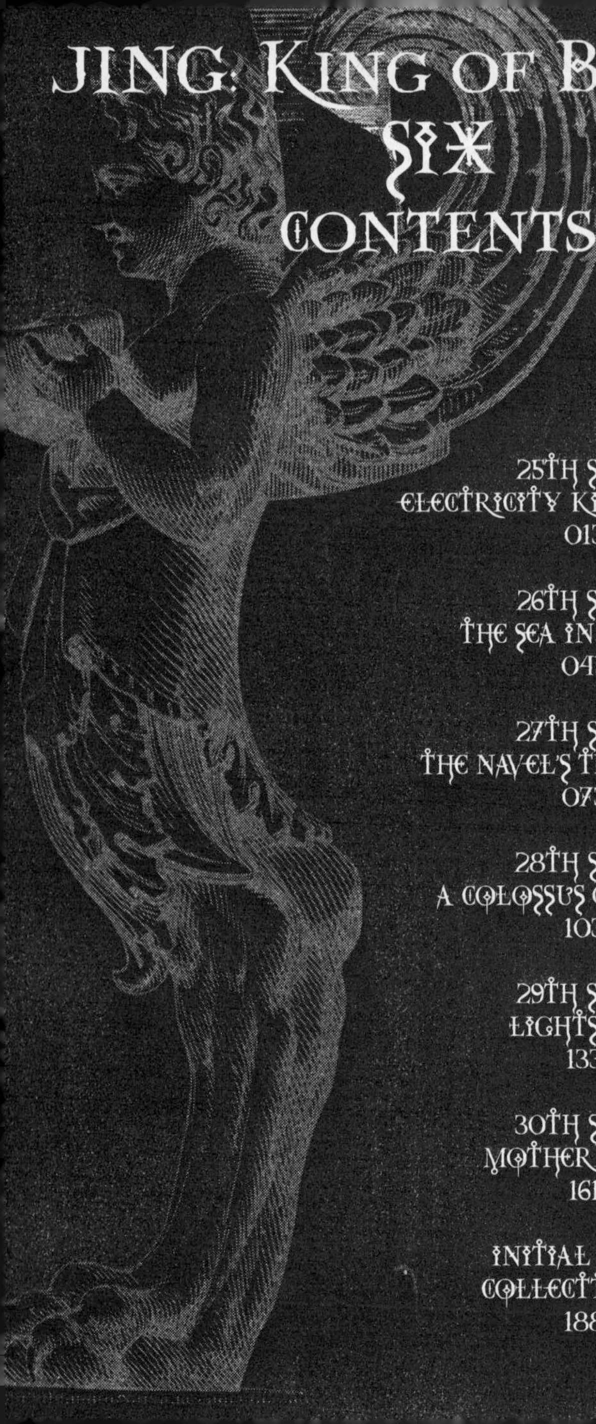

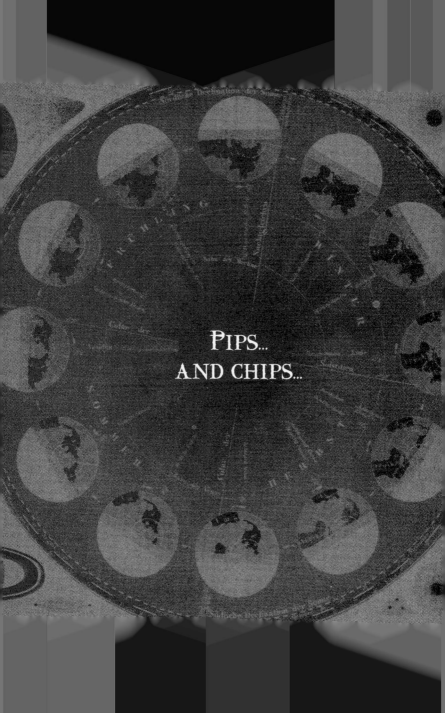

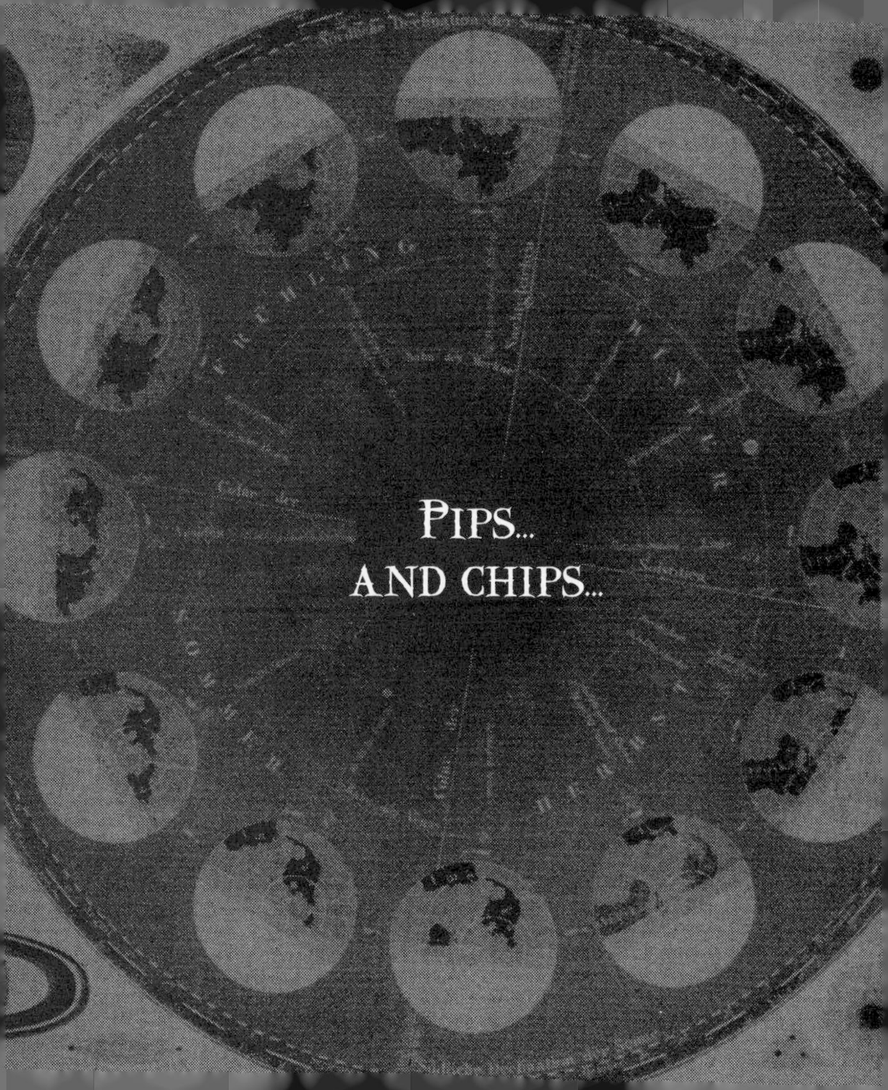
PIPS...
AND CHIPS...

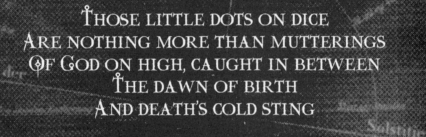

Those little dots on dice
Are nothing more than mutterings
Of God on high, caught in between
The dawn of birth
And death's cold sting

—Prayer often chanted by gamblers in Aviation
while playing Sugoroku.

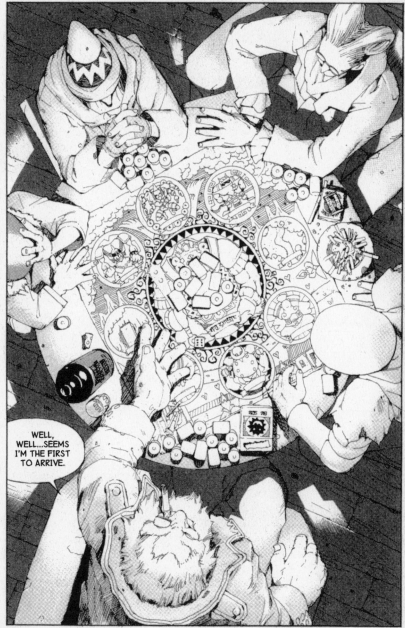

25th SHOT - ELECTRICITY KILLED THE CAT

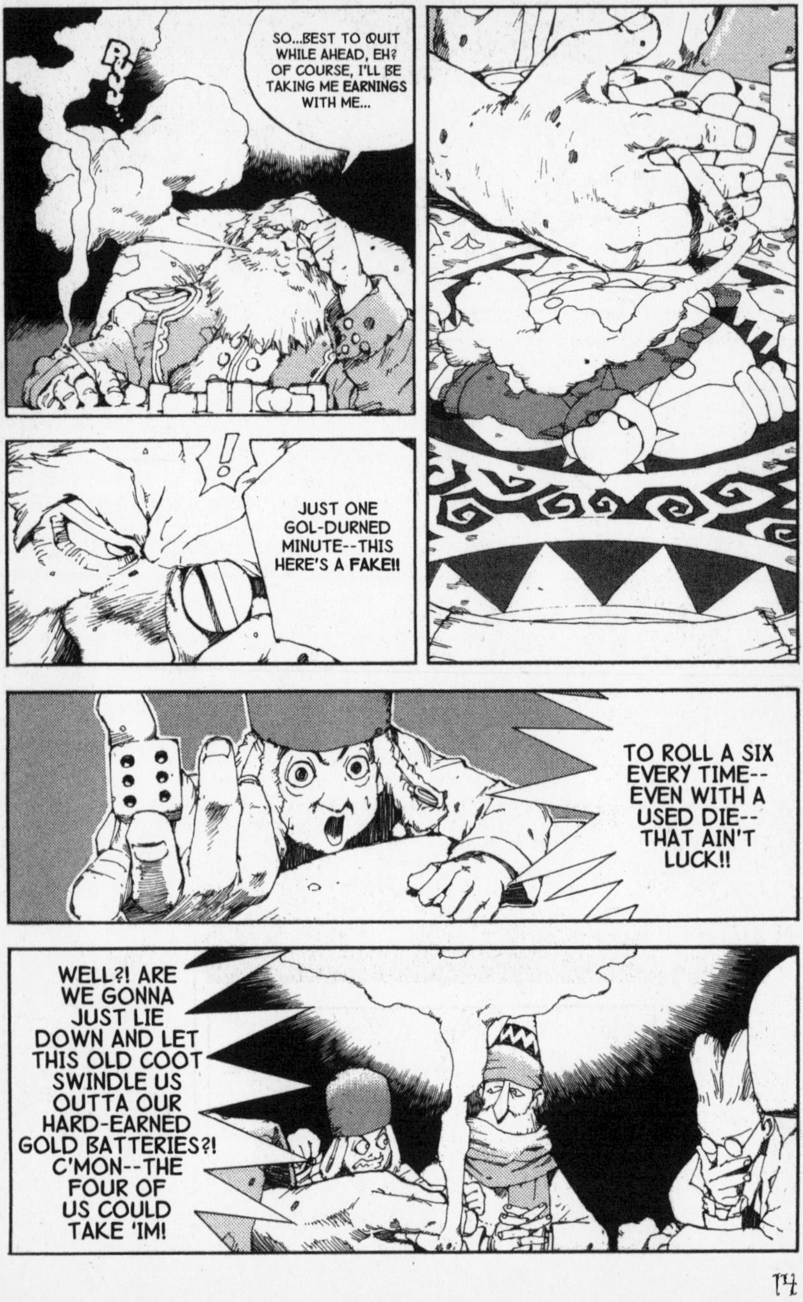
SO...BEST TO QUIT WHILE AHEAD, EH? OF COURSE, I'LL BE TAKING ME EARNINGS WITH ME...
!
JUST ONE GOL-DURNED MINUTE--THIS HERE'S A FAKE!!
TO ROLL A SIX EVERY TIME-- EVEN WITH A USED DIE-- THAT AIN'T LUCK!!
WELL?! ARE WE GONNA JUST LIE DOWN AND LET THIS OLD COOT SWINDLE US OUTTA OUR HARD-EARNED GOLD BATTERIES?! C'MON--THE FOUR OF US COULD TAKE 'IM!

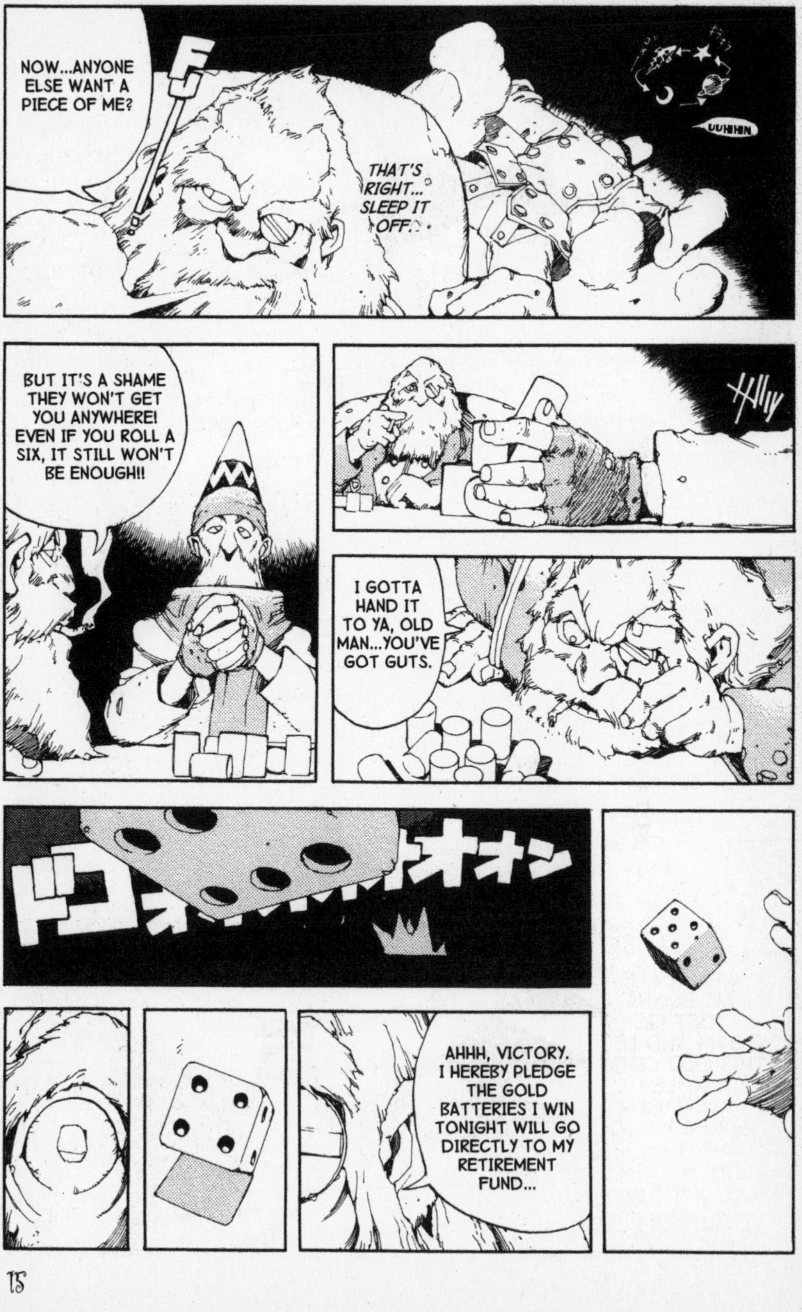
UUHHN
THAT'S RIGHT... SLEEP IT OFF...
NOW...ANYONE ELSE WANT A PIECE OF ME?
I GOTTA HAND IT TO YA, OLD MAN...YOU'VE GOT GUTS.
BUT IT'S A SHAME THEY WON'T GET YOU ANYWHERE! EVEN IF YOU ROLL A SIX, IT STILL WON'T BE ENOUGH!!
AHHH, VICTORY. I HEREBY PLEDGE THE GOLD BATTERIES I WIN TONIGHT WILL GO DIRECTLY TO MY RETIREMENT FUND...

SEVEN
?!!!

!?

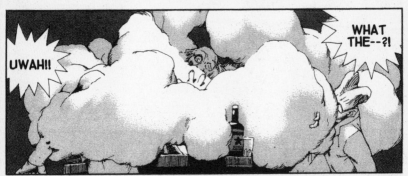

UWAH!!

WHAT
THE--?!

...RIGHT...
OLD MAN...
COME OUT
AND...

*COUGH COUGH

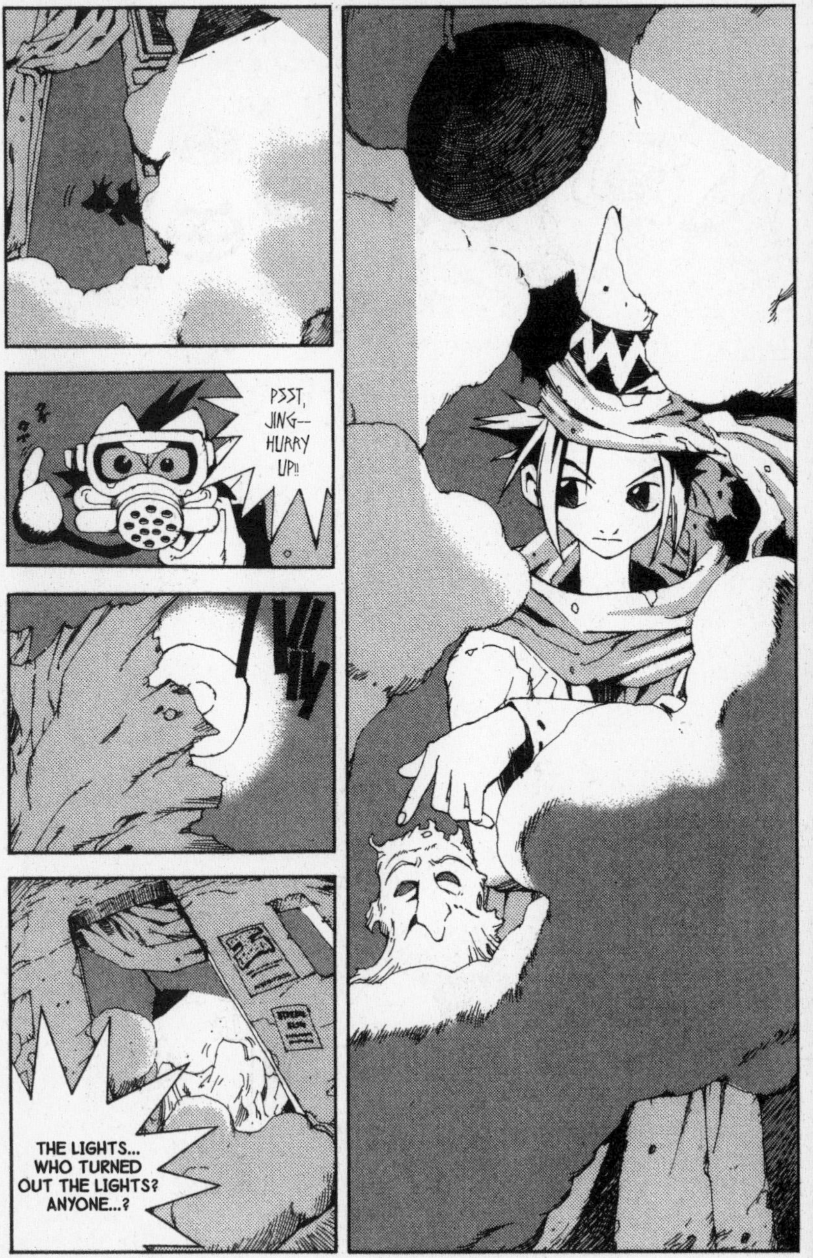
PSST, JING--HURRY UP!!
THE LIGHTS... WHO TURNED OUT THE LIGHTS? ANYONE...?

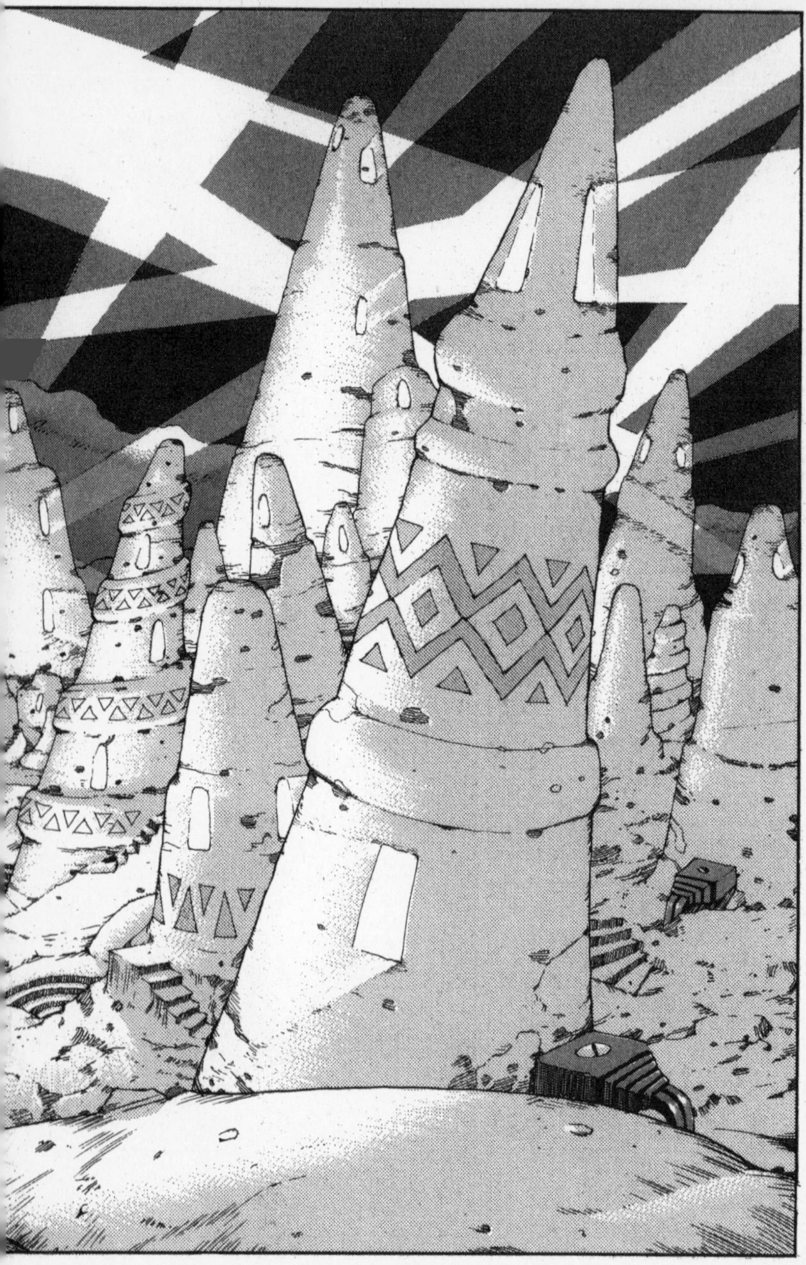

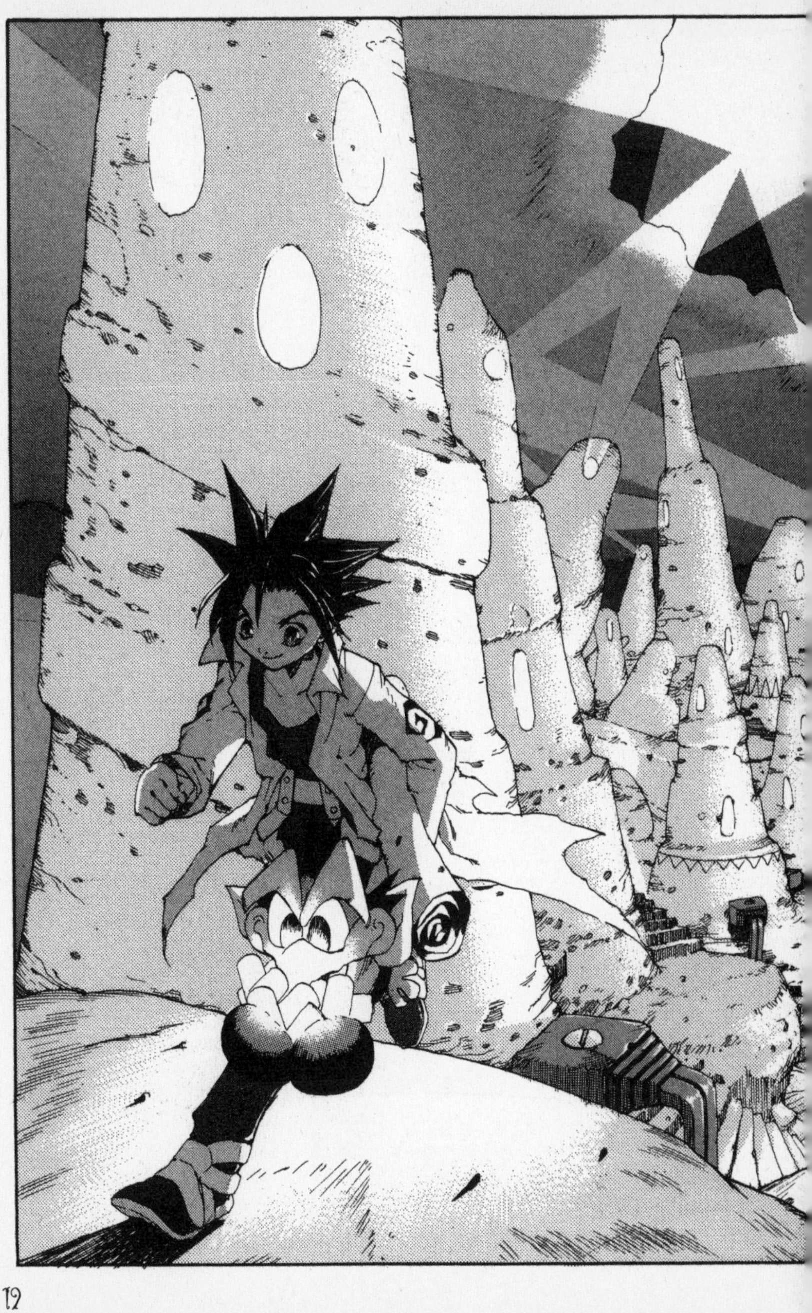

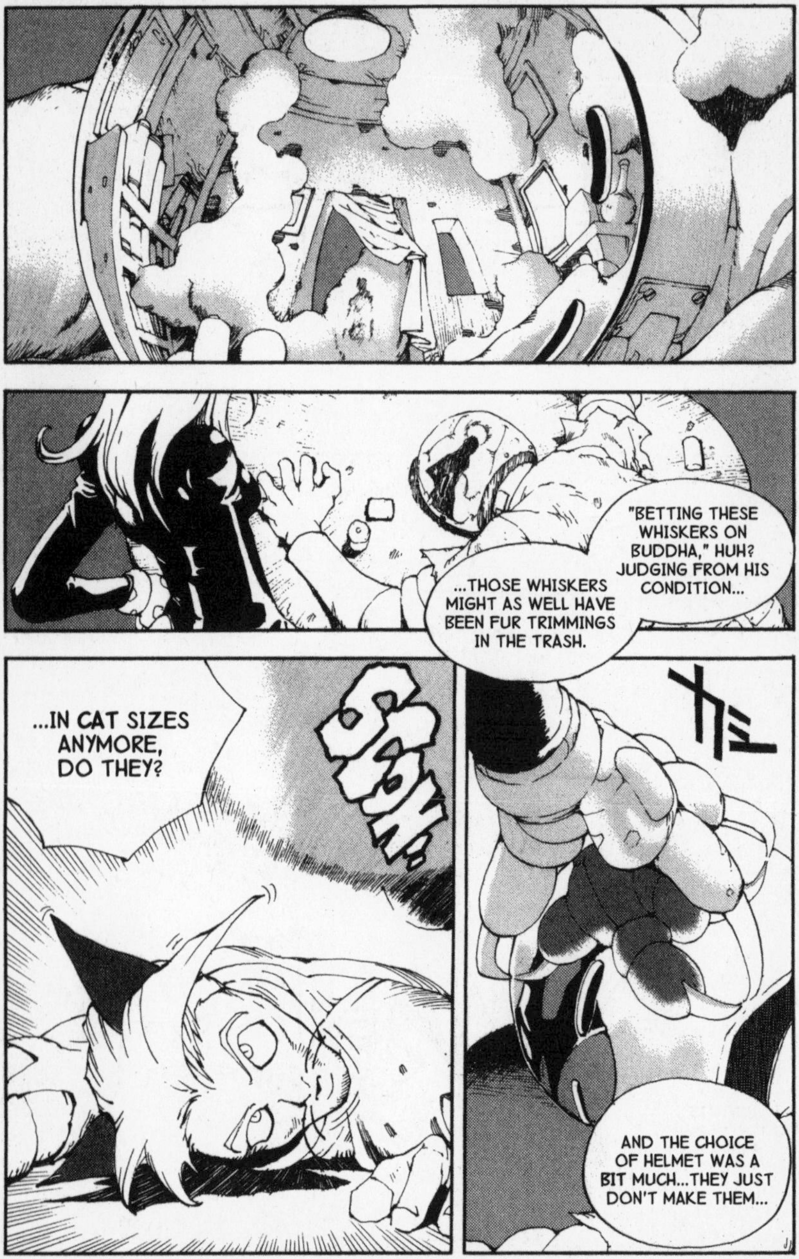
"BETTING THESE WHISKERS ON BUDDHA," HUH? JUDGING FROM HIS CONDITION...
...THOSE WHISKERS MIGHT AS WELL HAVE BEEN FUR TRIMMINGS IN THE TRASH.
AND THE CHOICE OF HELMET WAS A BIT MUCH...THEY JUST DON'T MAKE THEM...
...IN CAT SIZES ANYMORE, DO THEY?

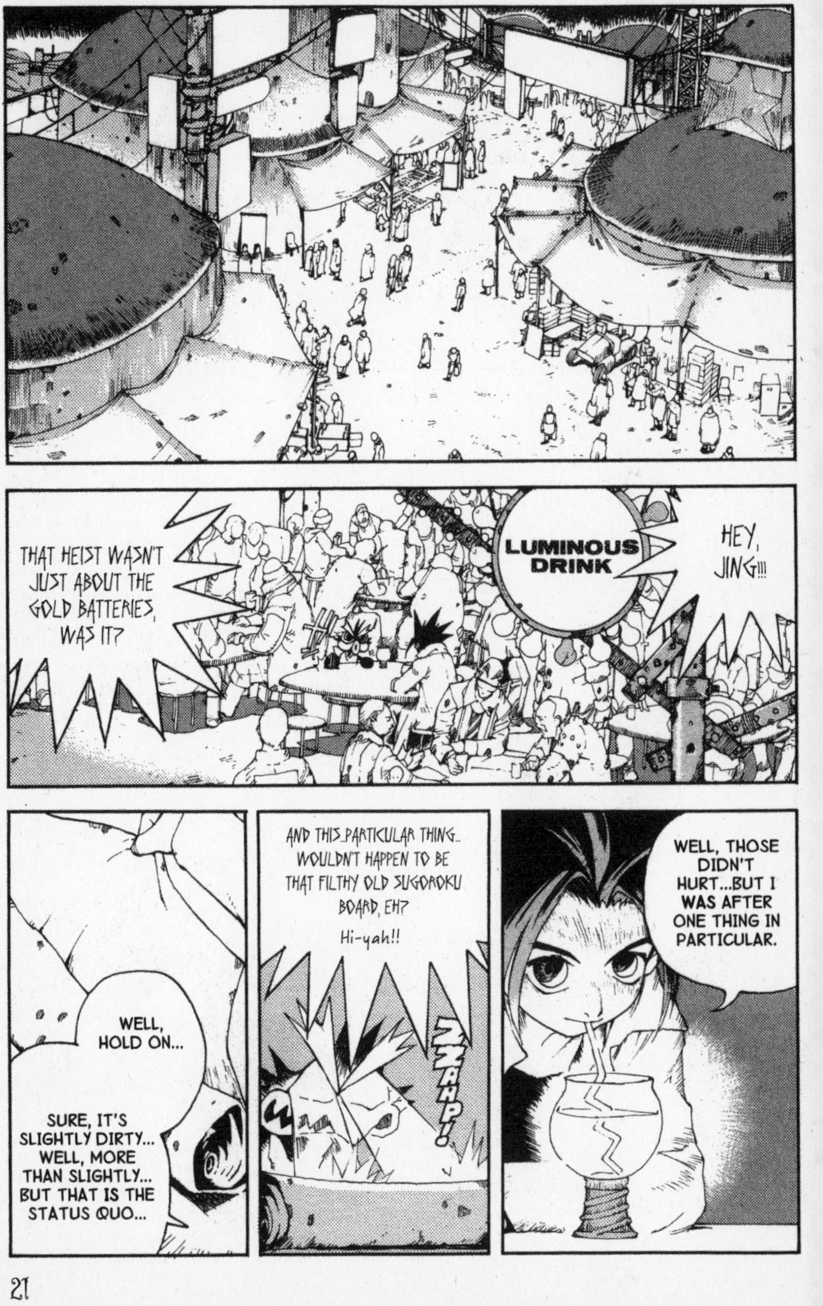
HEY, JING!!!
LUMINOUS DRINK
THAT HEIST WASN'T JUST ABOUT THE GOLD BATTERIES, WAS IT?
WELL, THOSE DIDN'T HURT...BUT I WAS AFTER ONE THING IN PARTICULAR.
AND THIS..PARTICULAR THING... WOULDN'T HAPPEN TO BE THAT FILTHY OLD SUGOROKU BOARD, EH?
Hi-yah!!
ZZAHP!
WELL, HOLD ON...
SURE, IT'S SLIGHTLY DIRTY... WELL, MORE THAN SLIGHTLY... BUT THAT IS THE STATUS QUO...

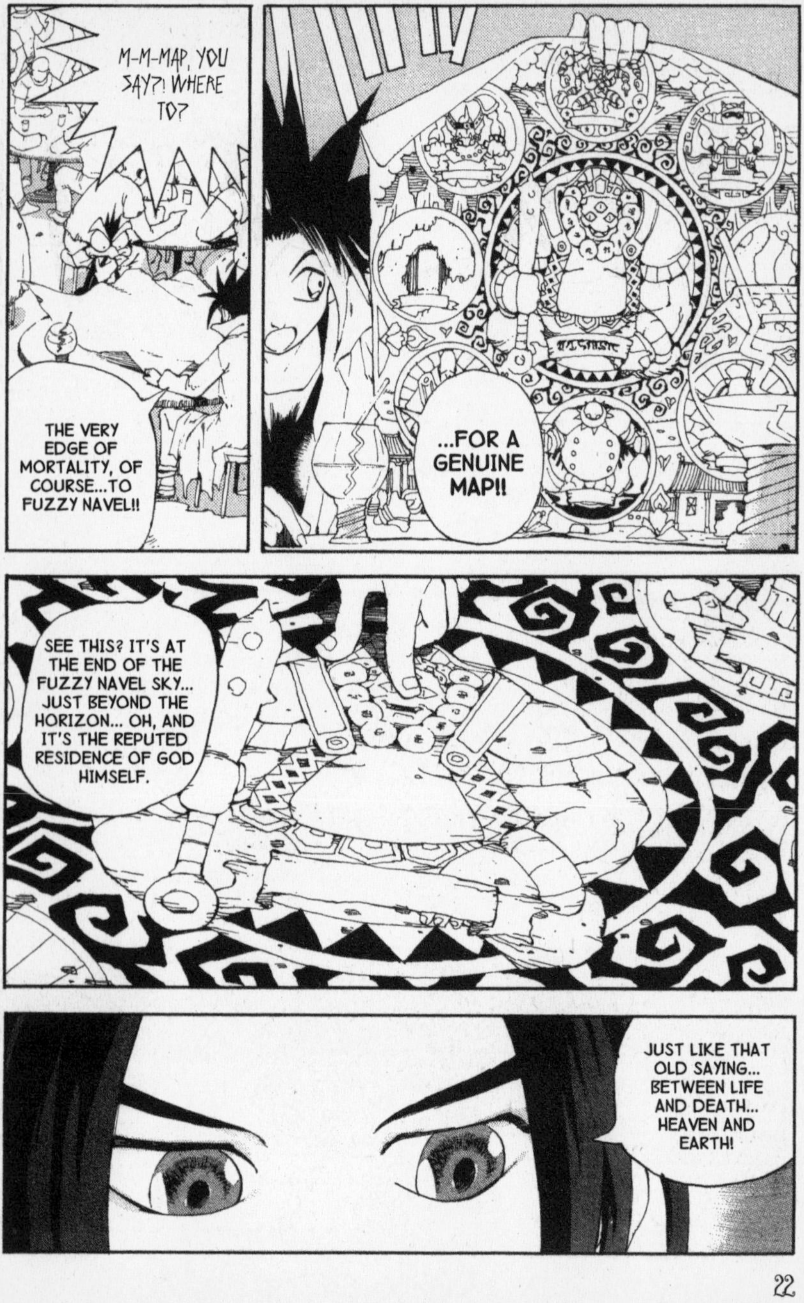
...FOR A GENUINE MAP!!
M-M-MAP, YOU SAY?! WHERE TO?
THE VERY EDGE OF MORTALITY, OF COURSE...TO FUZZY NAVEL!!
SEE THIS? IT'S AT THE END OF THE FUZZY NAVEL SKY... JUST BEYOND THE HORIZON... OH, AND IT'S THE REPUTED RESIDENCE OF GOD HIMSELF.
JUST LIKE THAT OLD SAYING... BETWEEN LIFE AND DEATH... HEAVEN AND EARTH!

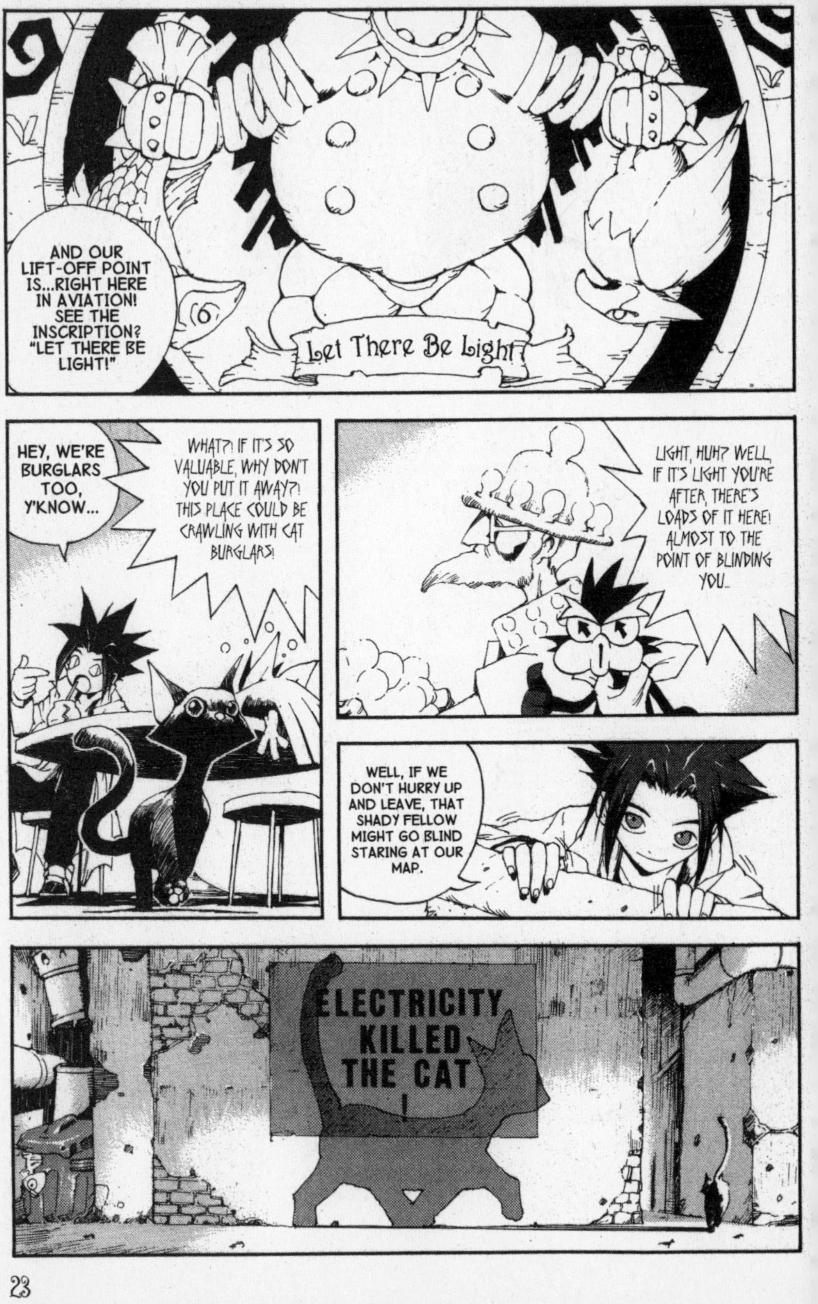
AND OUR LIFT-OFF POINT IS...RIGHT HERE IN AVIATION! SEE THE INSCRIPTION? "LET THERE BE LIGHT!"
Let There Be Light
LIGHT, HUH? WELL, IF IT'S LIGHT YOU'RE AFTER, THERE'S LOADS OF IT HERE! ALMOST TO THE POINT OF BLINDING YOU...
WELL, IF WE DON'T HURRY UP AND LEAVE, THAT SHADY FELLOW MIGHT GO BLIND STARING AT OUR MAP.
WHAT?! IF IT'S SO VALUABLE, WHY DON'T YOU PUT IT AWAY?! THIS PLACE COULD BE CRAWLING WITH CAT BURGLARS!
HEY, WE'RE BURGLARS TOO, Y'KNOW...
ELECTRICITY KILLED THE CAT!

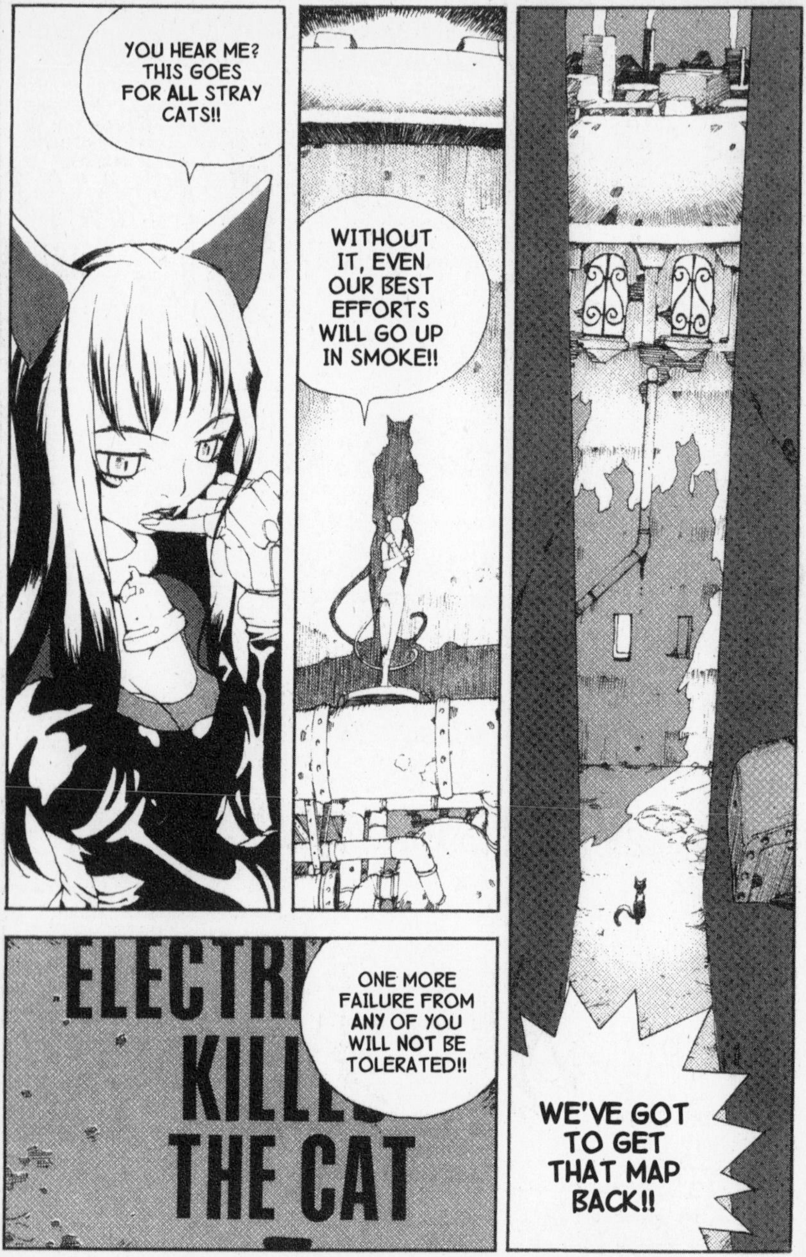
WE'VE GOT TO GET THAT MAP BACK!!
WITHOUT IT, EVEN OUR BEST EFFORTS WILL GO UP IN SMOKE!!
YOU HEAR ME? THIS GOES FOR **ALL** STRAY CATS!!
ELECTRI
KILL
THE CAT
ONE MORE FAILURE FROM ANY OF YOU WILL NOT BE TOLERATED!!

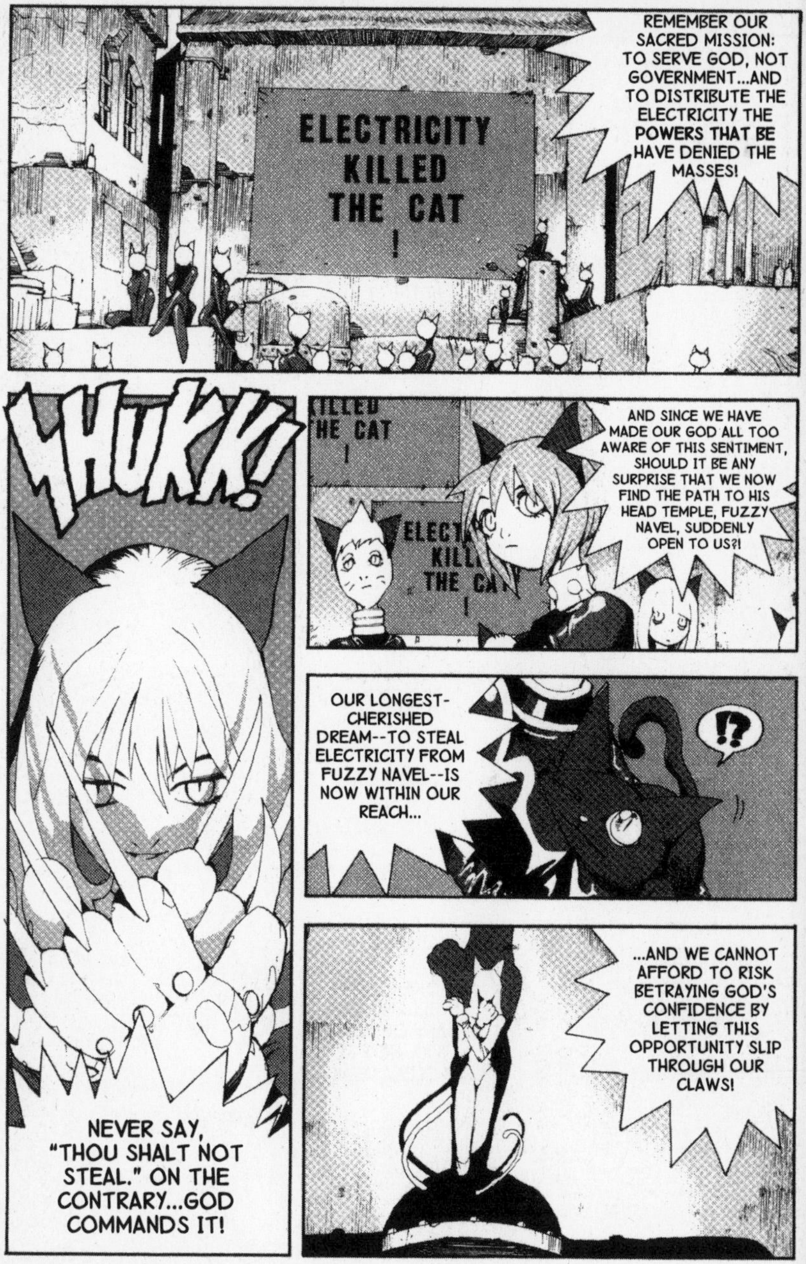

REMEMBER OUR SACRED MISSION: TO SERVE GOD, NOT GOVERNMENT...AND TO DISTRIBUTE THE ELECTRICITY THE POWERS THAT BE HAVE DENIED THE MASSES!
ELECTRICITY KILLED THE CAT !
AND SINCE WE HAVE MADE OUR GOD ALL TOO AWARE OF THIS SENTIMENT, SHOULD IT BE ANY SURPRISE THAT WE NOW FIND THE PATH TO HIS HEAD TEMPLE, FUZZY NAVEL, SUDDENLY OPEN TO US?!
!?
OUR LONGEST-CHERISHED DREAM--TO STEAL ELECTRICITY FROM FUZZY NAVEL--IS NOW WITHIN OUR REACH...
...AND WE CANNOT AFFORD TO RISK BETRAYING GOD'S CONFIDENCE BY LETTING THIS OPPORTUNITY SLIP THROUGH OUR CLAWS!
WHUKK!
NEVER SAY, "THOU SHALT NOT STEAL." ON THE CONTRARY...GOD COMMANDS IT!

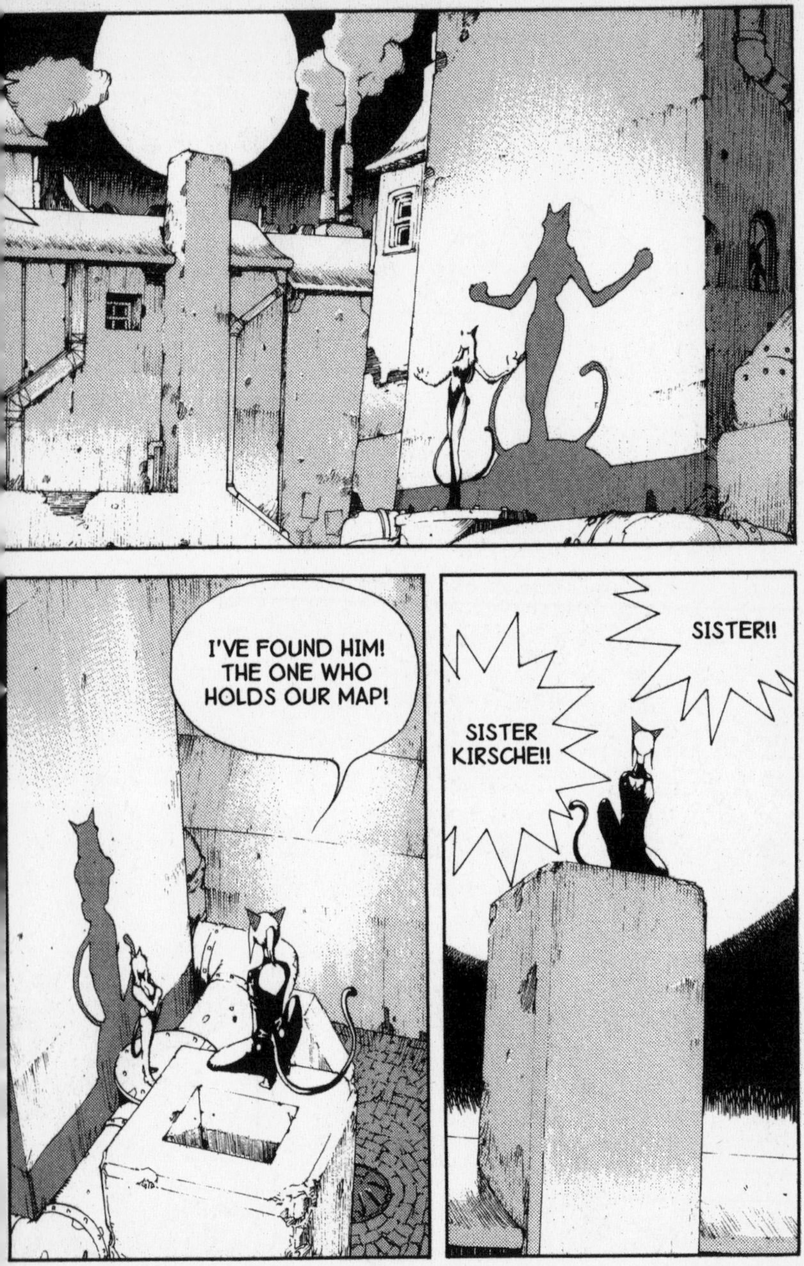
SISTER!!
SISTER KIRSCHE!!
I'VE FOUND HIM! THE ONE WHO HOLDS OUR MAP!

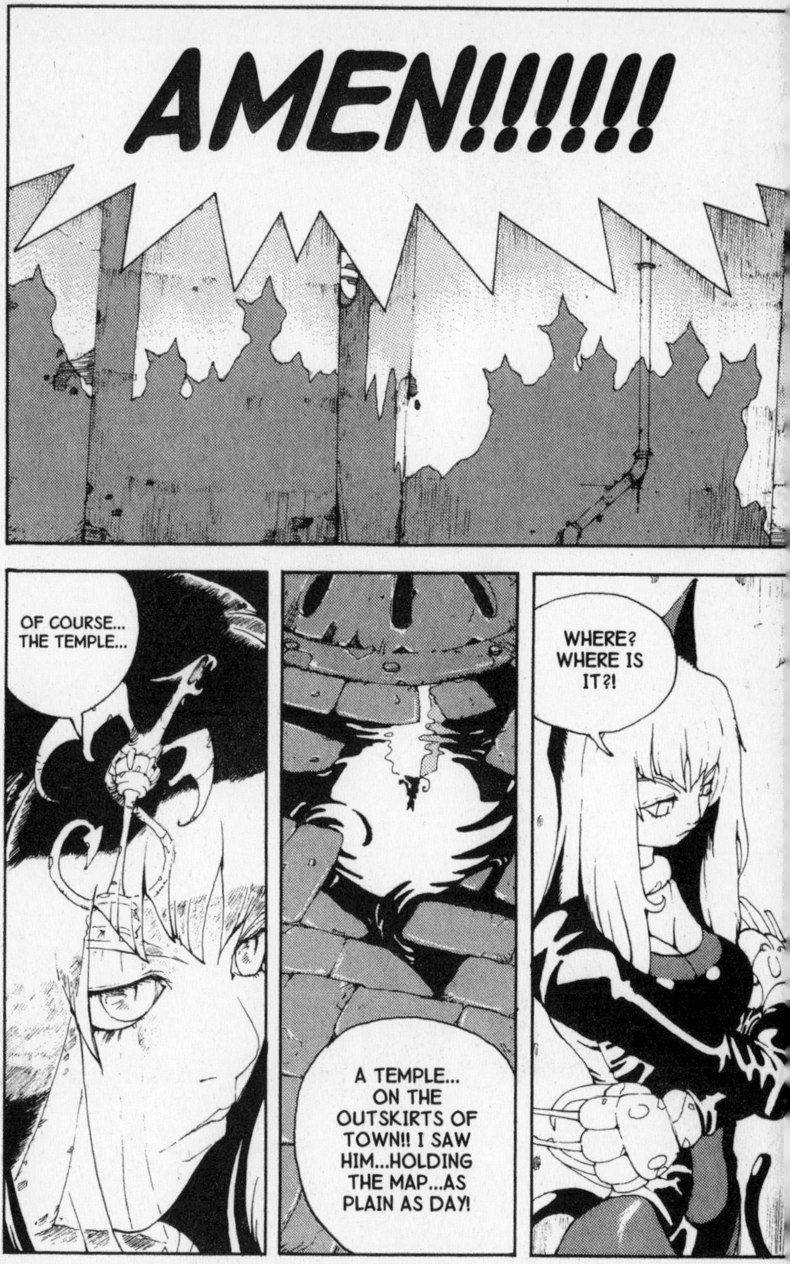
AMEN!!!!!!!
WHERE? WHERE IS IT?!
A TEMPLE... ON THE OUTSKIRTS OF TOWN!! I SAW HIM...HOLDING THE MAP...AS PLAIN AS DAY!
OF COURSE... THE TEMPLE...

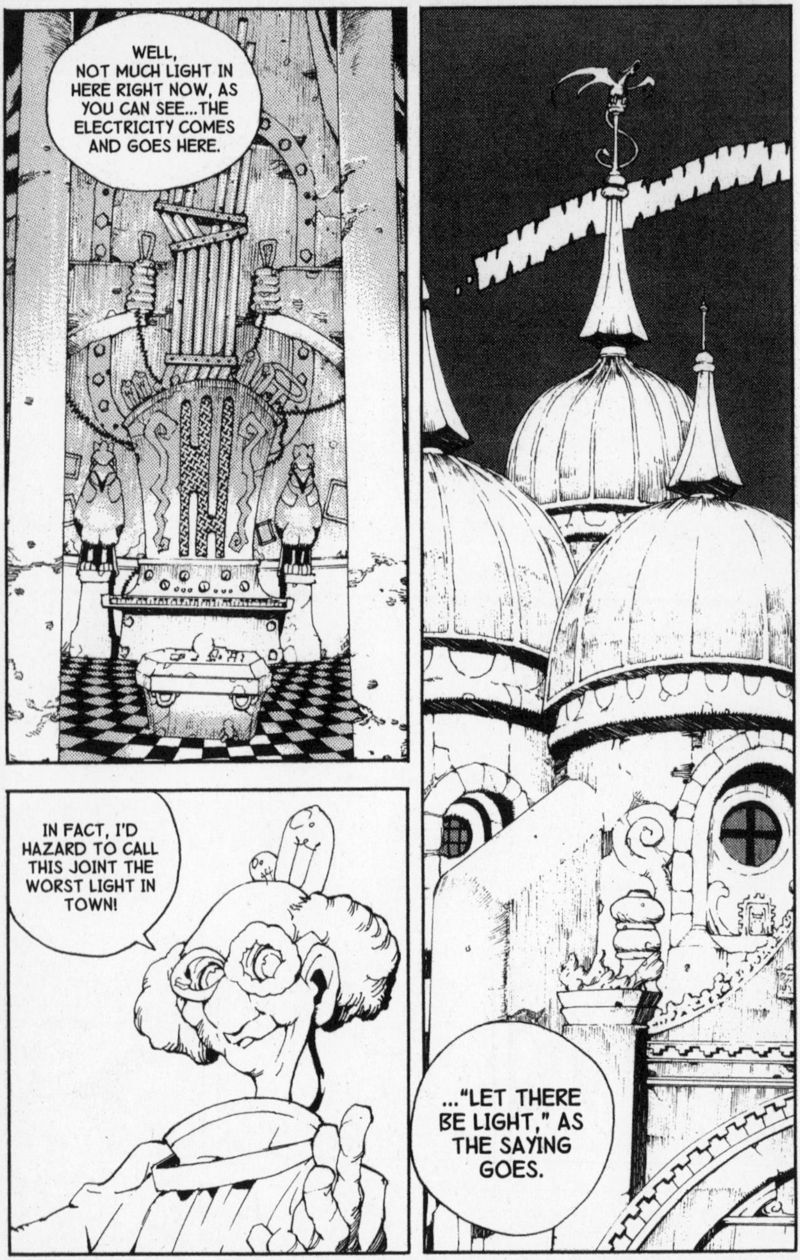

..."LET THERE BE LIGHT," AS THE SAYING GOES.
WELL, NOT MUCH LIGHT IN HERE RIGHT NOW, AS YOU CAN SEE...THE ELECTRICITY COMES AND GOES HERE.
IN FACT, I'D HAZARD TO CALL THIS JOINT THE WORST LIGHT IN TOWN!

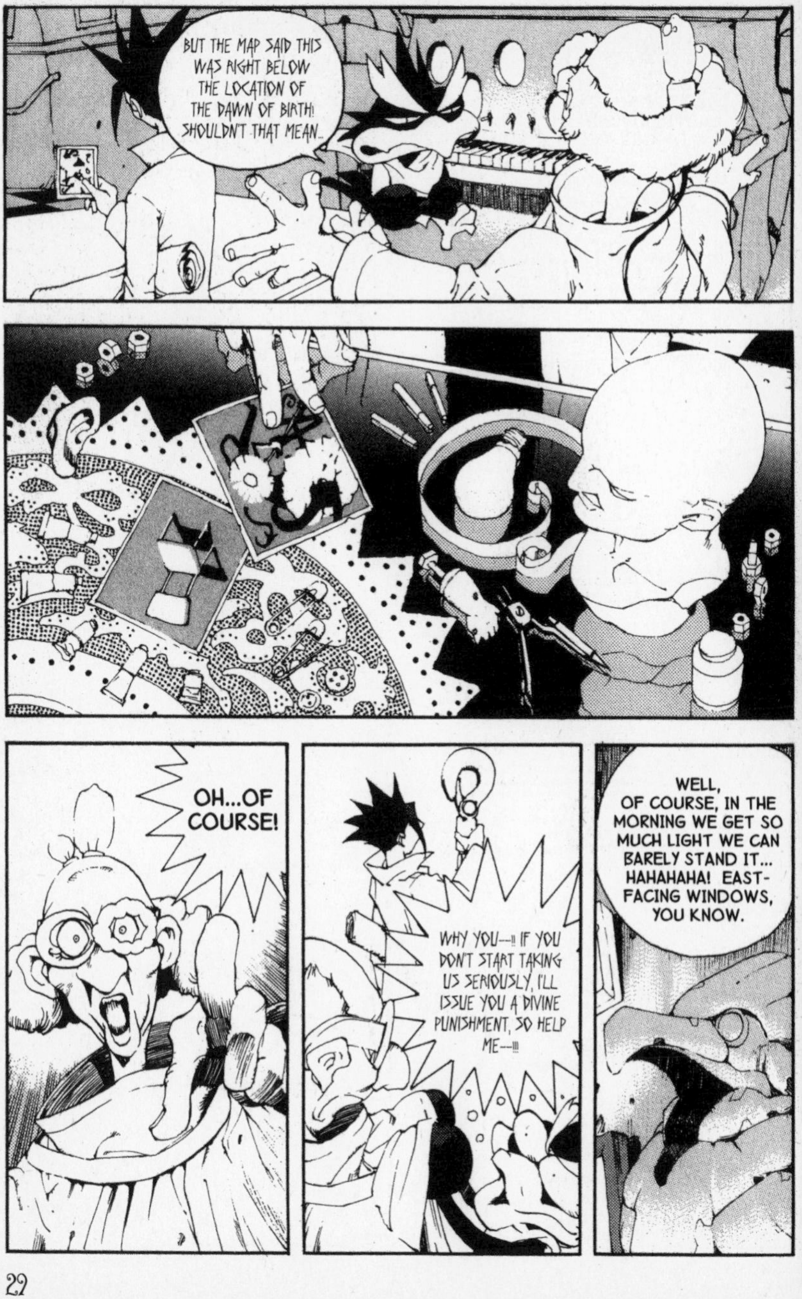
BUT THE MAP SAID THIS WAS RIGHT BELOW THE LOCATION OF THE DAWN OF BIRTH! SHOULDN'T THAT MEAN...
WELL, OF COURSE, IN THE MORNING WE GET SO MUCH LIGHT WE CAN BARELY STAND IT... HAHAHAHA! EAST-FACING WINDOWS, YOU KNOW.
WHY YOU--!! IF YOU DON'T START TAKING US SERIOUSLY, I'LL ISSUE YOU A DIVINE PUNISHMENT, SO HELP ME--!!!
OH...OF COURSE!

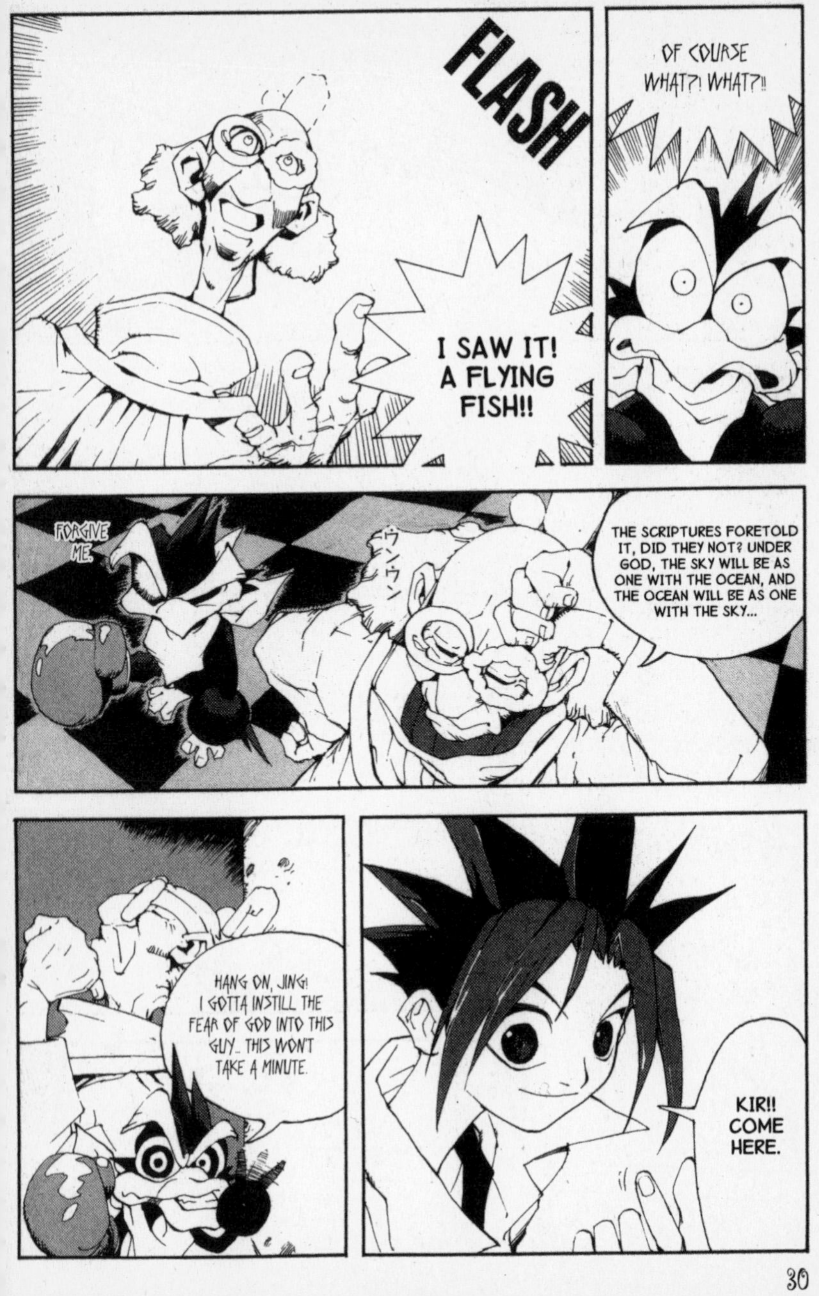
OF COURSE WHAT?! WHAT?!!
FLASH
I SAW IT! A FLYING FISH!!
THE SCRIPTURES FORETOLD IT, DID THEY NOT? UNDER GOD, THE SKY WILL BE AS ONE WITH THE OCEAN, AND THE OCEAN WILL BE AS ONE WITH THE SKY...
ウンウン
FORGIVE ME.
KIR!! COME HERE.
HANG ON, JING! I GOTTA INSTILL THE FEAR OF GOD INTO THIS GUY.. THIS WON'T TAKE A MINUTE.

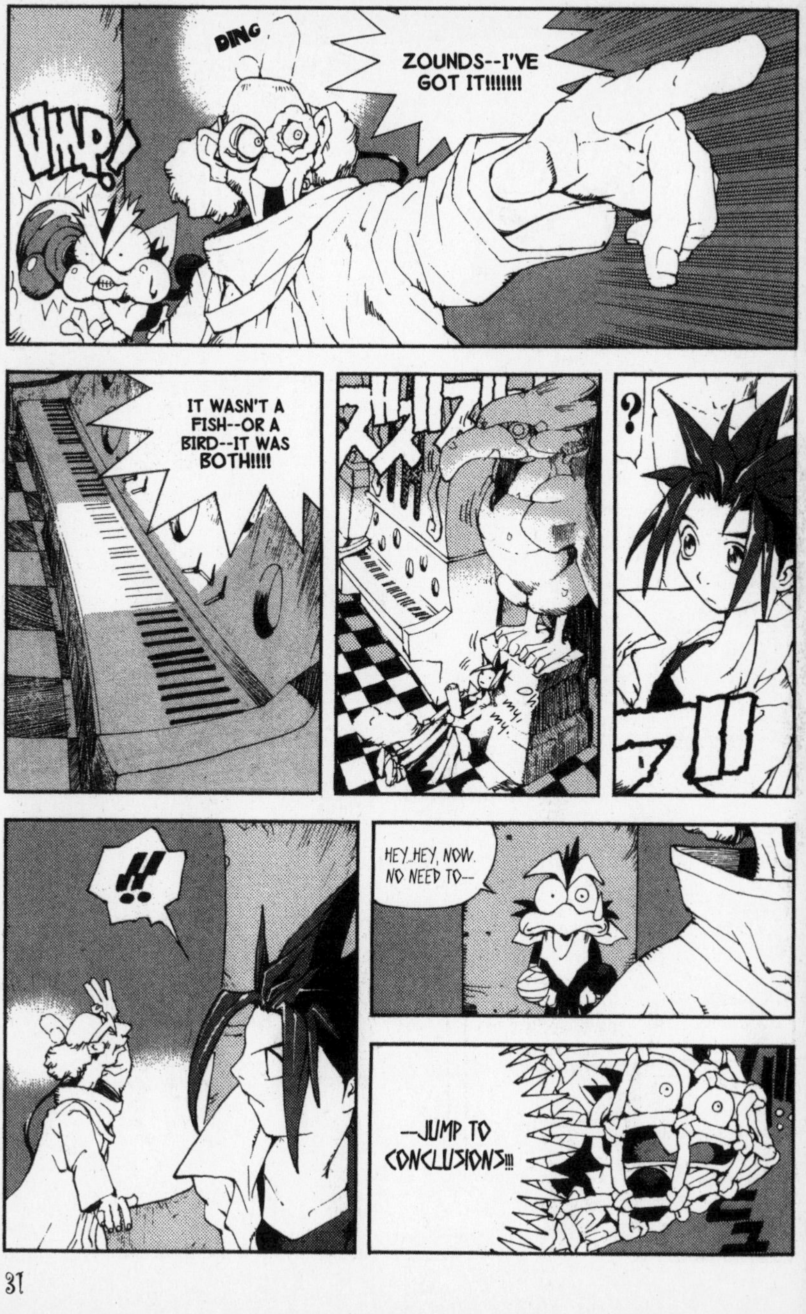
DING
ZOUNDS--I'VE GOT IT!!!!!!!
UHP!
?
Oh my, my.
IT WASN'T A FISH--OR A BIRD--IT WAS BOTH!!!!
HEY...HEY, NOW. NO NEED TO--
--JUMP TO CONCLUSIONS!!!
!!

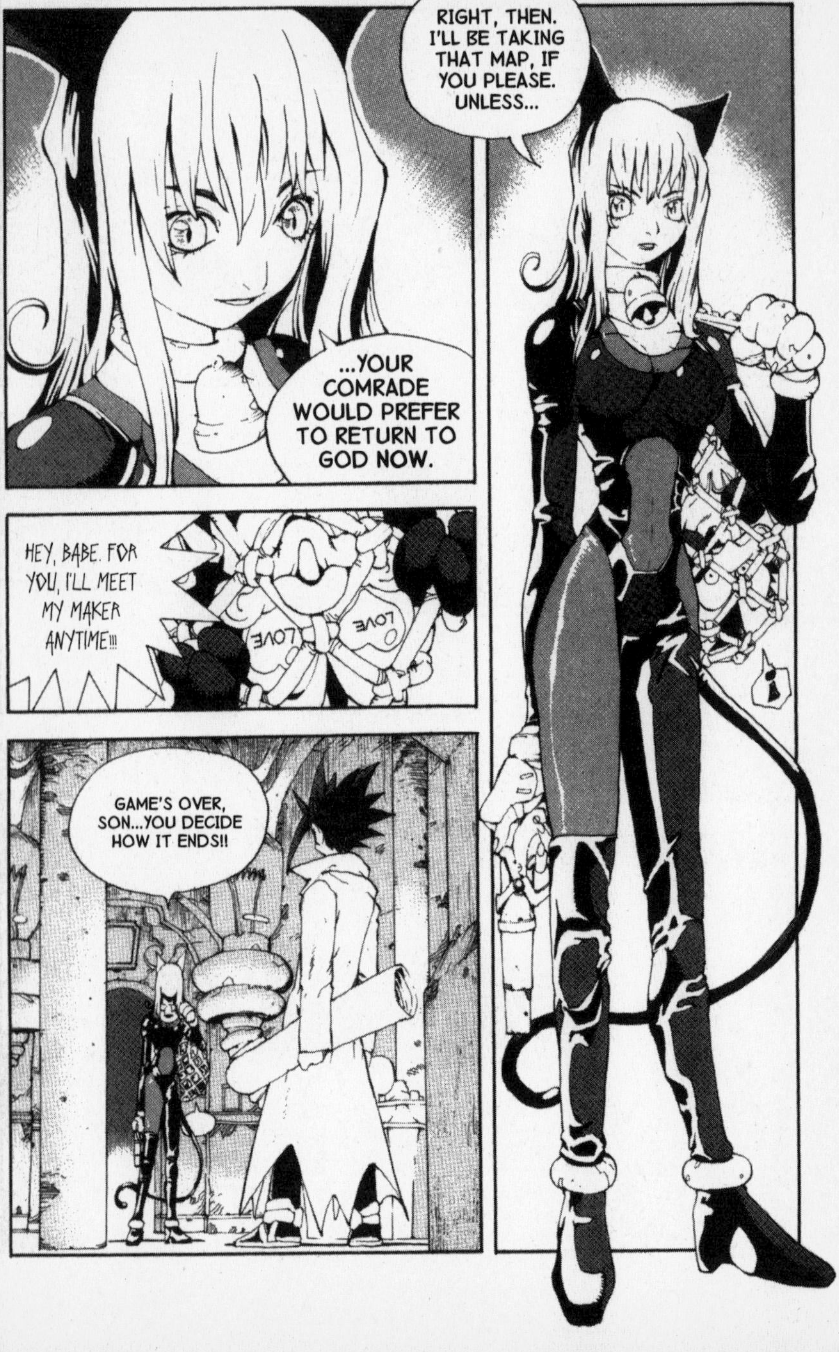
RIGHT, THEN. I'LL BE TAKING THAT MAP, IF YOU PLEASE. UNLESS...
...YOUR COMRADE WOULD PREFER TO RETURN TO GOD NOW.
HEY, BABE. FOR YOU, I'LL MEET MY MAKER ANYTIME!!!
LOVE
GAME'S OVER, SON...YOU DECIDE HOW IT ENDS!!

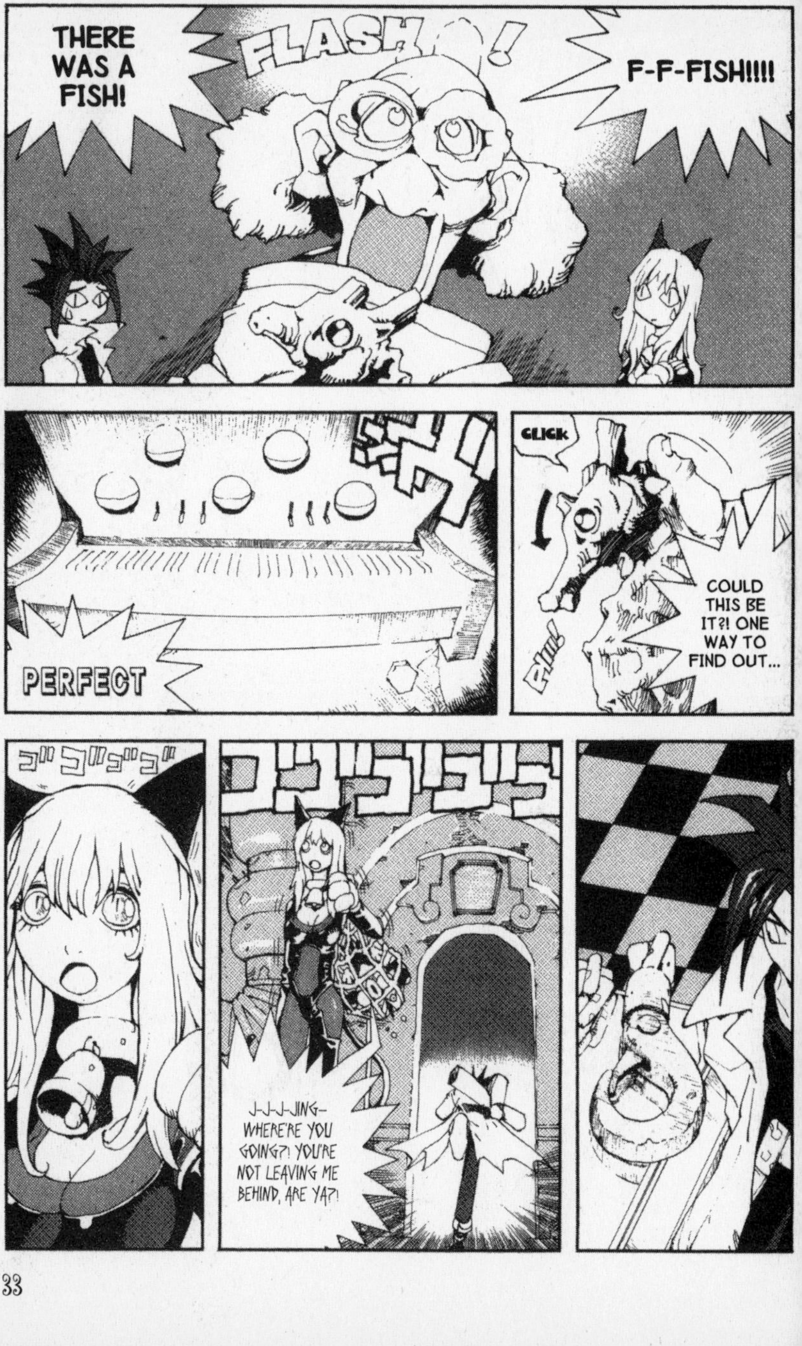
F-F-FISH!!!!
FLASH!
THERE WAS A FISH!
CLICK
COULD THIS BE IT?! ONE WAY TO FIND OUT...
PERFECT
J-J-J-JING—
WHERE'RE YOU GOING?! YOU'RE NOT LEAVING ME BEHIND, ARE YA?!

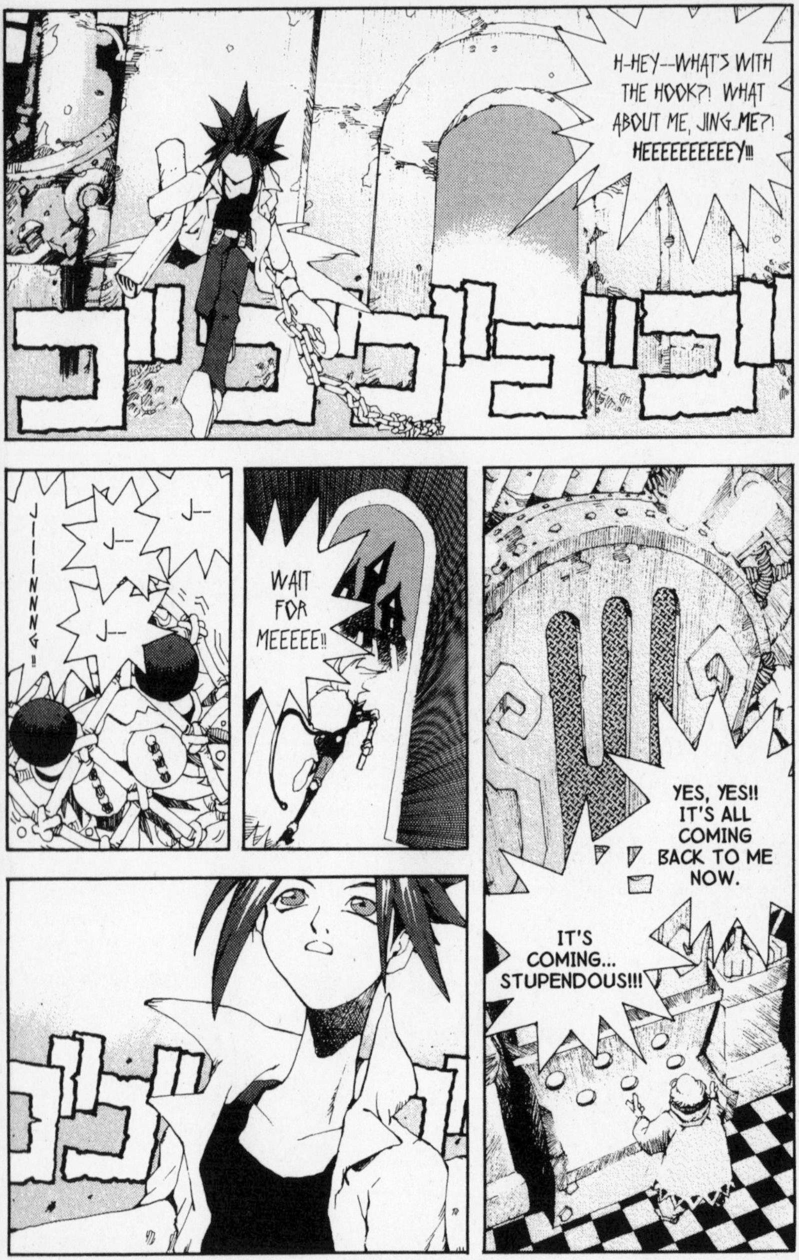
H-HEY--WHAT'S WITH THE HOOK?! WHAT ABOUT ME, JING...ME?! HEEEEEEEEEEY!!!
YES, YES!! IT'S ALL COMING BACK TO ME NOW.
IT'S COMING... STUPENDOUS!!!
WAIT FOR MEEEEE!!
J--
J--
J--
JIIIINNNG!!

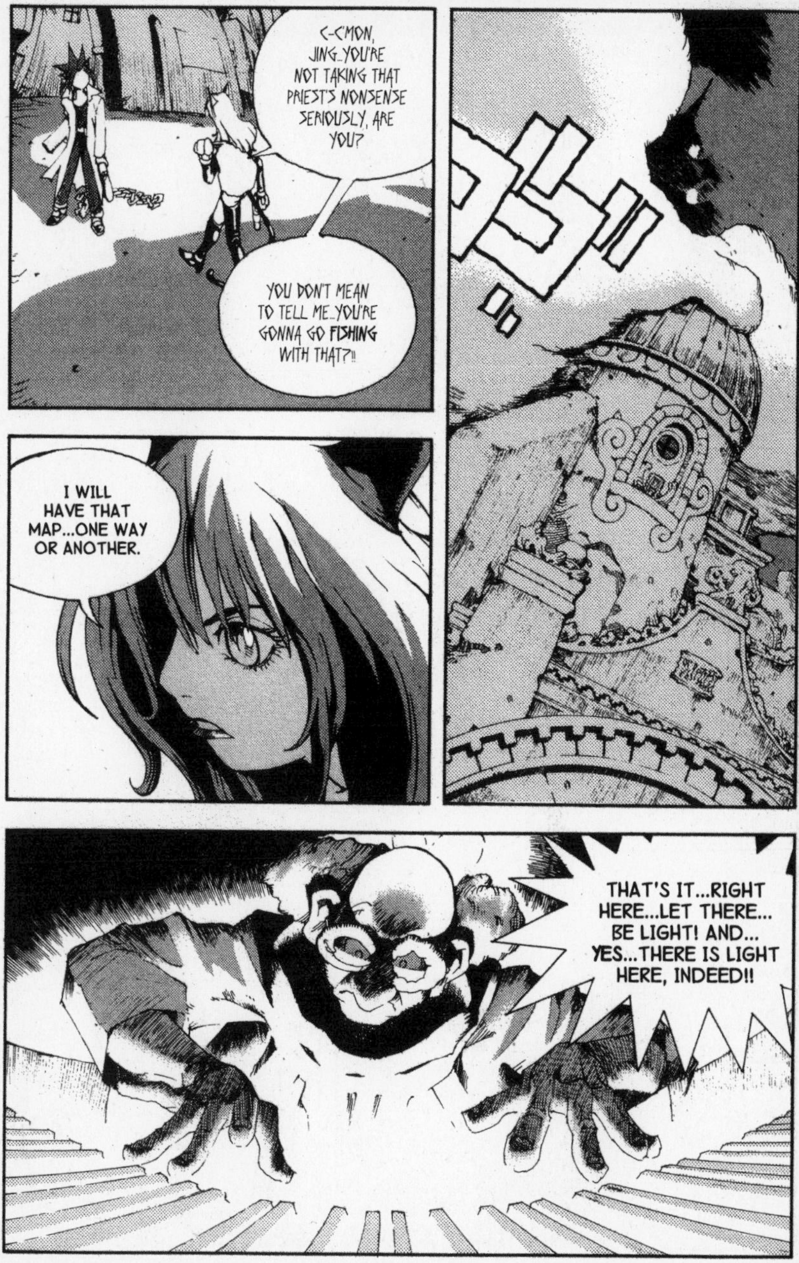
C-C'MON, JING...YOU'RE NOT TAKING THAT PRIEST'S NONSENSE SERIOUSLY, ARE YOU?
YOU DON'T MEAN TO TELL ME...YOU'RE GONNA GO FISHING WITH THAT?!!
I WILL HAVE THAT MAP...ONE WAY OR ANOTHER.
THAT'S IT...RIGHT HERE...LET THERE... BE LIGHT! AND... YES...THERE IS LIGHT HERE, INDEED!!

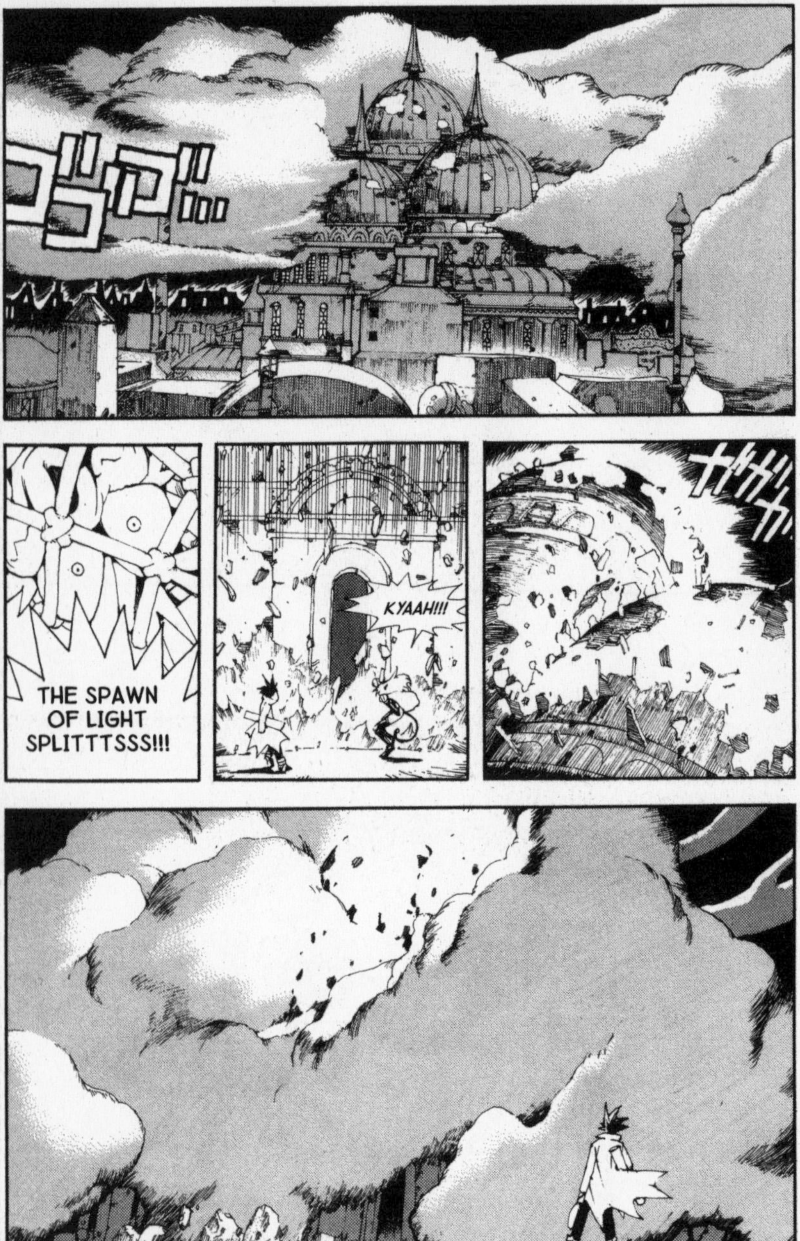
KYAAH!!!
THE SPAWN OF LIGHT SPLITTTSSS!!!

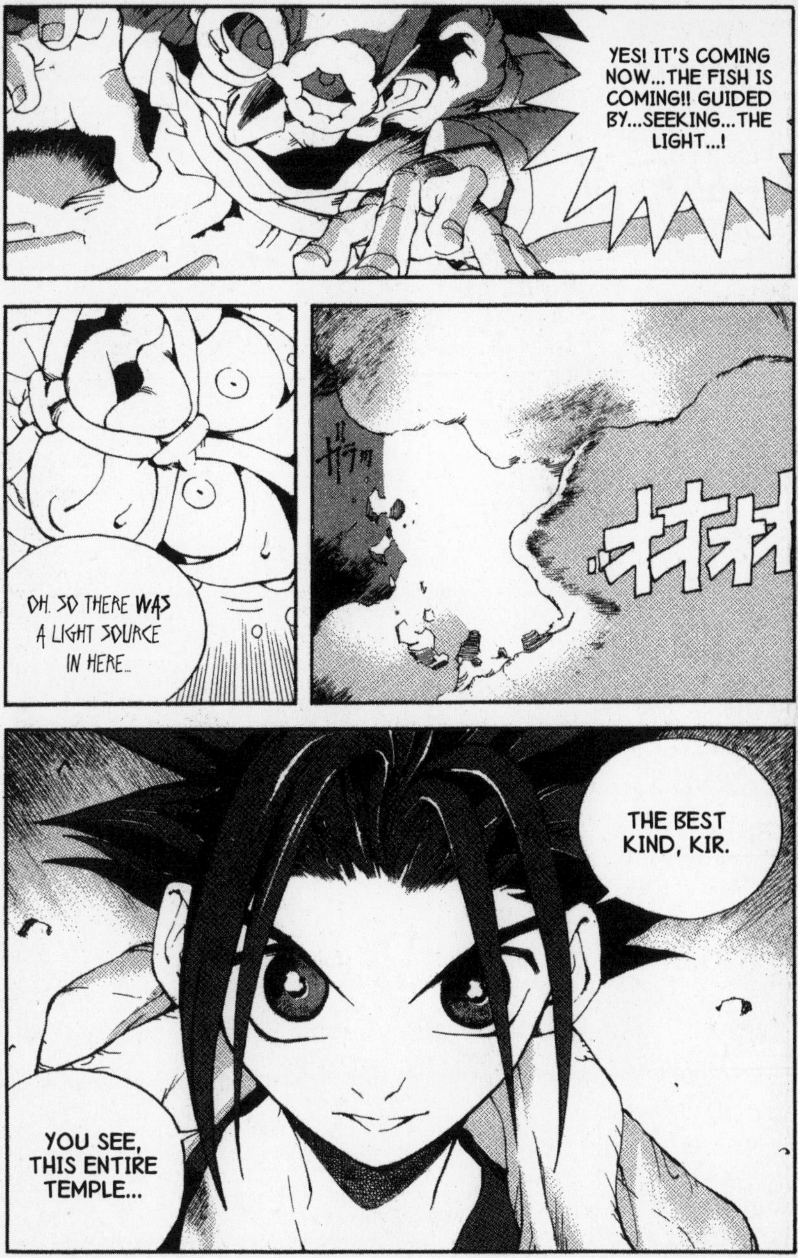
YES! IT'S COMING NOW...THE FISH IS COMING!! GUIDED BY...SEEKING...THE LIGHT...!
オオオ
OH. SO THERE WAS A LIGHT SOURCE IN HERE...
THE BEST KIND, KIR.
YOU SEE, THIS ENTIRE TEMPLE...

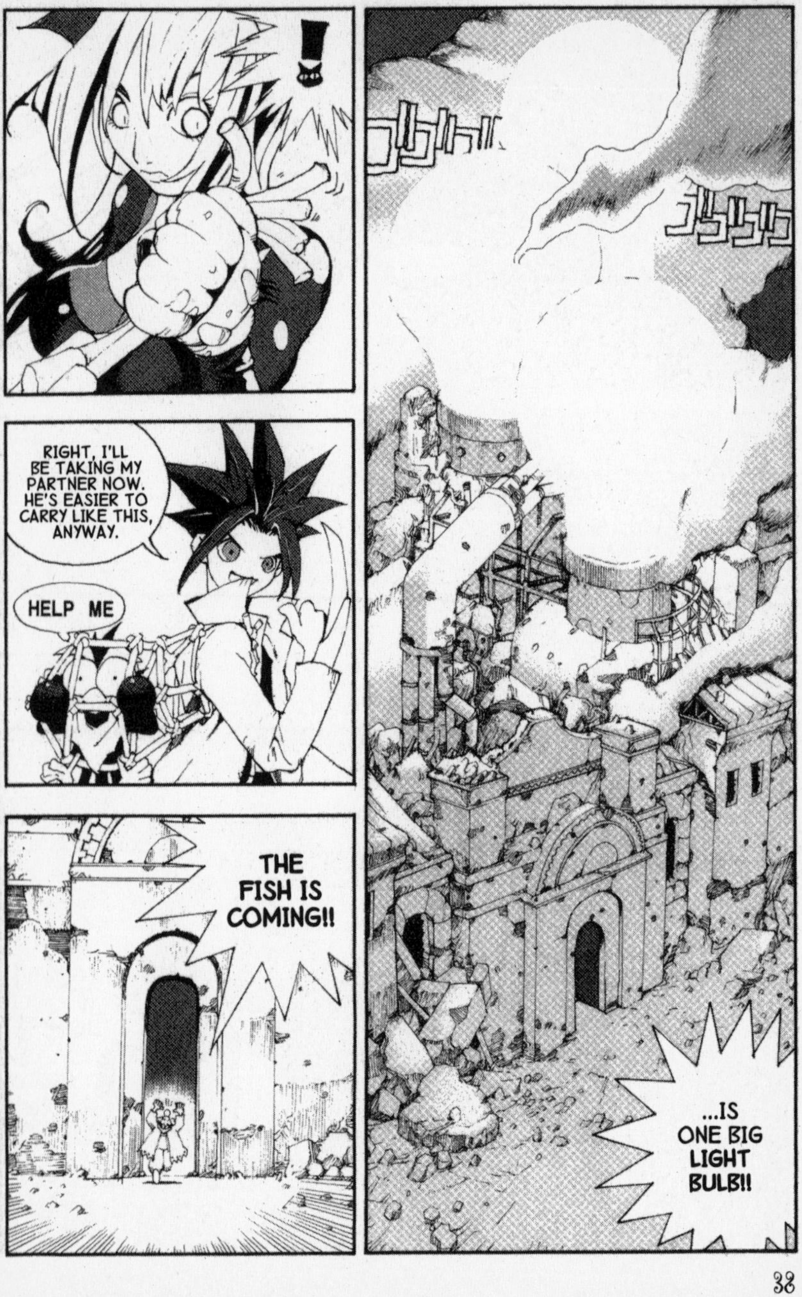
...IS ONE BIG LIGHT BULB!!
!
RIGHT, I'LL BE TAKING MY PARTNER NOW. HE'S EASIER TO CARRY LIKE THIS, ANYWAY.
HELP ME
THE FISH IS COMING!!

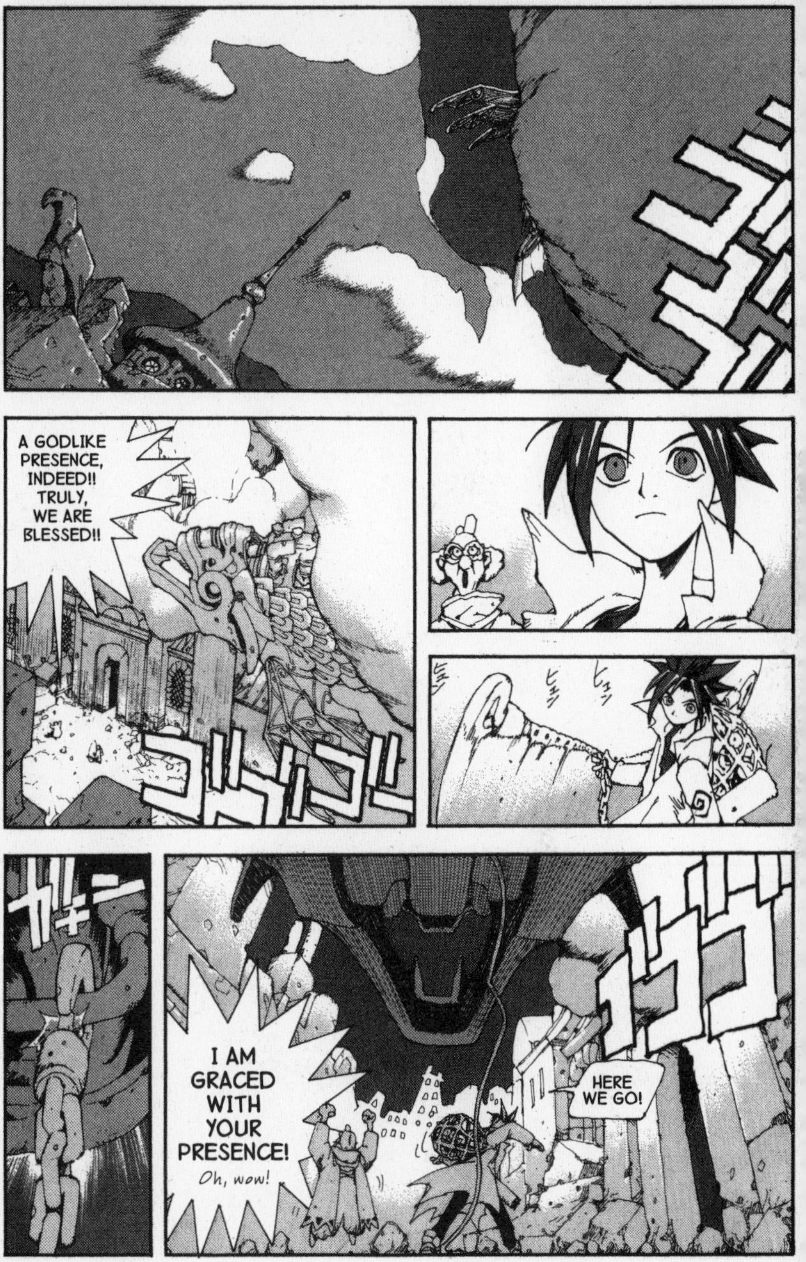
A GODLIKE PRESENCE, INDEED!! TRULY, WE ARE BLESSED!!
I AM GRACED WITH YOUR PRESENCE!
Oh, wow!
HERE WE GO!

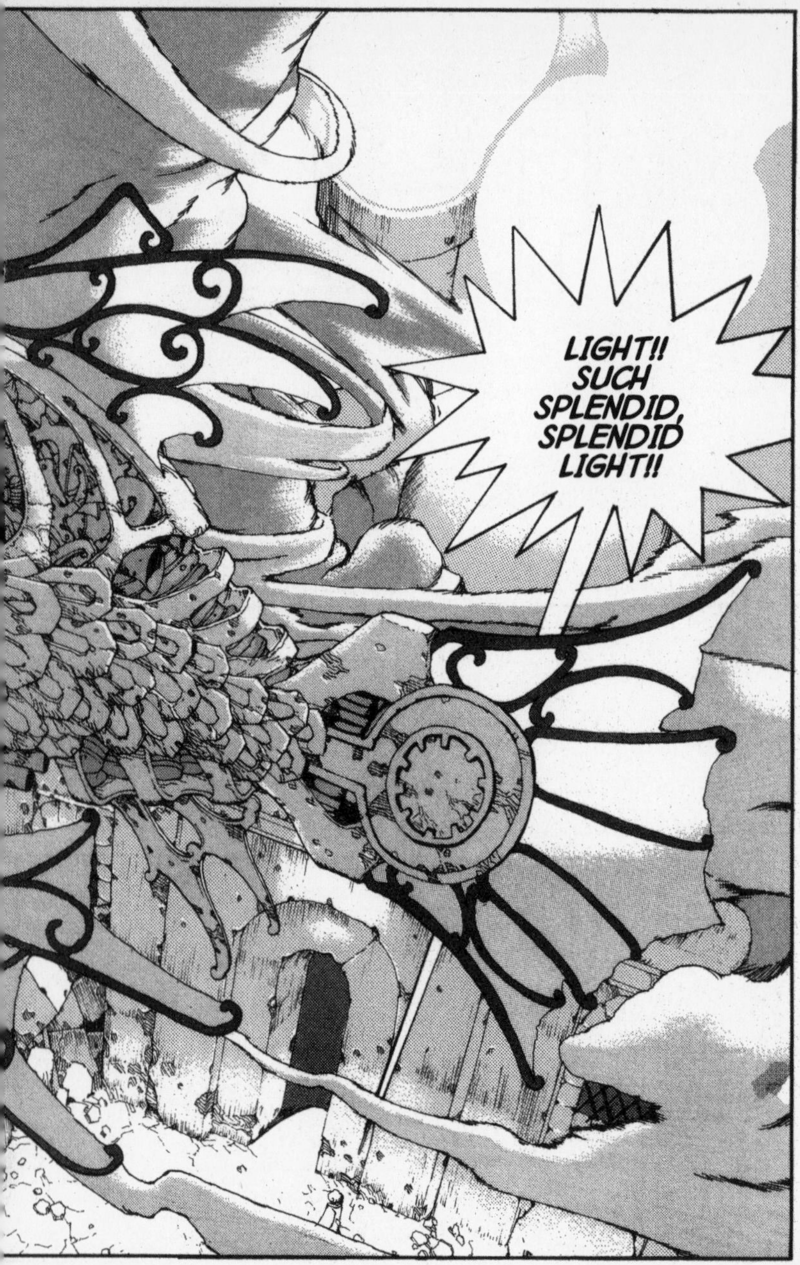
LIGHT!! SUCH SPLENDID, SPLENDID LIGHT!!

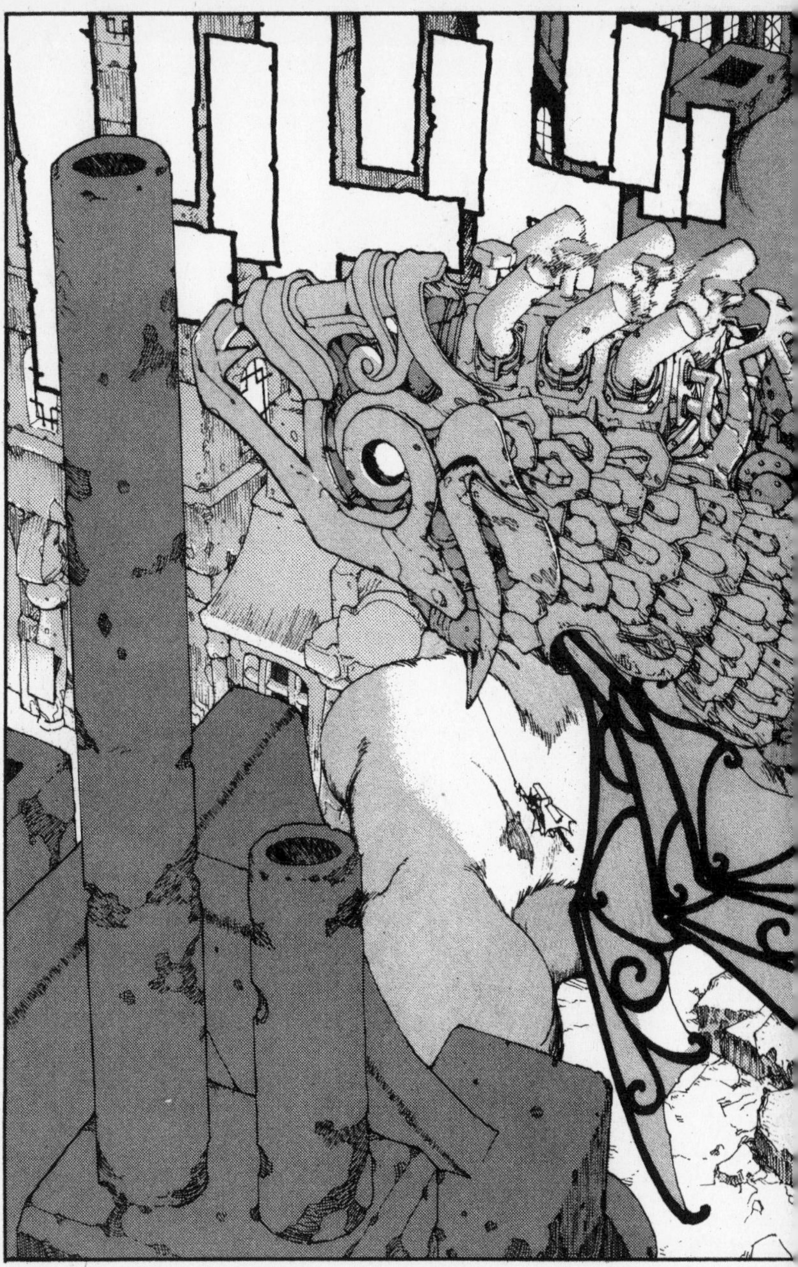

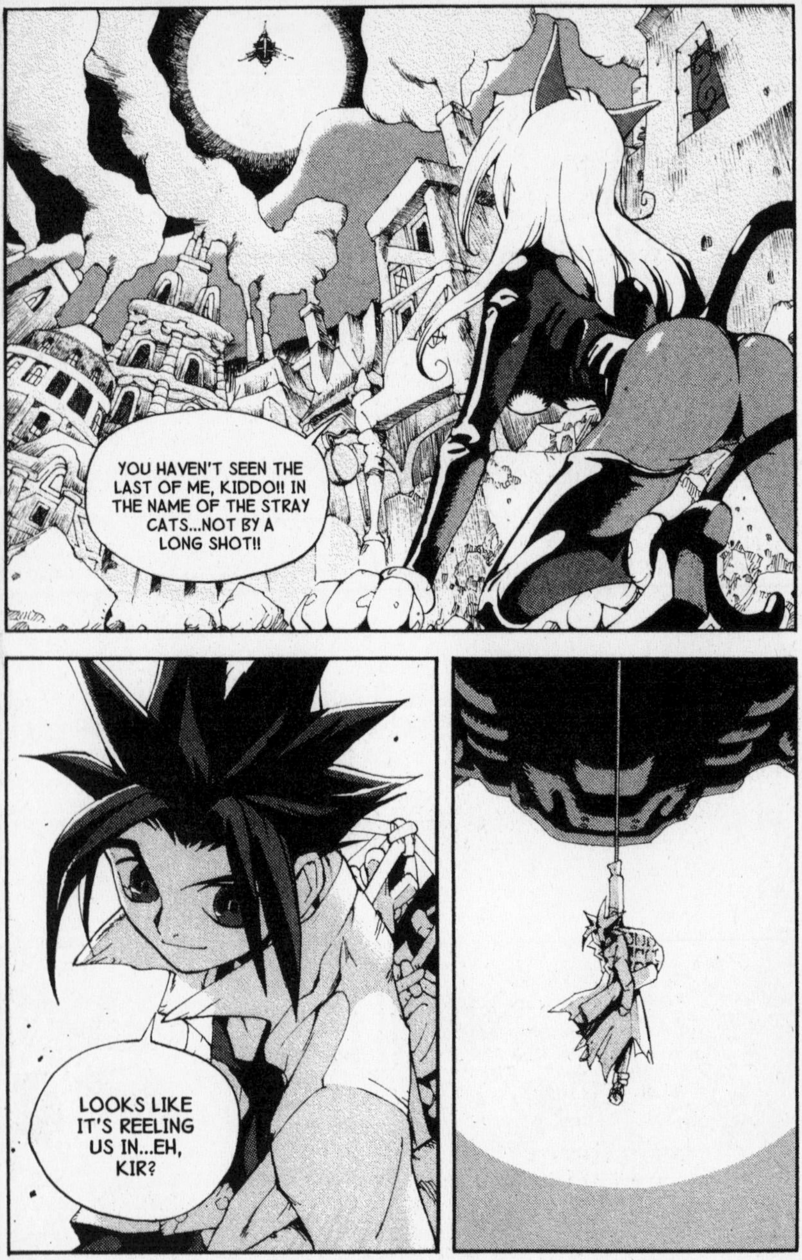
YOU HAVEN'T SEEN THE LAST OF ME, KIDDO!! IN THE NAME OF THE STRAY CATS...NOT BY A LONG SHOT!!
LOOKS LIKE IT'S REELING US IN...EH, KIR?

SWING
SWING
Swing low, sweet chariot Comin for to carry me home—
I looked over Jordan — and
SWING
JING..I HAD THIS DREAM.
THERE WAS THIS EERIE.. MYSTERIOUS.. UNUSUALLY BIG..FISH. FROM THE SKY.
AND IT SNAPPED US UP LIKE SO MUCH BAIT, AND--
What — did I see
OH!
OH!
OH!
Comin for to carry me Home—

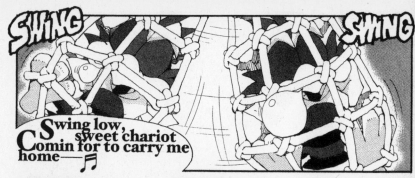

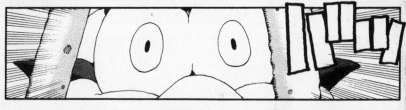

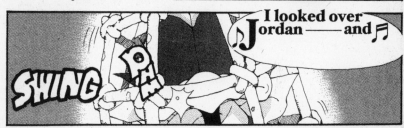

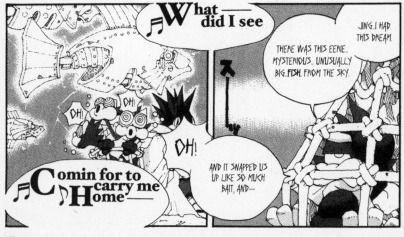

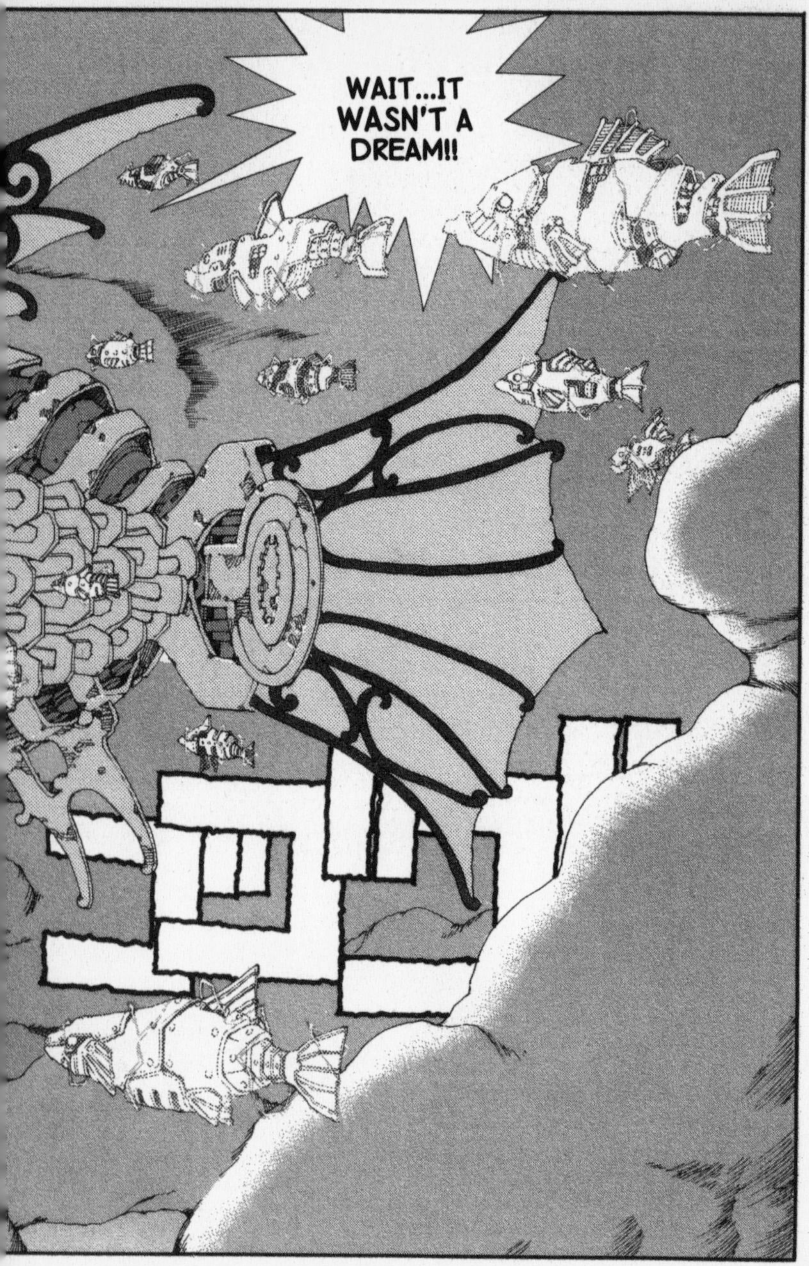
WAIT...IT WASN'T A DREAM!!

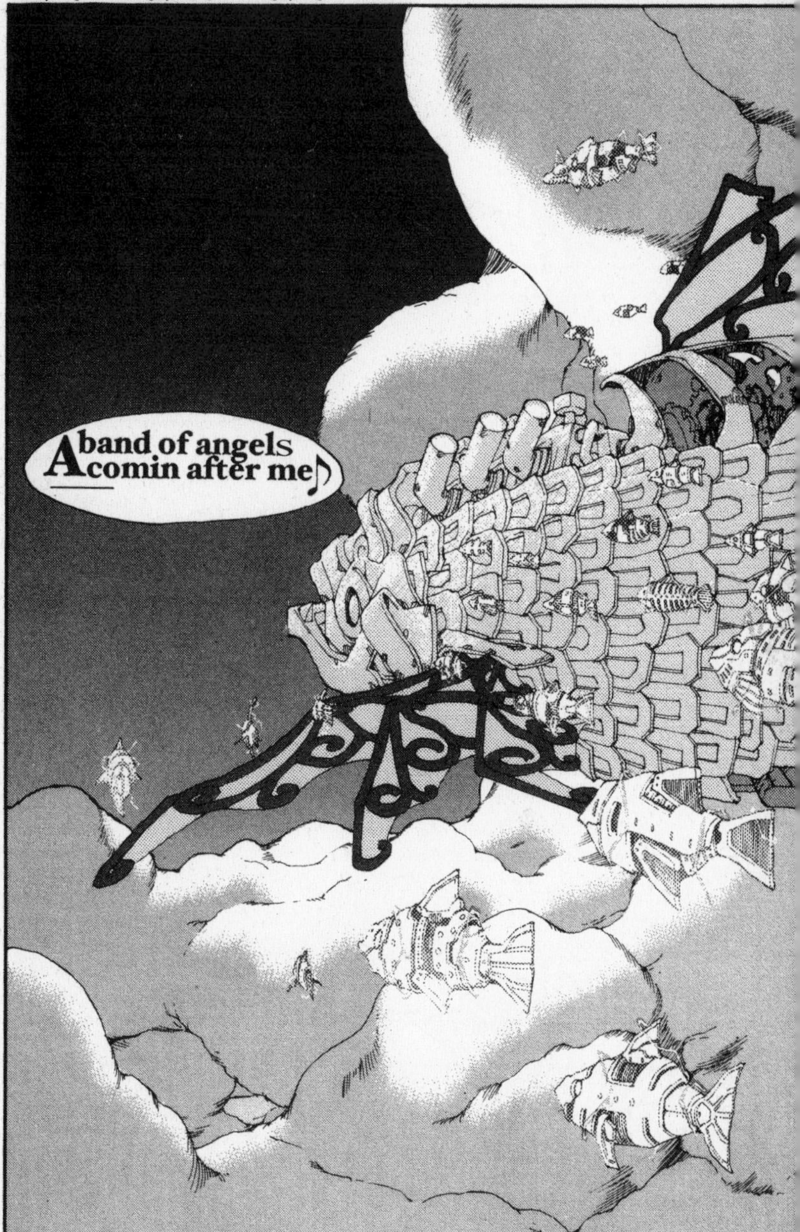
A band of angels comin after me♪

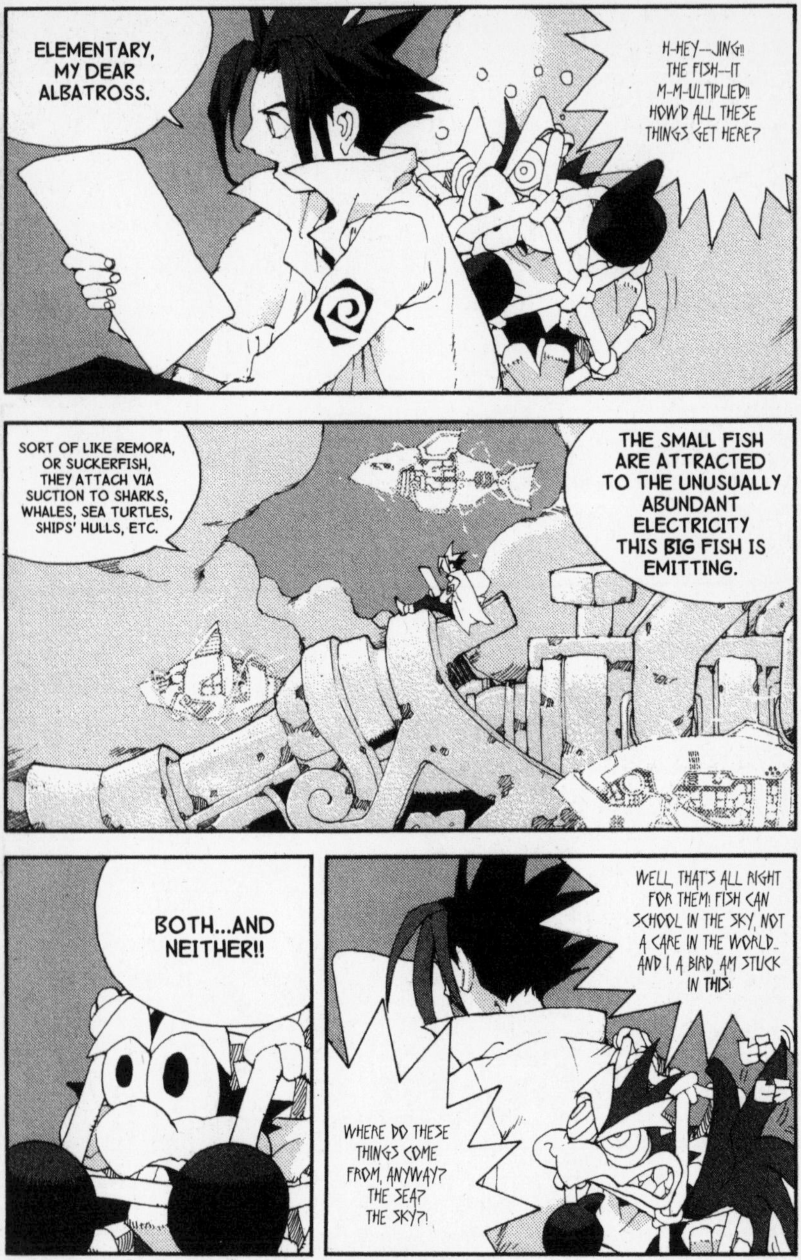
H-HEY--JING!! THE FISH--IT M-M-ULTIPLIED!! HOW'D ALL THESE THINGS GET HERE?
ELEMENTARY, MY DEAR ALBATROSS.
THE SMALL FISH ARE ATTRACTED TO THE UNUSUALLY ABUNDANT ELECTRICITY THIS BIG FISH IS EMITTING.
SORT OF LIKE REMORA, OR SUCKERFISH, THEY ATTACH VIA SUCTION TO SHARKS, WHALES, SEA TURTLES, SHIPS' HULLS, ETC.
WELL, THAT'S ALL RIGHT FOR THEM! FISH CAN SCHOOL IN THE SKY, NOT A CARE IN THE WORLD... AND I, A BIRD, AM STUCK IN THIS!
WHERE DO THESE THINGS COME FROM, ANYWAY? THE SEA? THE SKY?!
BOTH...AND NEITHER!!

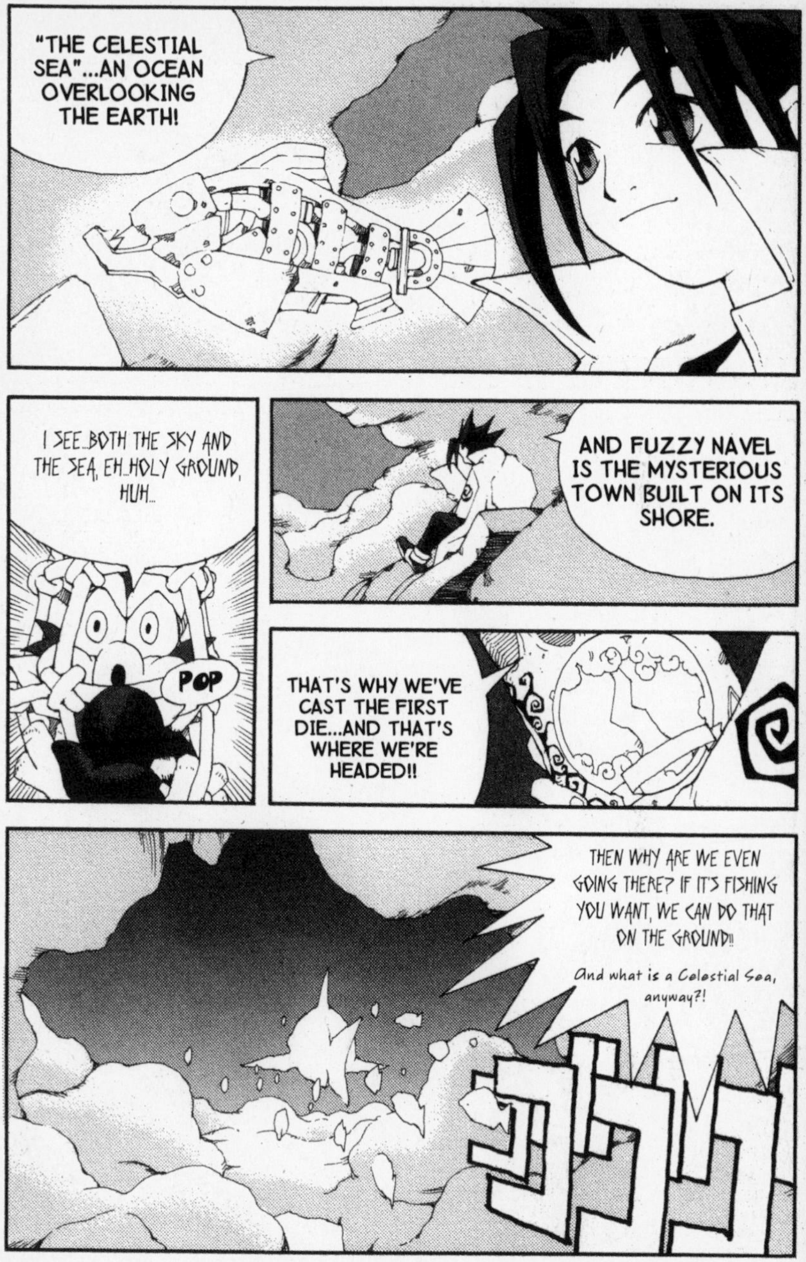
"THE CELESTIAL SEA"...AN OCEAN OVERLOOKING THE EARTH!
AND FUZZY NAVEL IS THE MYSTERIOUS TOWN BUILT ON ITS SHORE.
THAT'S WHY WE'VE CAST THE FIRST DIE...AND THAT'S WHERE WE'RE HEADED!!
I SEE...BOTH THE SKY AND THE SEA, EH...HOLY GROUND, HUH...
POP
THEN WHY ARE WE EVEN GOING THERE? IF IT'S FISHING YOU WANT, WE CAN DO THAT ON THE GROUND!!
And what is a Celestial Sea, anyway?!

THEY'RE HEADED FOR THE CELESTIAL SEA--I'D BET MY LIFE ON IT!!

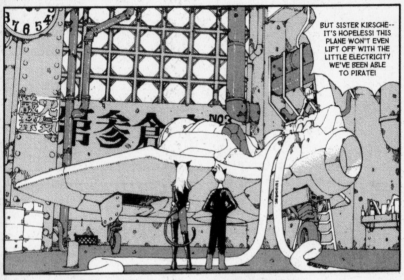

BUT SISTER KIRSCHE-- IT'S HOPELESS! THIS PLANE WON'T EVEN LIFT OFF WITH THE LITTLE ELECTRICITY WE'VE BEEN ABLE TO PIRATE!

UM...

GREAT! AND AS WE SIT HERE HELPLESSLY ON THE GROUND... THAT FISH IS ON ITS WAY TO FUZZY NAVEL!!

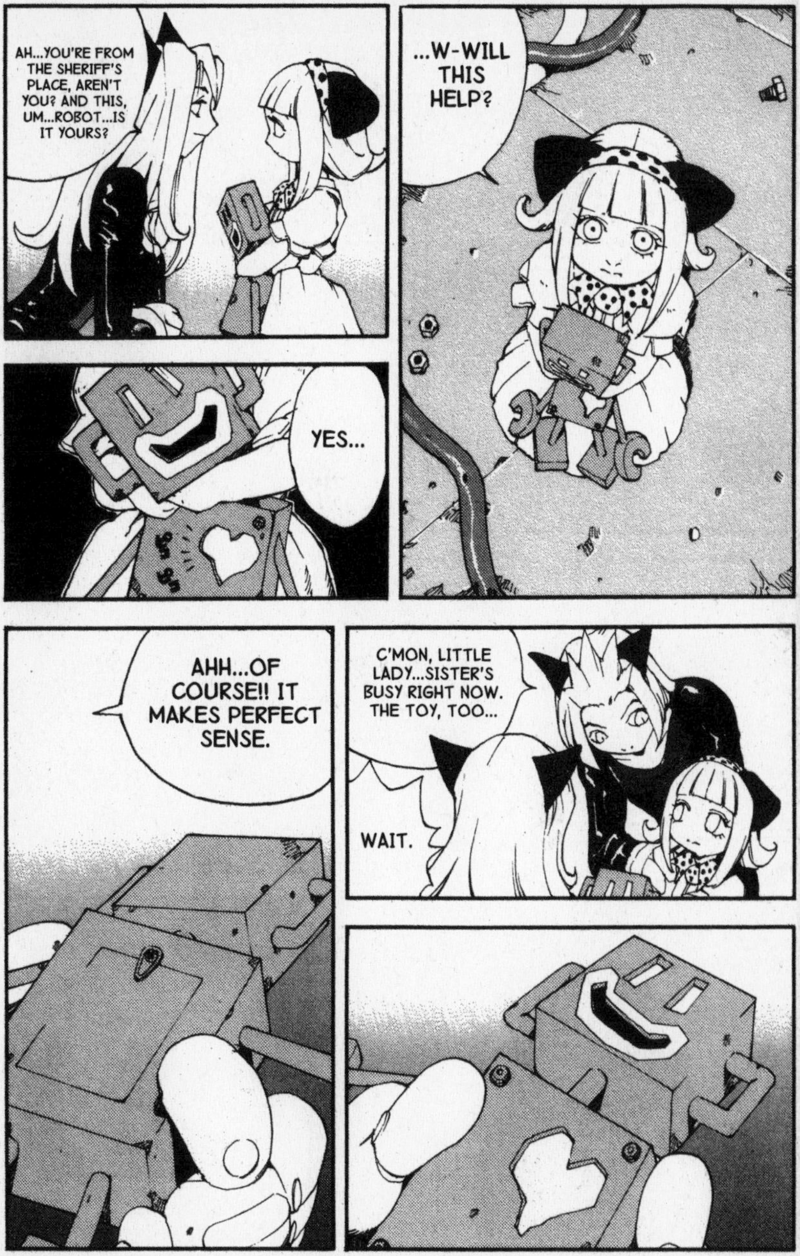
...W-WILL THIS HELP?
AH...YOU'RE FROM THE SHERIFF'S PLACE, AREN'T YOU? AND THIS, UM...ROBOT...IS IT YOURS?
YES...
C'MON, LITTLE LADY...SISTER'S BUSY RIGHT NOW. THE TOY, TOO...
WAIT.
AHH...OF COURSE!! IT MAKES PERFECT SENSE.

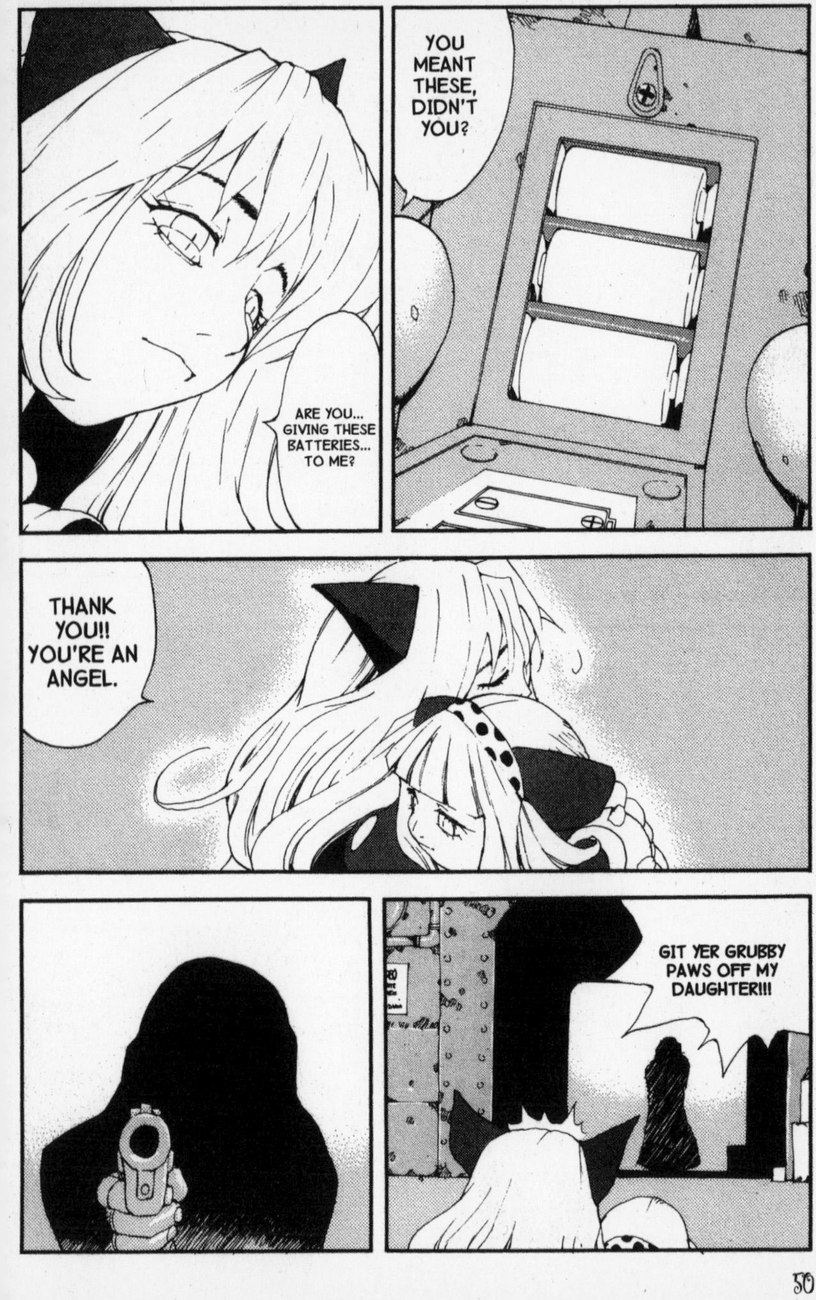
YOU MEANT THESE, DIDN'T YOU?
ARE YOU... GIVING THESE BATTERIES... TO ME?
THANK YOU!! YOU'RE AN ANGEL.
GIT YER GRUBBY PAWS OFF MY DAUGHTER!!!

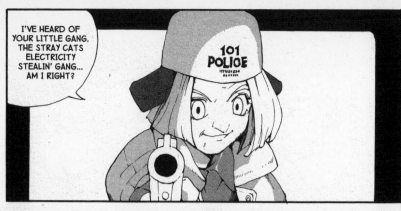

I'VE HEARD OF YOUR LITTLE GANG. THE STRAY CATS ELECTRICITY STEALIN' GANG... AM I RIGHT?
101 POLICE
BUT STEALING ELECTRICITY WASN'T ENOUGH FOR YOU THIS TIME, WAS IT? THOUGHT YOU'D TRY AN' STEAL MY ONLY DAUGHTER TOO!
NO, MAMA...
DON'T MATTER. I'M PUTTIN' YOU ALL UNDER ARREST...IT IS MY JOB.
ALTHOUGH...I DO KNOW WHAT Y'ALL HAVE BEEN DOIN' FOR THE POOR FOLKS OF THIS TOWN. HECK...MY OWN DAUGHTER'S A FAN, IT SEEMS. SO, IN LIGHT OF ALL THAT...
101 POLICE

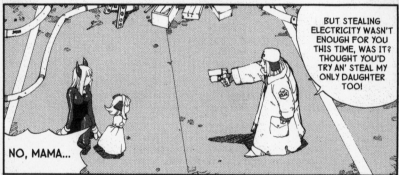

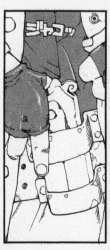

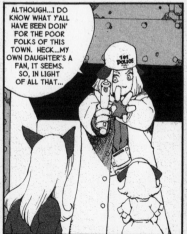

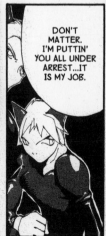

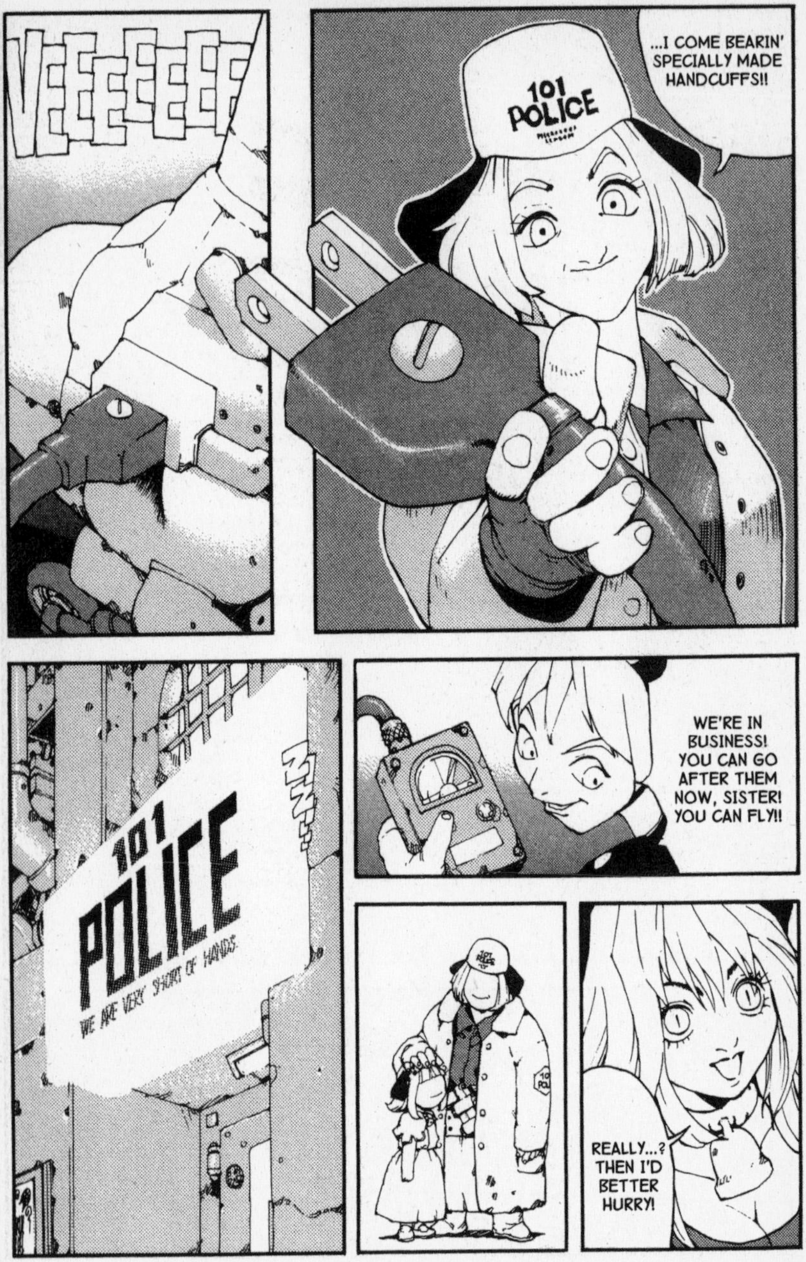
...I COME BEARIN' SPECIALLY MADE HANDCUFFS!!
101 POLICE
VEEEEEEE
WE'RE IN BUSINESS! YOU CAN GO AFTER THEM NOW, SISTER! YOU CAN FLY!!
REALLY...? THEN I'D BETTER HURRY!
101 POLICE
101 POLICE
WE ARE VERY SHORT OF HANDS

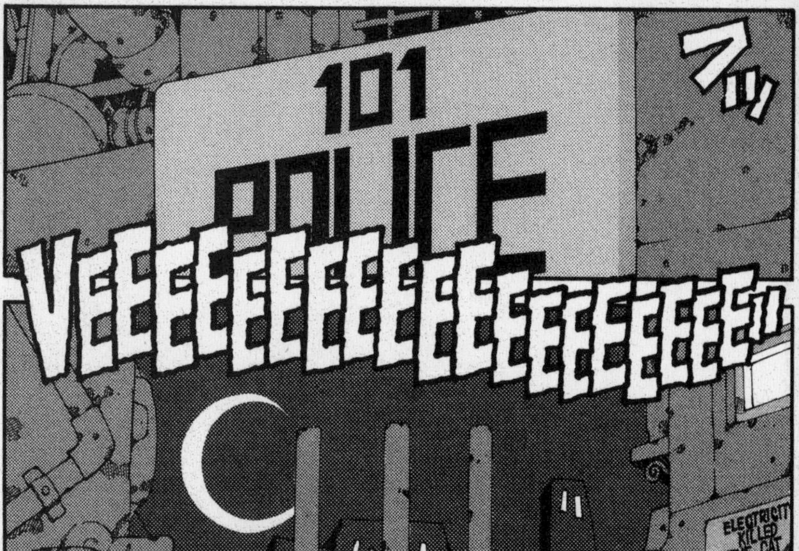
101 POLICE
フッ
VEEEEEEEEEEEEEEEEEEE!!
ELECTRICITY KILLED THE CAT

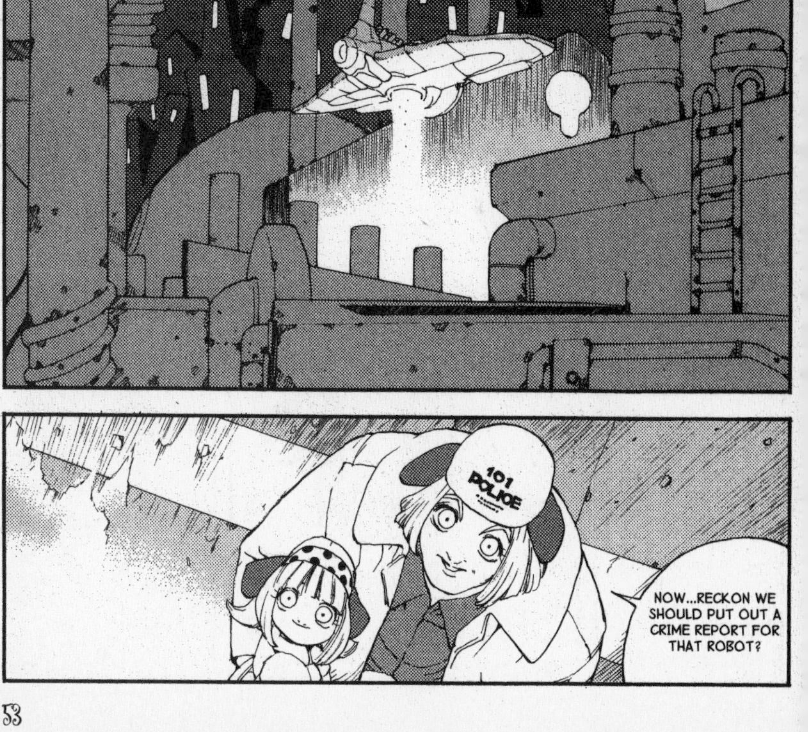
101 POLICE
NOW...RECKON WE SHOULD PUT OUT A CRIME REPORT FOR THAT ROBOT?

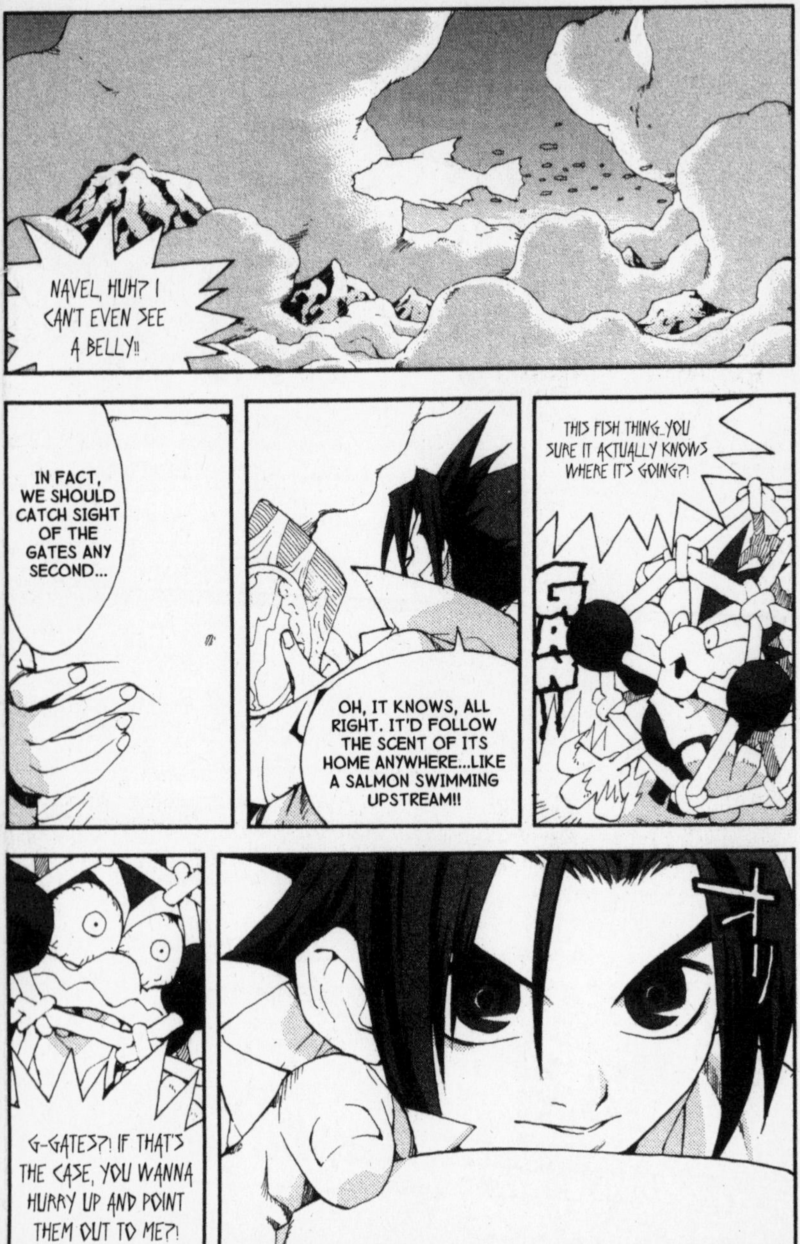
NAVEL, HUH? I CAN'T EVEN SEE A BELLY!!
THIS FISH THING...YOU SURE IT ACTUALLY KNOWS WHERE IT'S GOING?!
GAN
OH, IT KNOWS, ALL RIGHT. IT'D FOLLOW THE SCENT OF ITS HOME ANYWHERE...LIKE A SALMON SWIMMING UPSTREAM!!
IN FACT, WE SHOULD CATCH SIGHT OF THE GATES ANY SECOND...
G-GATES?! IF THAT'S THE CASE, YOU WANNA HURRY UP AND POINT THEM OUT TO ME?!

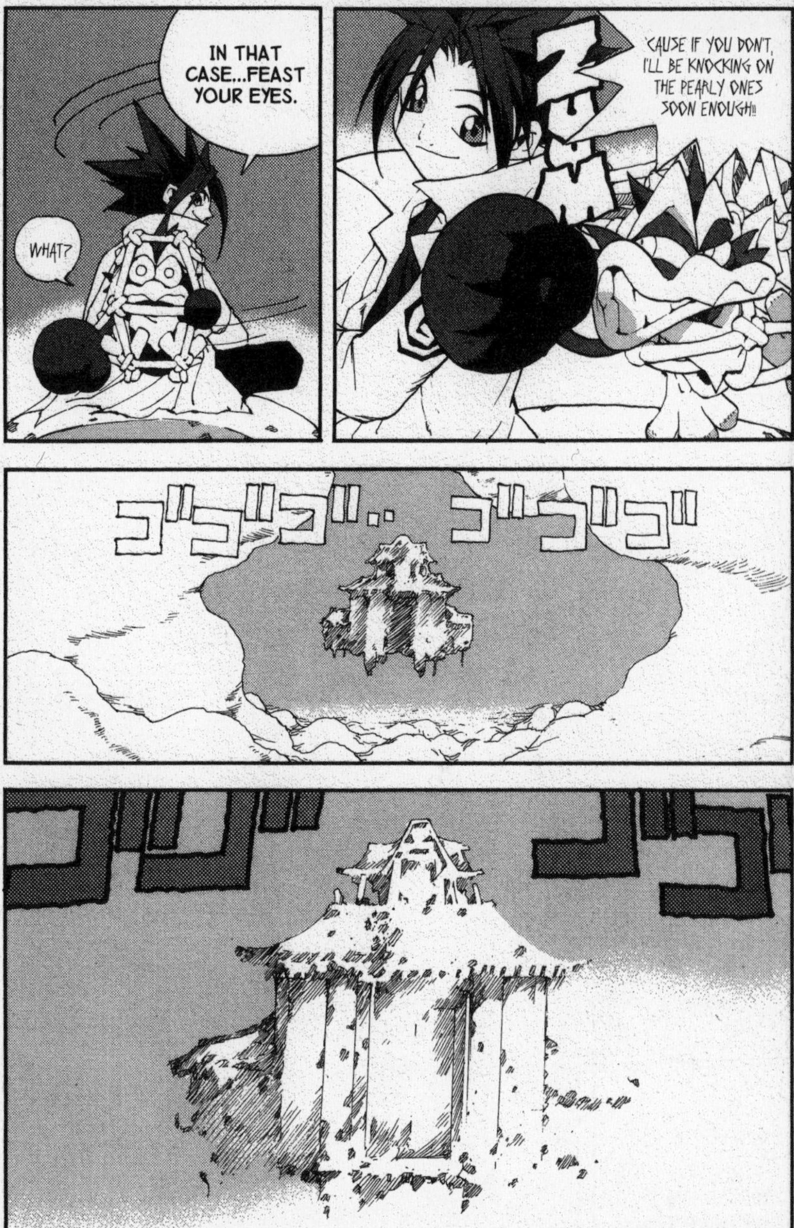
'CAUSE IF YOU DON'T, I'LL BE KNOCKING ON THE PEARLY ONES SOON ENOUGH!!
IN THAT CASE...FEAST YOUR EYES.
WHAT?
ゴゴゴ.. ゴゴゴ

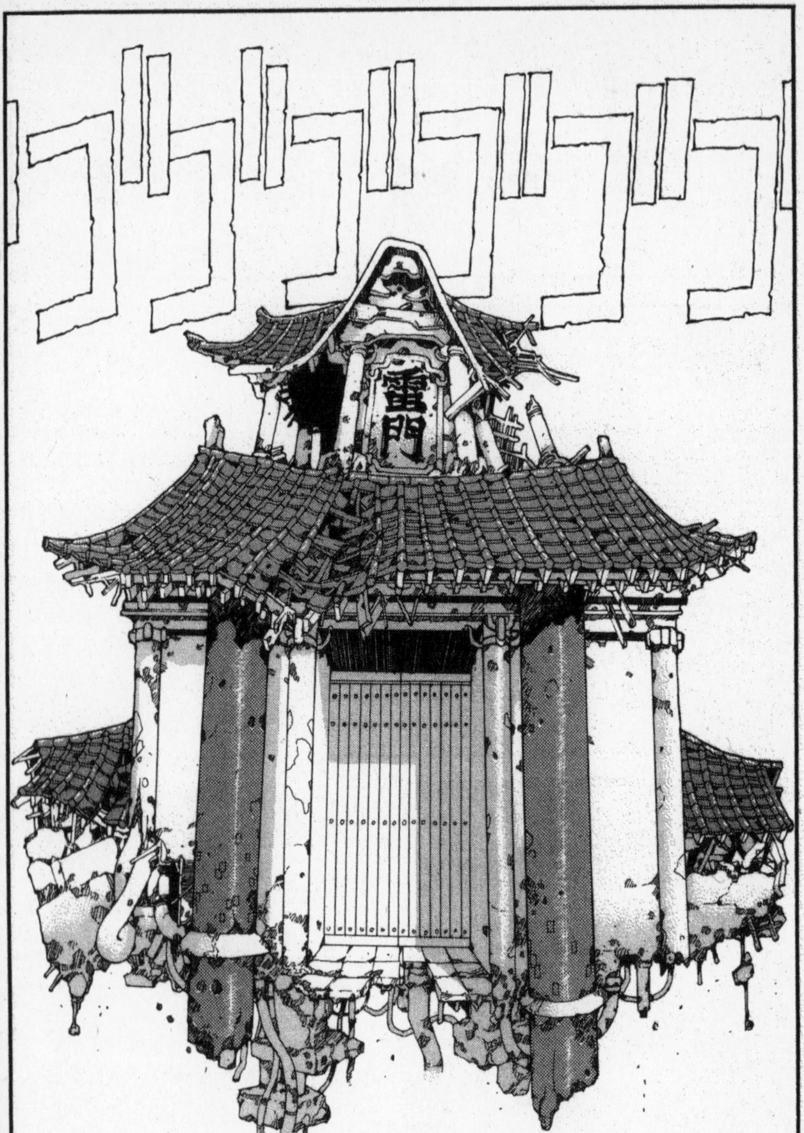
ゴゴゴゴゴゴ

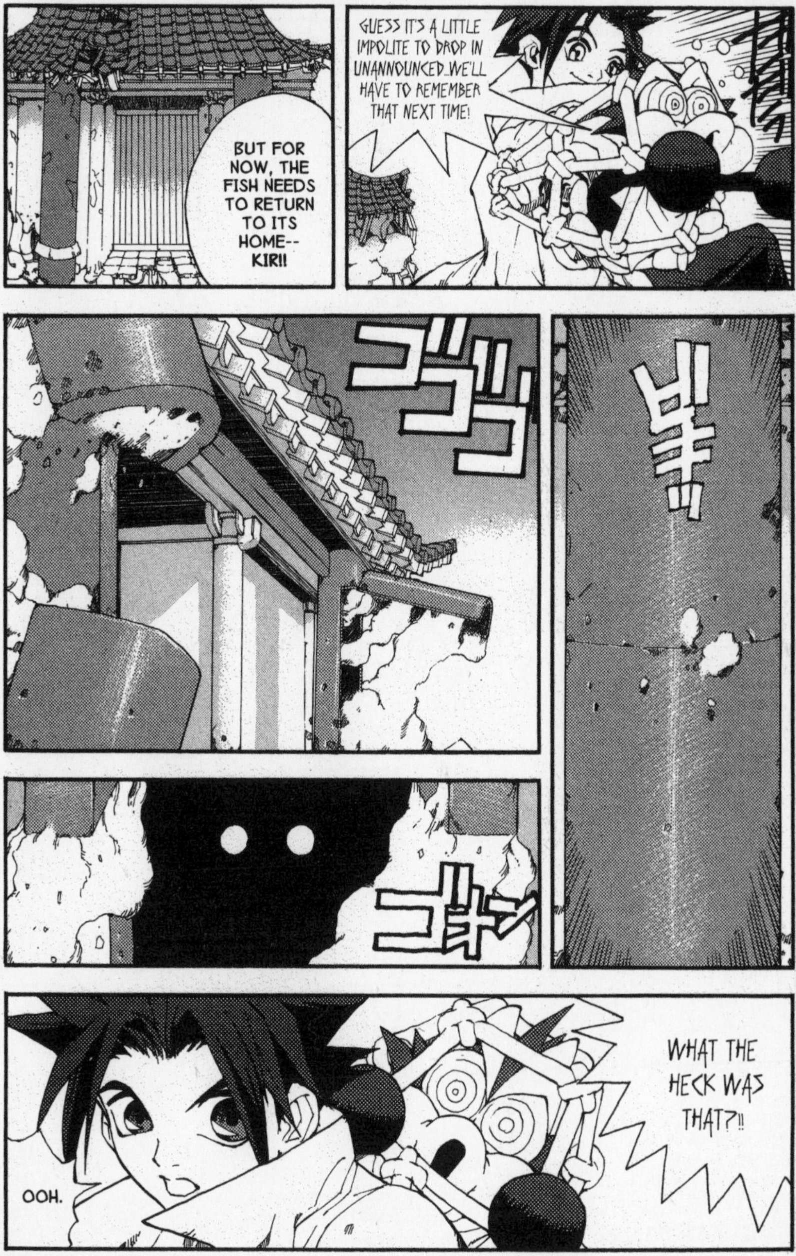
GUESS IT'S A LITTLE IMPOLITE TO DROP IN UNANNOUNCED...WE'LL HAVE TO REMEMBER THAT NEXT TIME!
BUT FOR NOW, THE FISH NEEDS TO RETURN TO ITS HOME-- KIR!!
ゴゴゴ
ゴオン
WHAT THE HECK WAS THAT?!!
OOH.

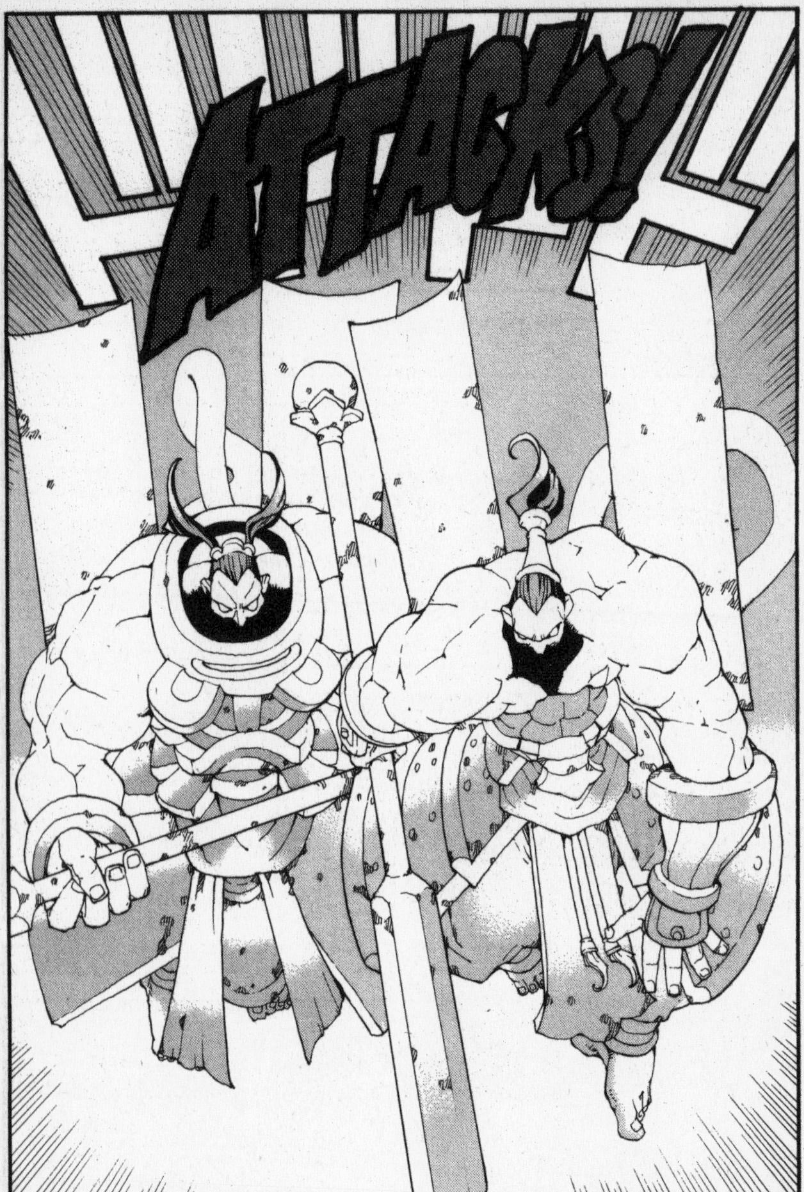
ATTACKS!!

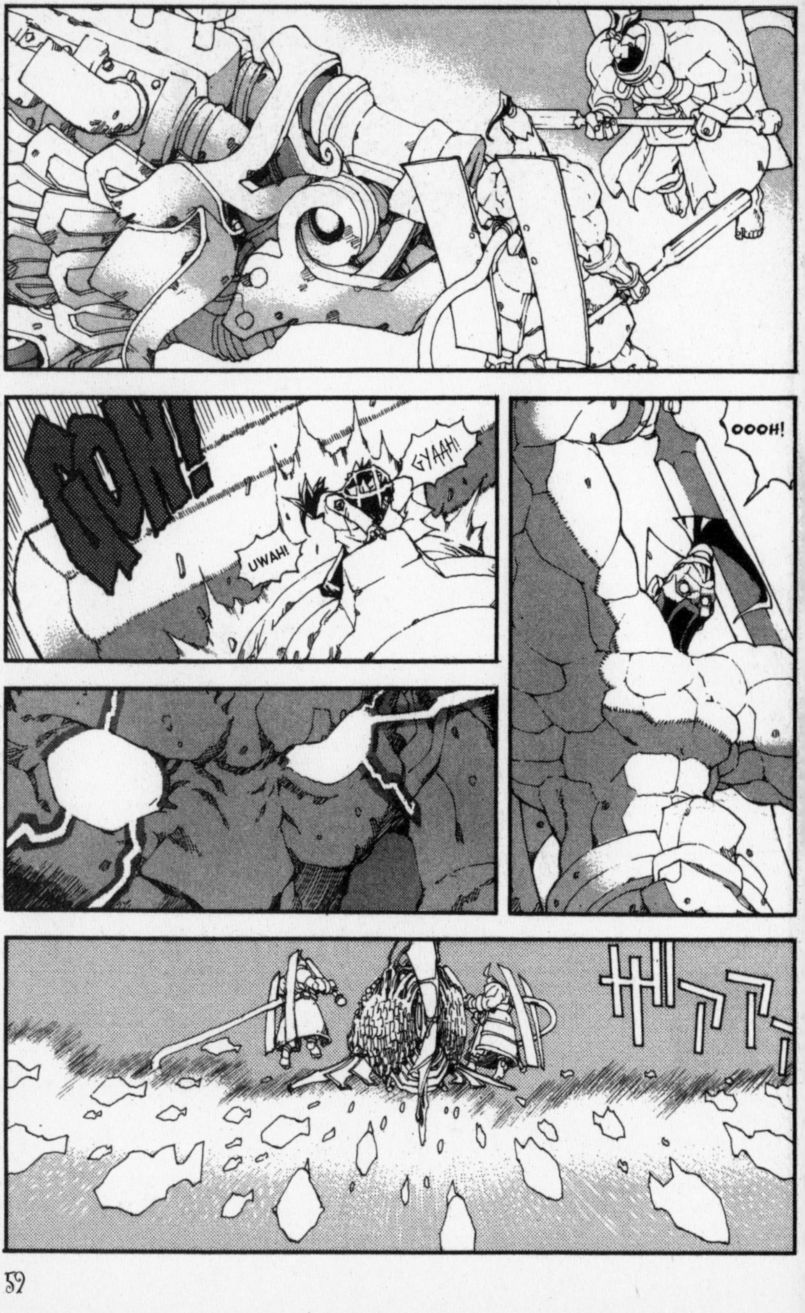
OOOH!
GYAAH!
UWAH!

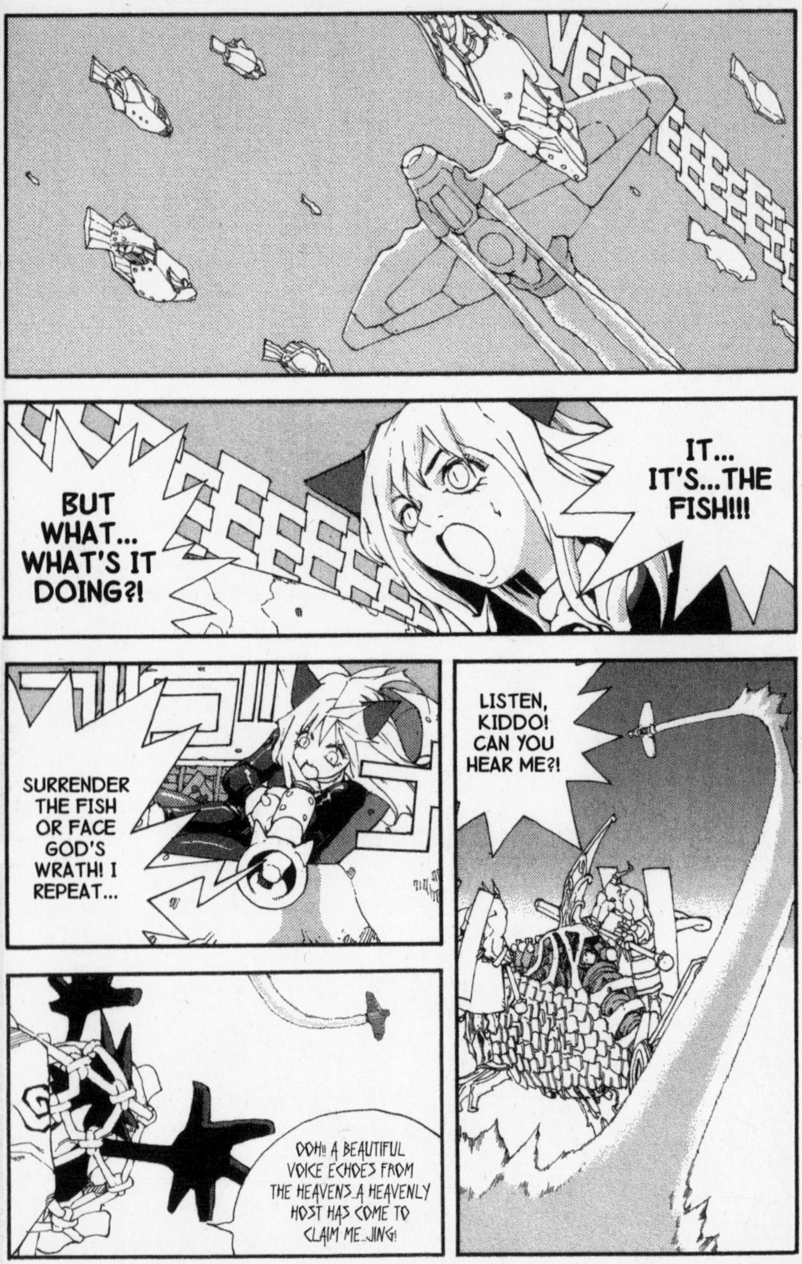
IT... IT'S...THE FISH!!!
BUT WHAT... WHAT'S IT DOING?!
LISTEN, KIDDO! CAN YOU HEAR ME?!
SURRENDER THE FISH OR FACE GOD'S WRATH! I REPEAT...
OOH!! A BEAUTIFUL VOICE ECHOES FROM THE HEAVENS...A HEAVENLY HOST HAS COME TO CLAIM ME...JING!

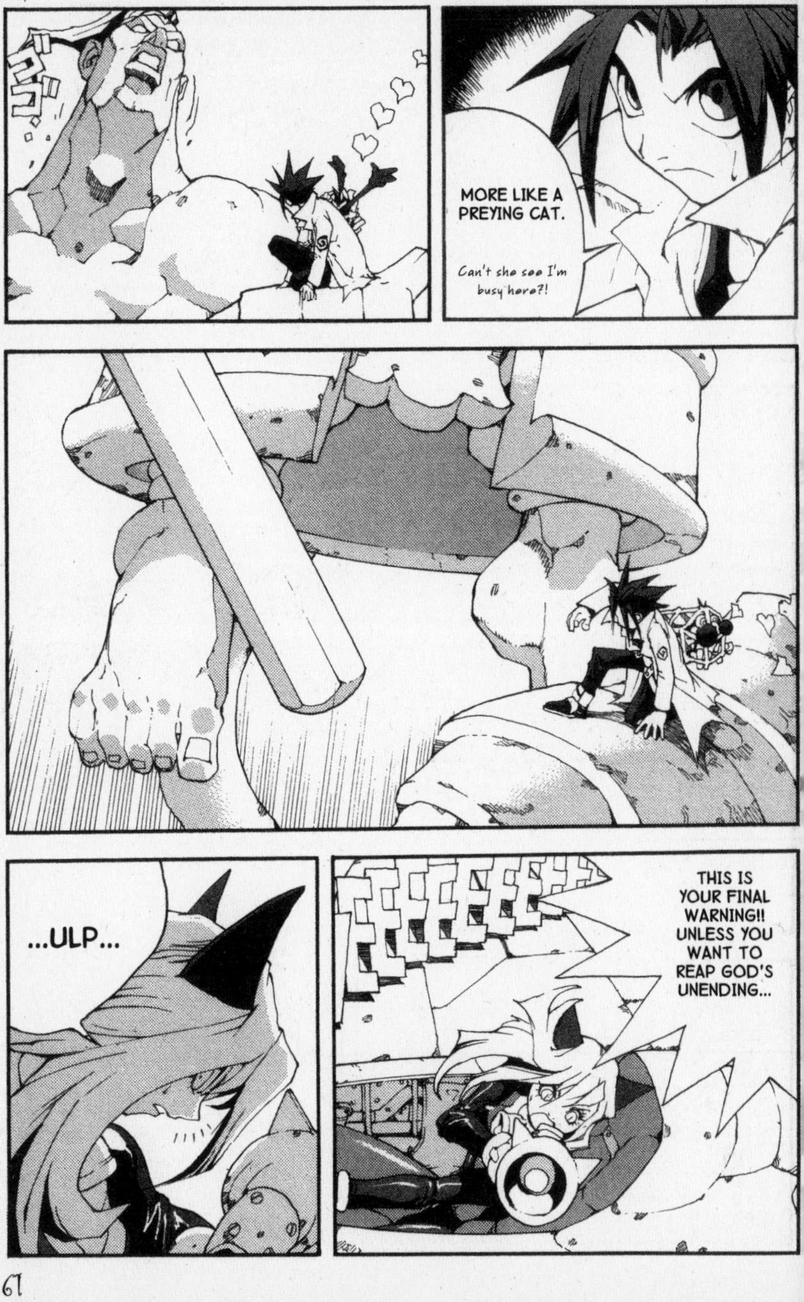
MORE LIKE A PREYING CAT.
Can't she see I'm busy here?!
THIS IS YOUR FINAL WARNING!! UNLESS YOU WANT TO REAP GOD'S UNENDING...
...ULP...

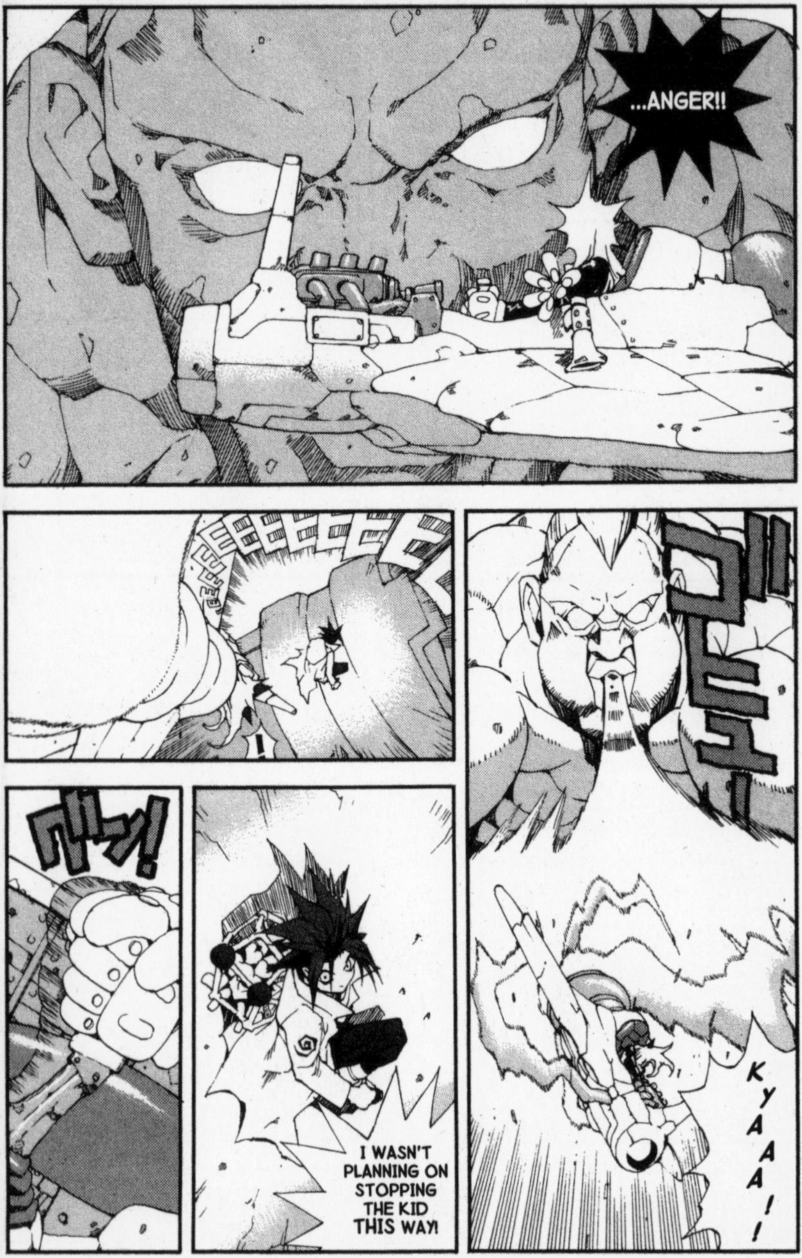
...ANGER!!
KYAAAA!!
I WASN'T PLANNING ON STOPPING THE KID THIS WAY!

PHEEEEEEWWW.

FORGIVE THE INTRUSION...

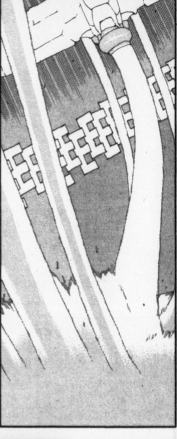

...BUT IT LOOKS LIKE GOD'S UNENDING ANGER ISN'T TOO PICKY!

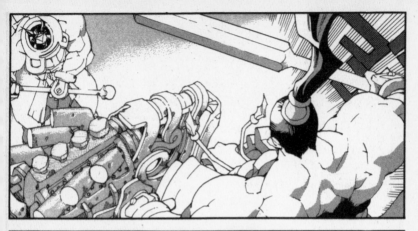

I SWEAR THIS FISH'S HOME IS **GONNA** BE THE AFTERLIFE WHEN I GET THROUGH WITH IT!!

...THERE!!

NNNNN...

ZING

KIIIIIRRRRR!

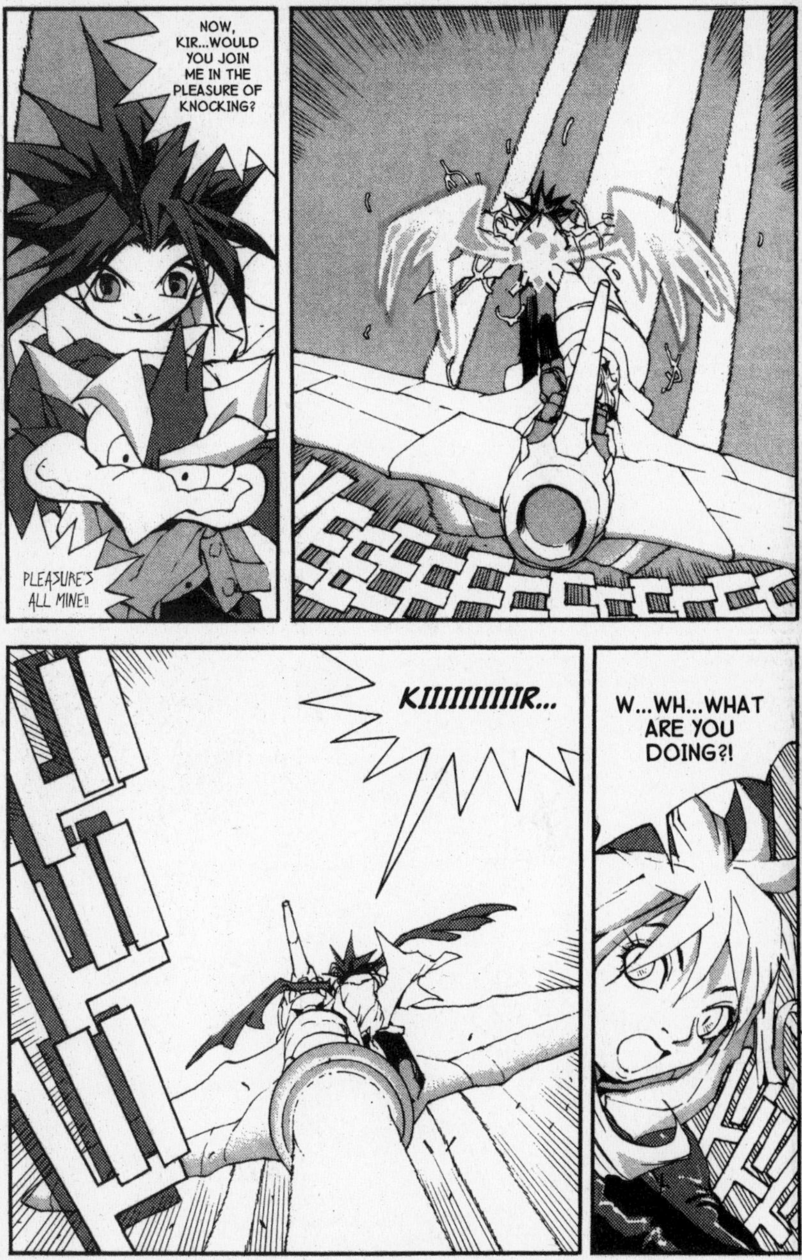
NOW, KIR...WOULD YOU JOIN ME IN THE PLEASURE OF KNOCKING?
PLEASURE'S ALL MINE!!
W...WH...WHAT ARE YOU DOING?!
KIIIIIIIIIIR...

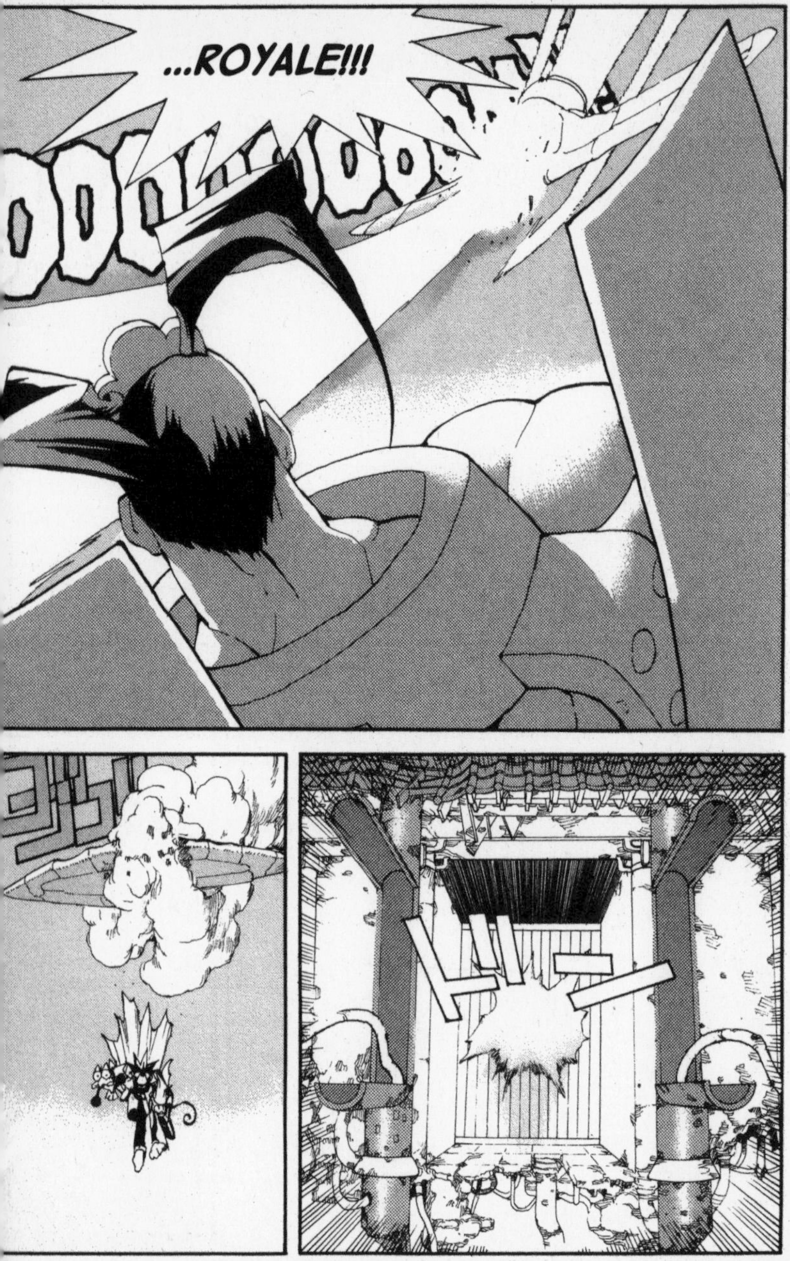
...ROYALE!!!

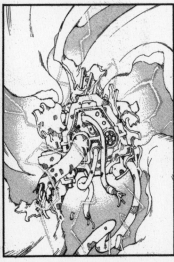

WAIT--WHAT
ARE YOU--?!!

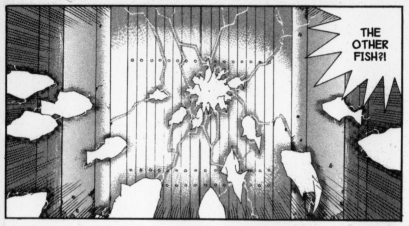

THE OTHER FISH?!

THEY DO LOVE THEIR ELECTRICITY...AND WE AIM TO PLEASE!!

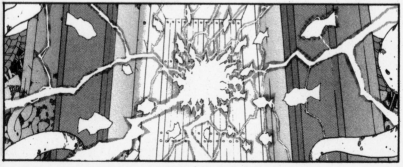

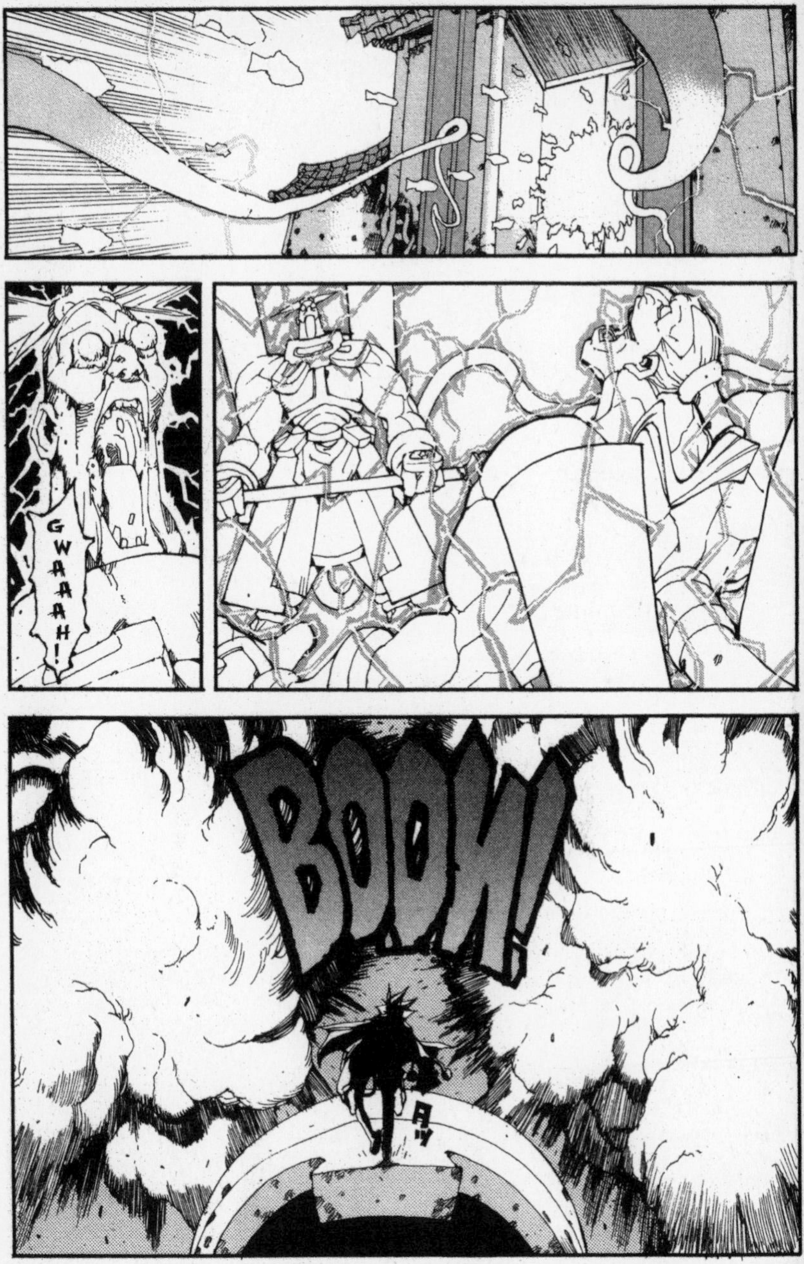
GWAAAH!
BOOM!

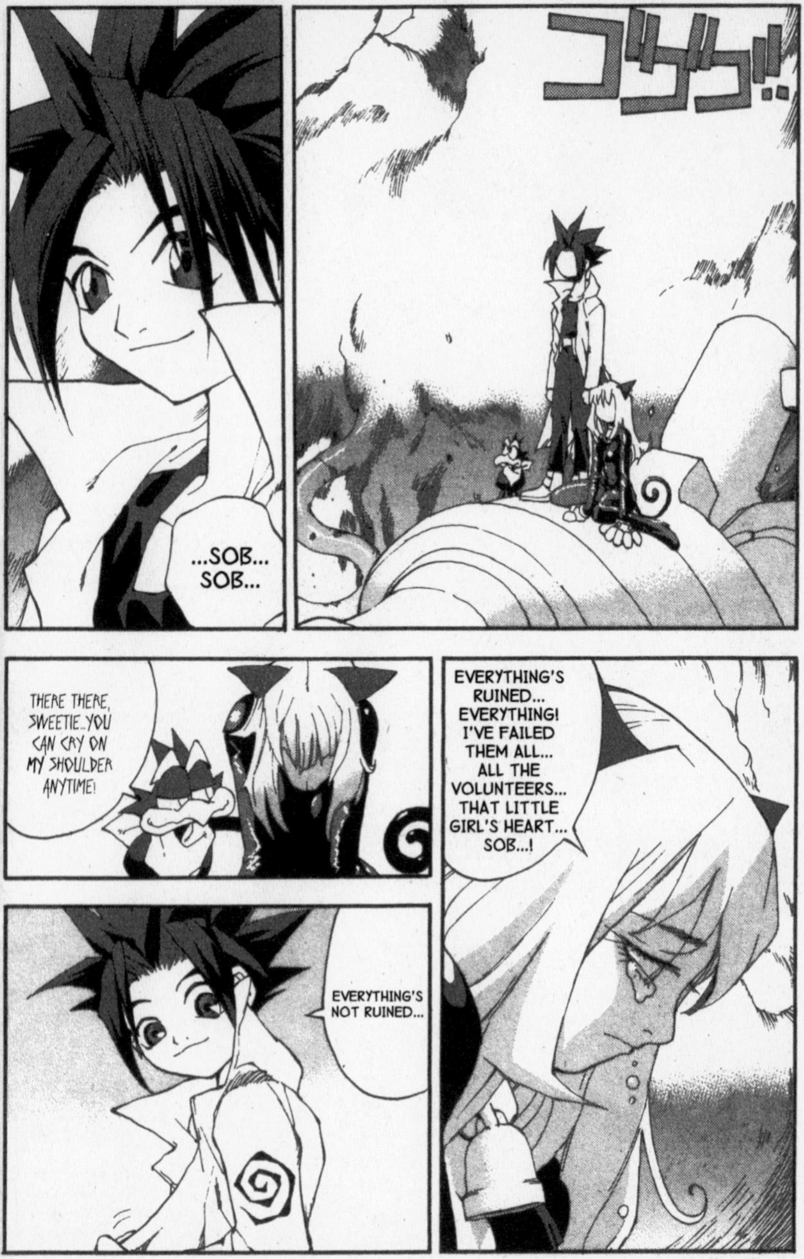
...SOB... SOB...
EVERYTHING'S RUINED... EVERYTHING! I'VE FAILED THEM ALL... ALL THE VOLUNTEERS... THAT LITTLE GIRL'S HEART... SOB...!
THERE THERE, SWEETIE...YOU CAN CRY ON MY SHOULDER ANYTIME!
EVERYTHING'S NOT RUINED...

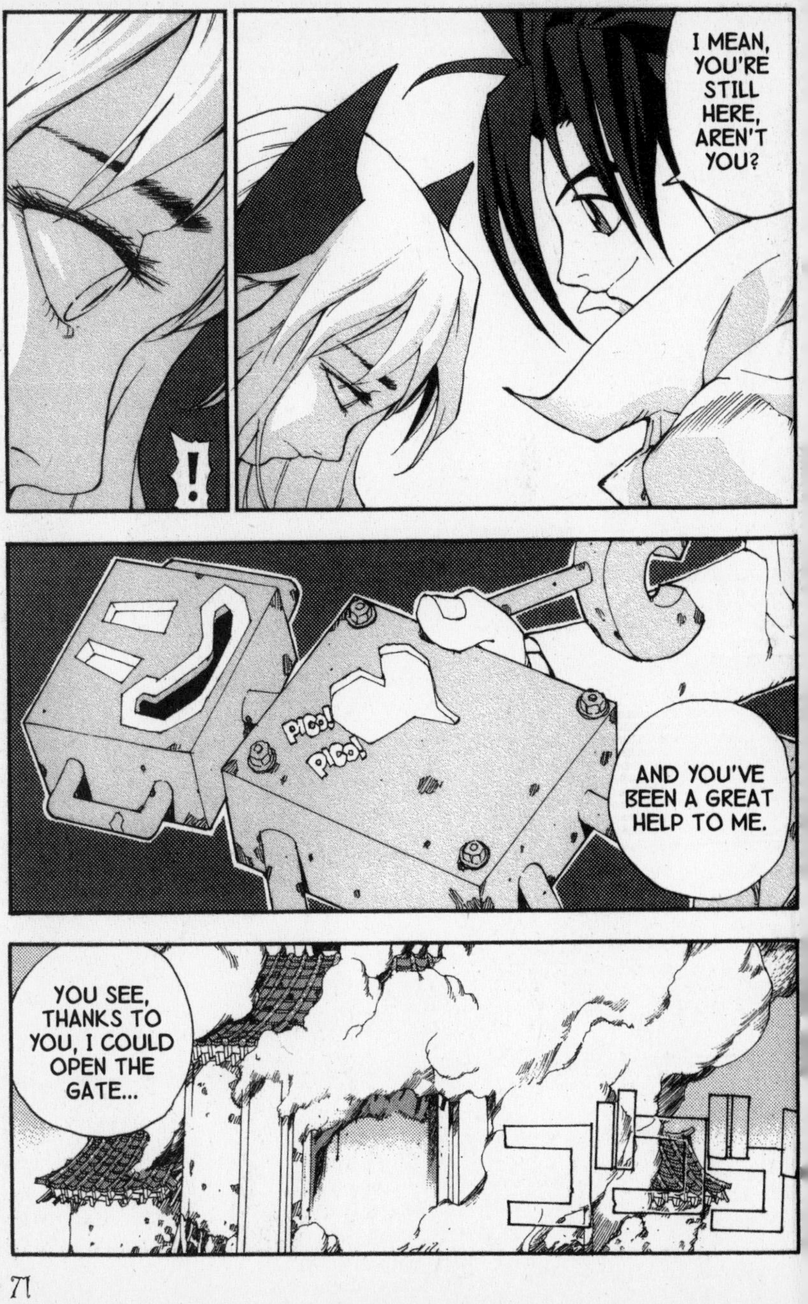
I MEAN, YOU'RE STILL HERE, AREN'T YOU?
!
AND YOU'VE BEEN A GREAT HELP TO ME.
PICO!
PICO!
YOU SEE, THANKS TO YOU, I COULD OPEN THE GATE...

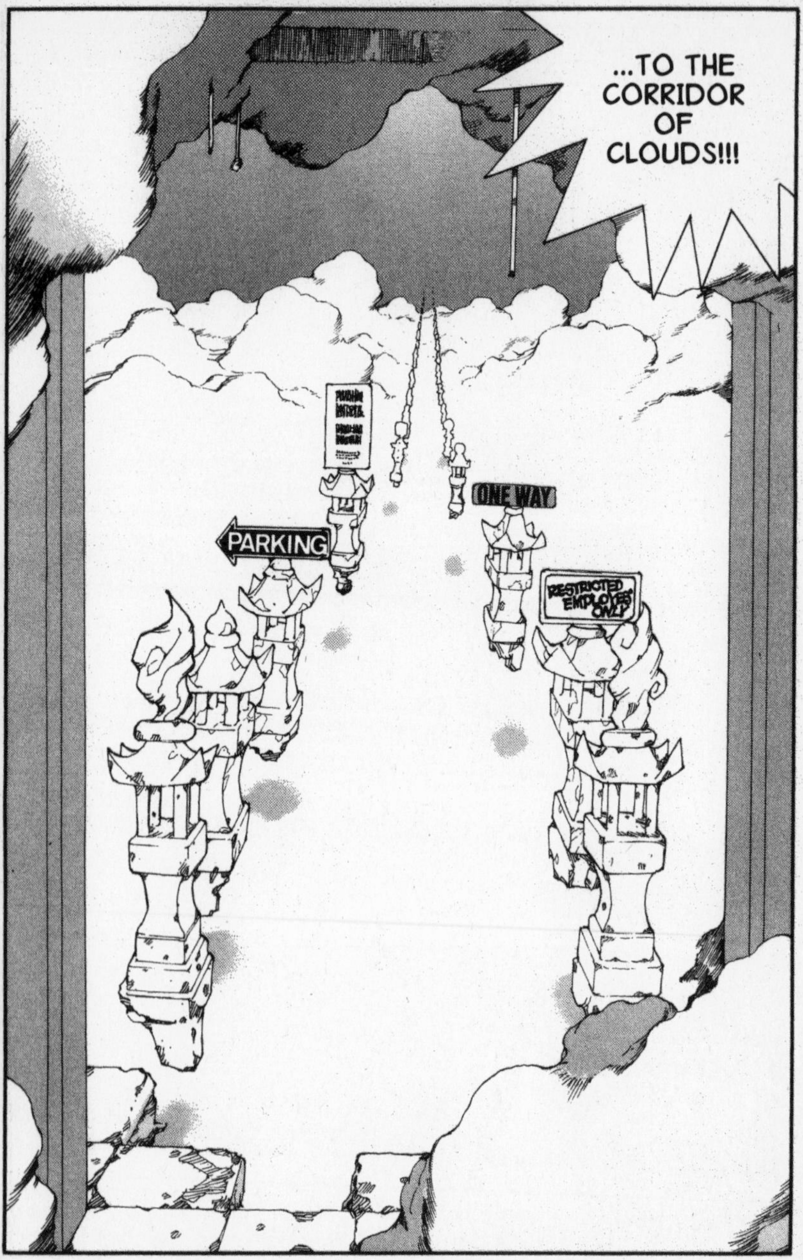
...TO THE CORRIDOR OF CLOUDS!!!
ONE WAY
PARKING
RESTRICTED EMPLOYEES' ONLY

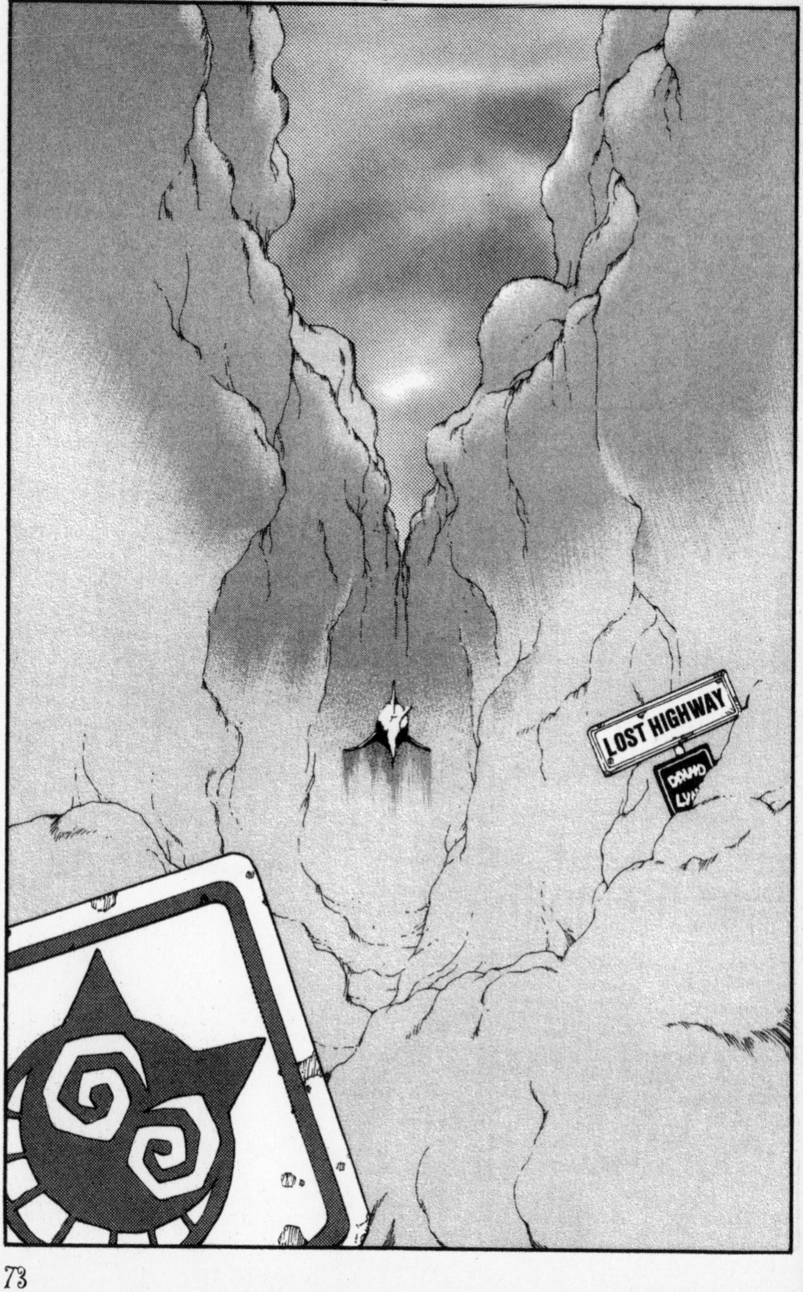
LOST HIGHWAY

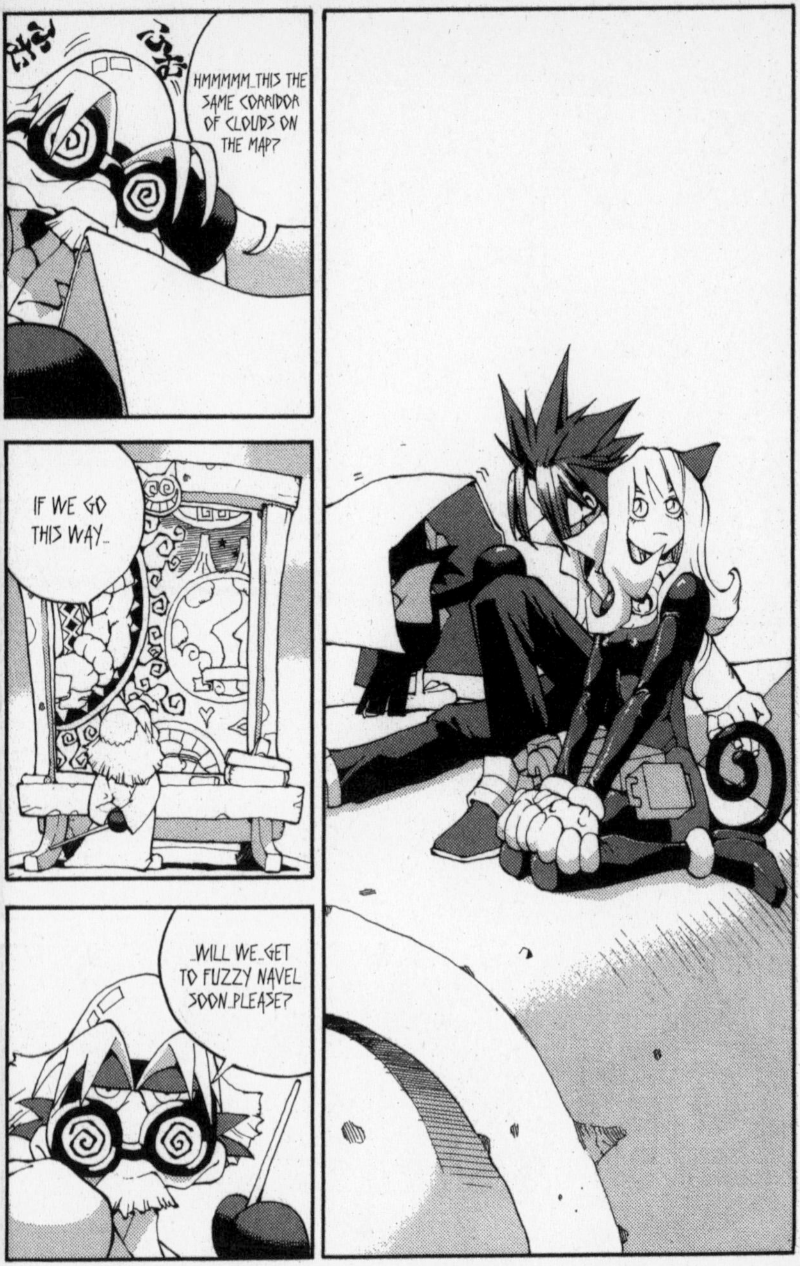
HMMMMM...THIS THE SAME CORRIDOR OF CLOUDS ON THE MAP?
IF WE GO THIS WAY...
...WILL WE...GET TO FUZZY NAVEL SOON...PLEASE?

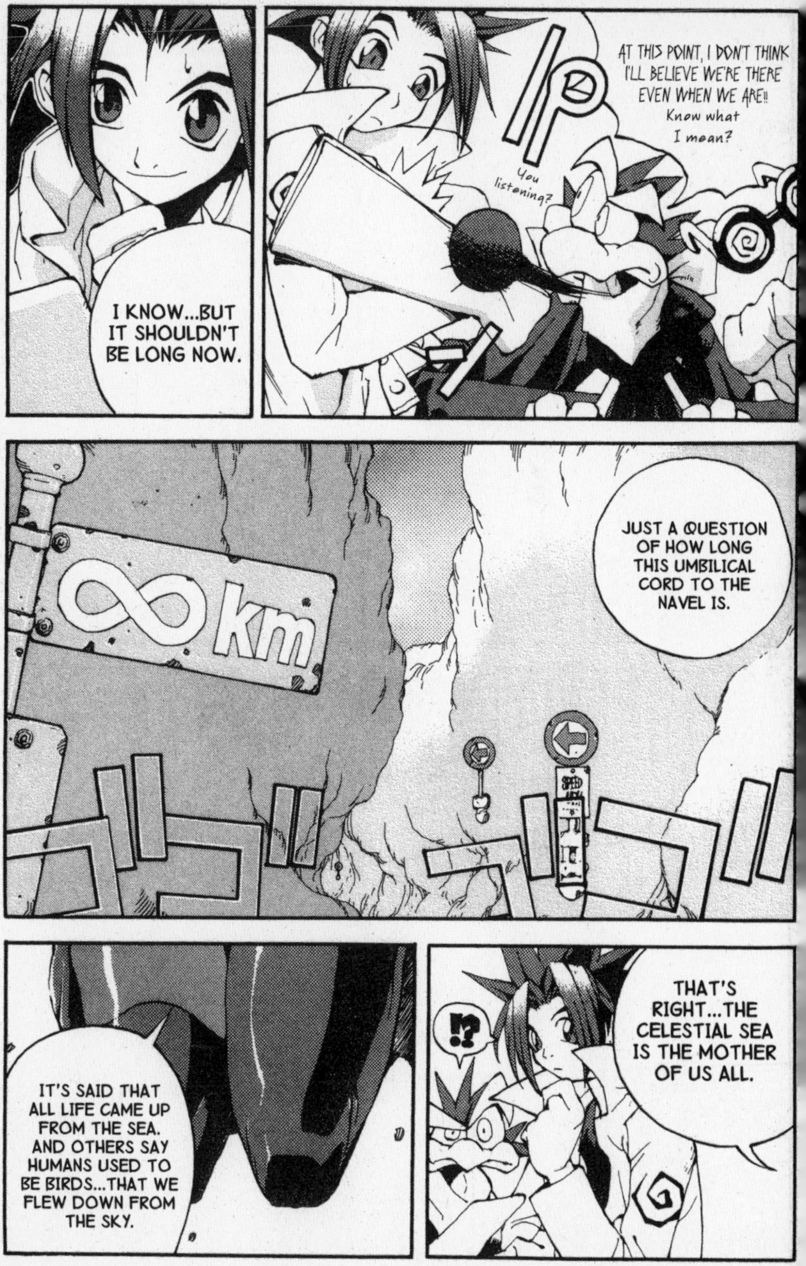
AT THIS POINT, I DON'T THINK I'LL BELIEVE WE'RE THERE EVEN WHEN WE ARE!!
Know what I mean?
You listening?
I KNOW...BUT IT SHOULDN'T BE LONG NOW.
JUST A QUESTION OF HOW LONG THIS UMBILICAL CORD TO THE NAVEL IS.
∞km
!?
THAT'S RIGHT...THE CELESTIAL SEA IS THE MOTHER OF US ALL.
IT'S SAID THAT ALL LIFE CAME UP FROM THE SEA. AND OTHERS SAY HUMANS USED TO BE BIRDS...THAT WE FLEW DOWN FROM THE SKY.

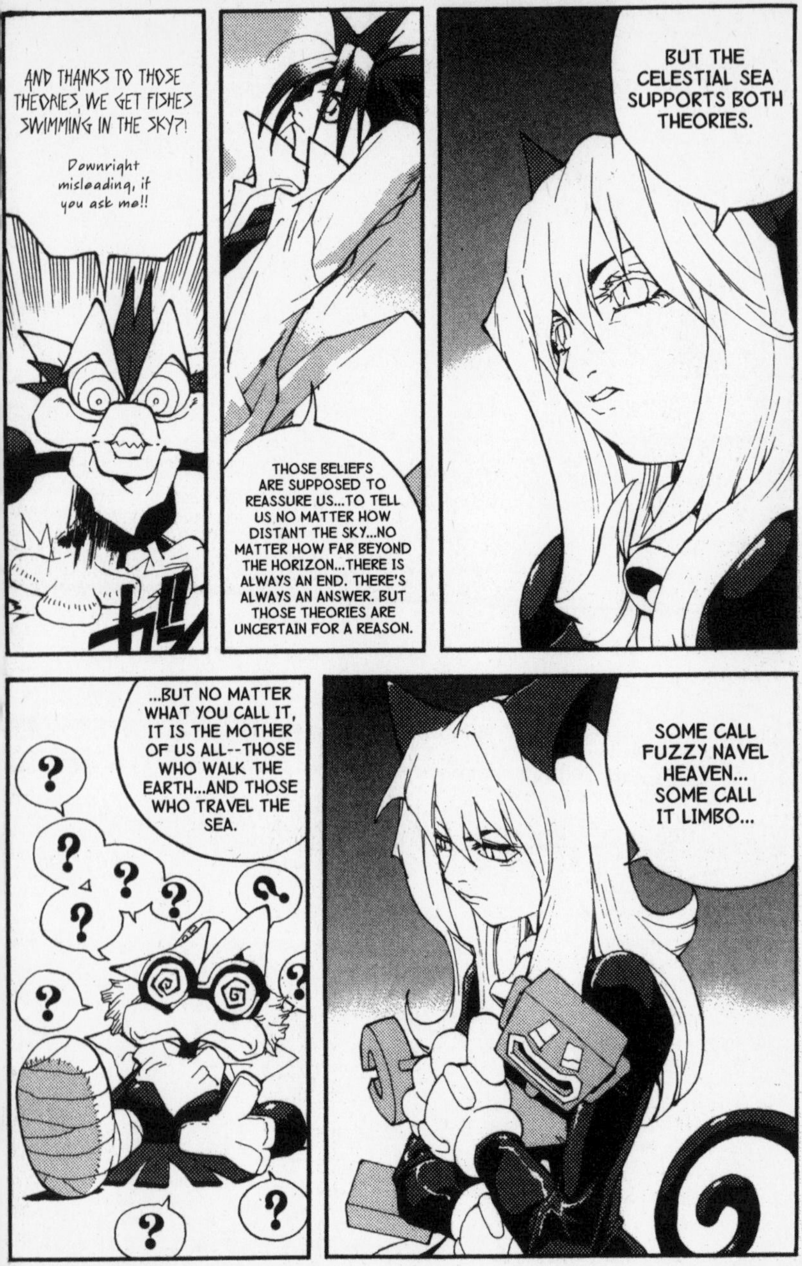
BUT THE CELESTIAL SEA SUPPORTS BOTH THEORIES.
THOSE BELIEFS ARE SUPPOSED TO REASSURE US...TO TELL US NO MATTER HOW DISTANT THE SKY...NO MATTER HOW FAR BEYOND THE HORIZON...THERE IS ALWAYS AN END. THERE'S ALWAYS AN ANSWER. BUT THOSE THEORIES ARE UNCERTAIN FOR A REASON.
AND THANKS TO THOSE THEORIES, WE GET FISHES SWIMMING IN THE SKY?!
Downright misleading, if you ask me!!
SOME CALL FUZZY NAVEL HEAVEN... SOME CALL IT LIMBO...
...BUT NO MATTER WHAT YOU CALL IT, IT IS THE MOTHER OF US ALL--THOSE WHO WALK THE EARTH...AND THOSE WHO TRAVEL THE SEA.

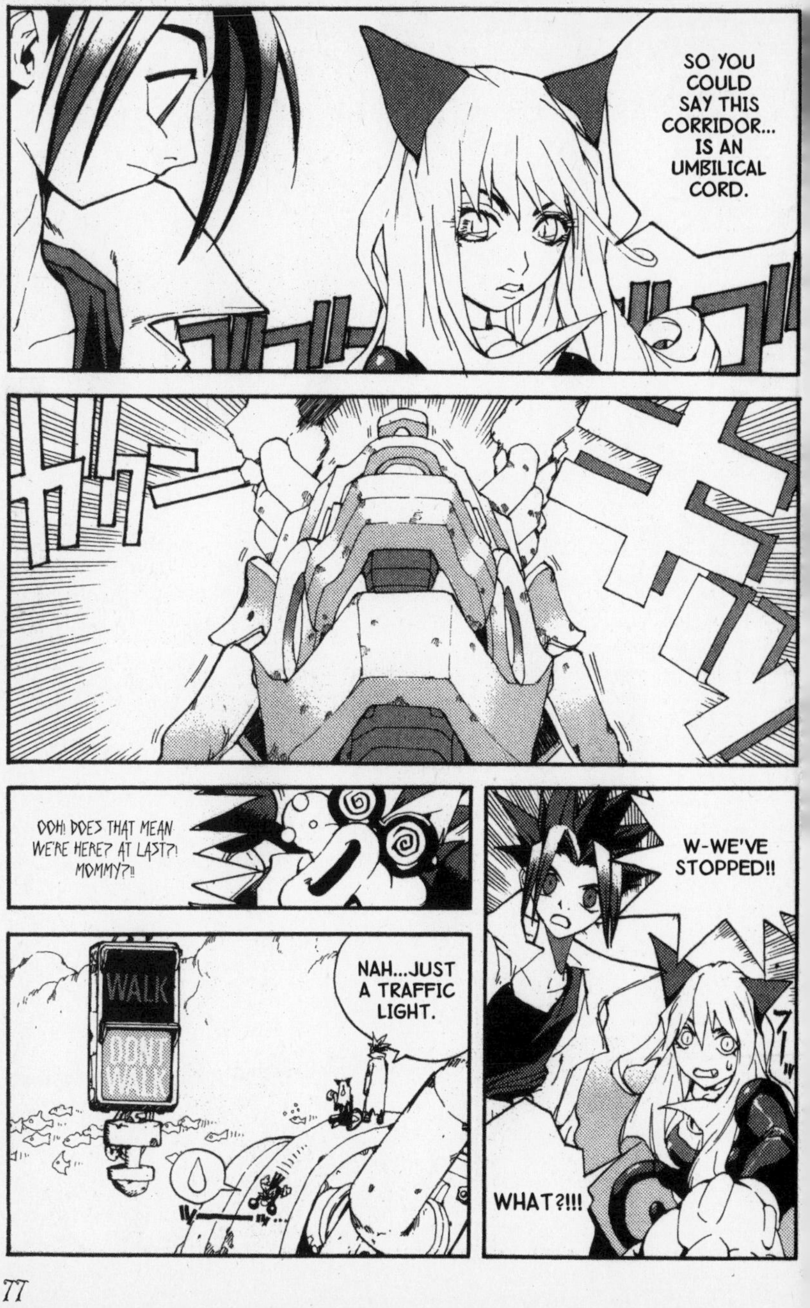
SO YOU COULD SAY THIS CORRIDOR... IS AN UMBILICAL CORD.
W-WE'VE STOPPED!!
WHAT?!!!
OOH! DOES THAT MEAN WE'RE HERE? AT LAST?! MOMMY?!!
WALK
DONT WALK
NAH...JUST A TRAFFIC LIGHT.

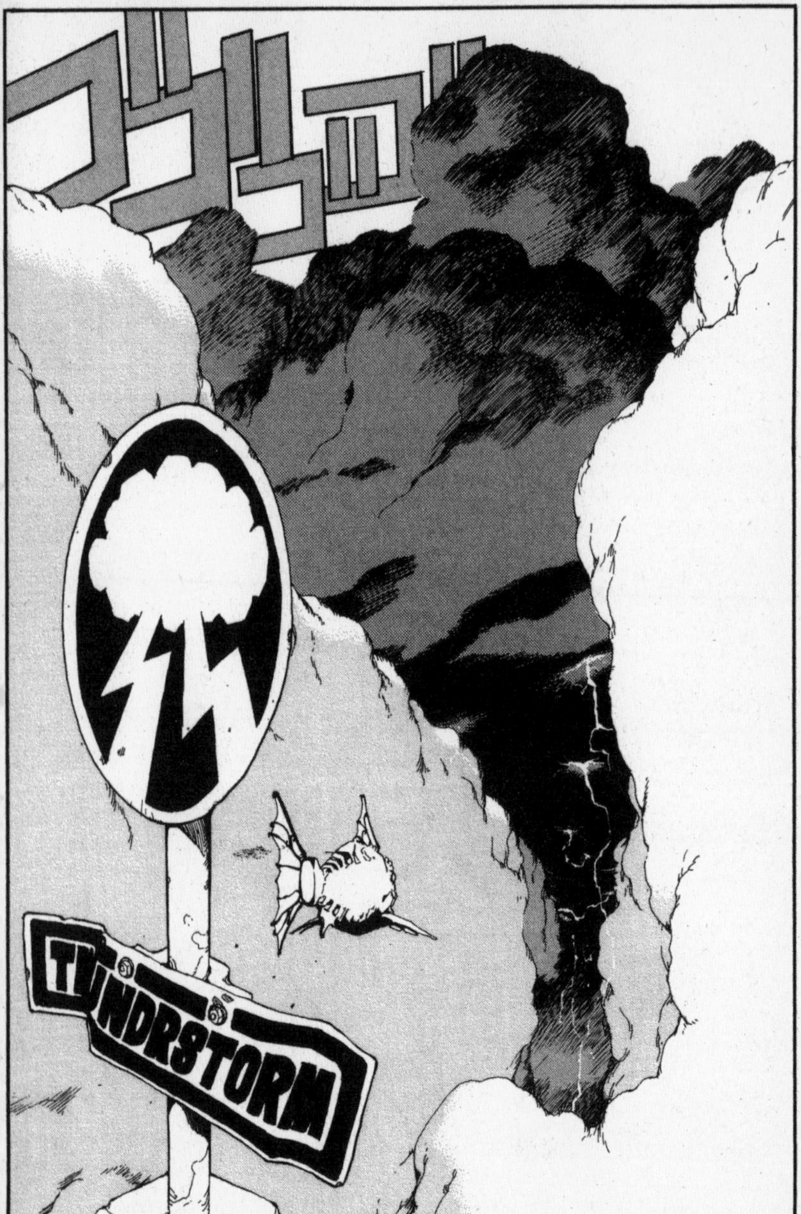
ゴゴゴゴ
TH
UNDRSTORM

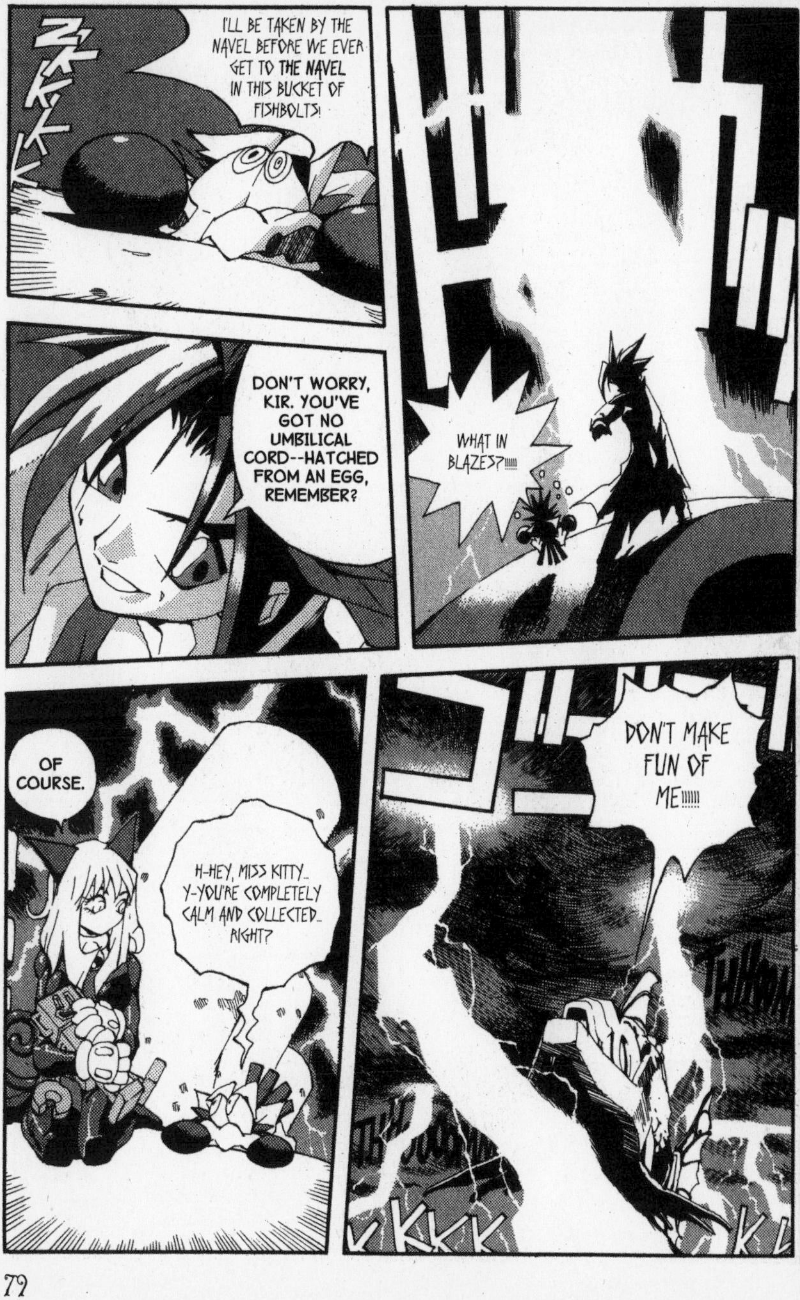
WHAT IN BLAZES?!!!!!!
I'LL BE TAKEN BY THE NAVEL BEFORE WE EVER GET TO THE NAVEL IN THIS BUCKET OF FISHBOLTS!
DON'T WORRY, KIR. YOU'VE GOT NO UMBILICAL CORD--HATCHED FROM AN EGG, REMEMBER?
DON'T MAKE FUN OF ME!!!!!!
H-HEY, MISS KITTY... Y-YOU'RE COMPLETELY CALM AND COLLECTED... RIGHT?
OF COURSE.

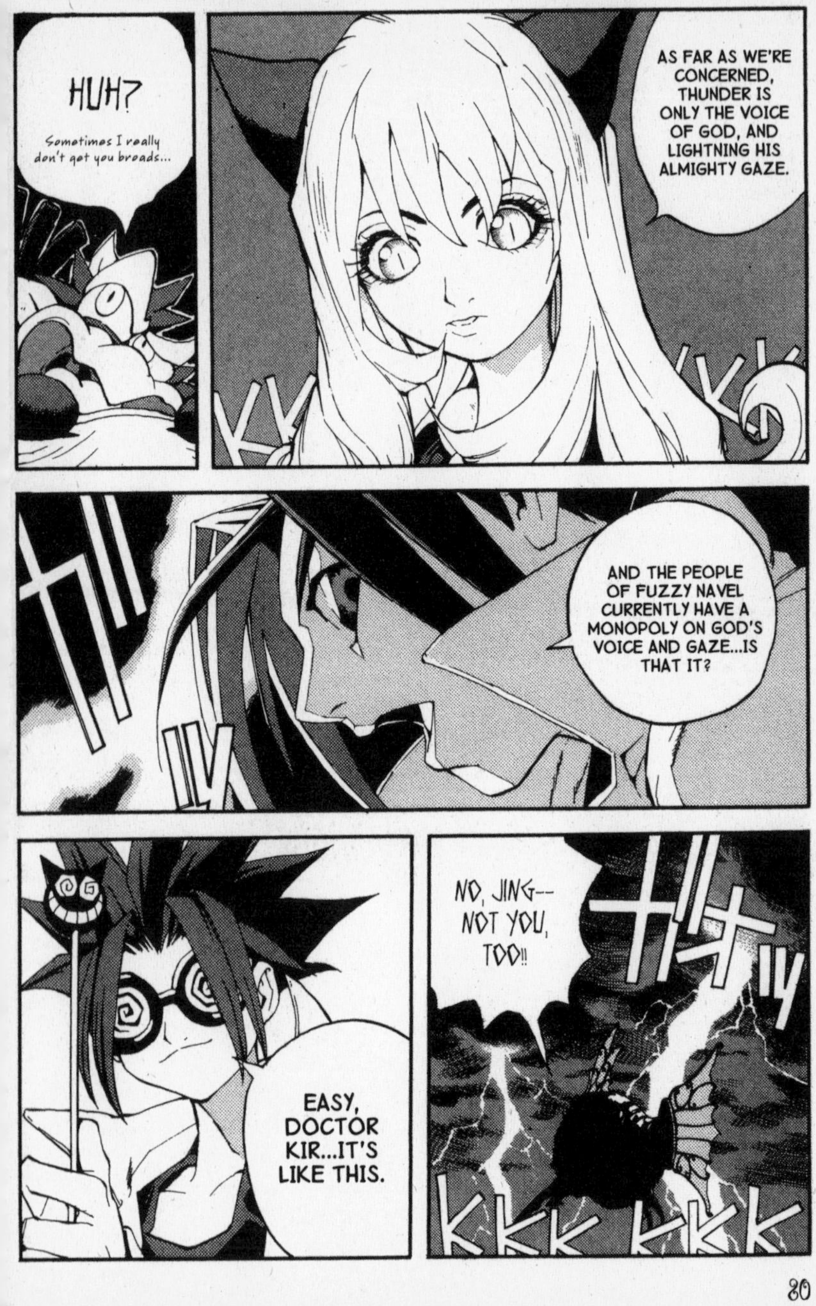
AS FAR AS WE'RE CONCERNED, THUNDER IS ONLY THE VOICE OF GOD, AND LIGHTNING HIS ALMIGHTY GAZE.
HUH?
Sometimes I really don't get you broads...
AND THE PEOPLE OF FUZZY NAVEL CURRENTLY HAVE A MONOPOLY ON GOD'S VOICE AND GAZE...IS THAT IT?
NO, JING-- NOT YOU, TOO!!
EASY, DOCTOR KIR...IT'S LIKE THIS.

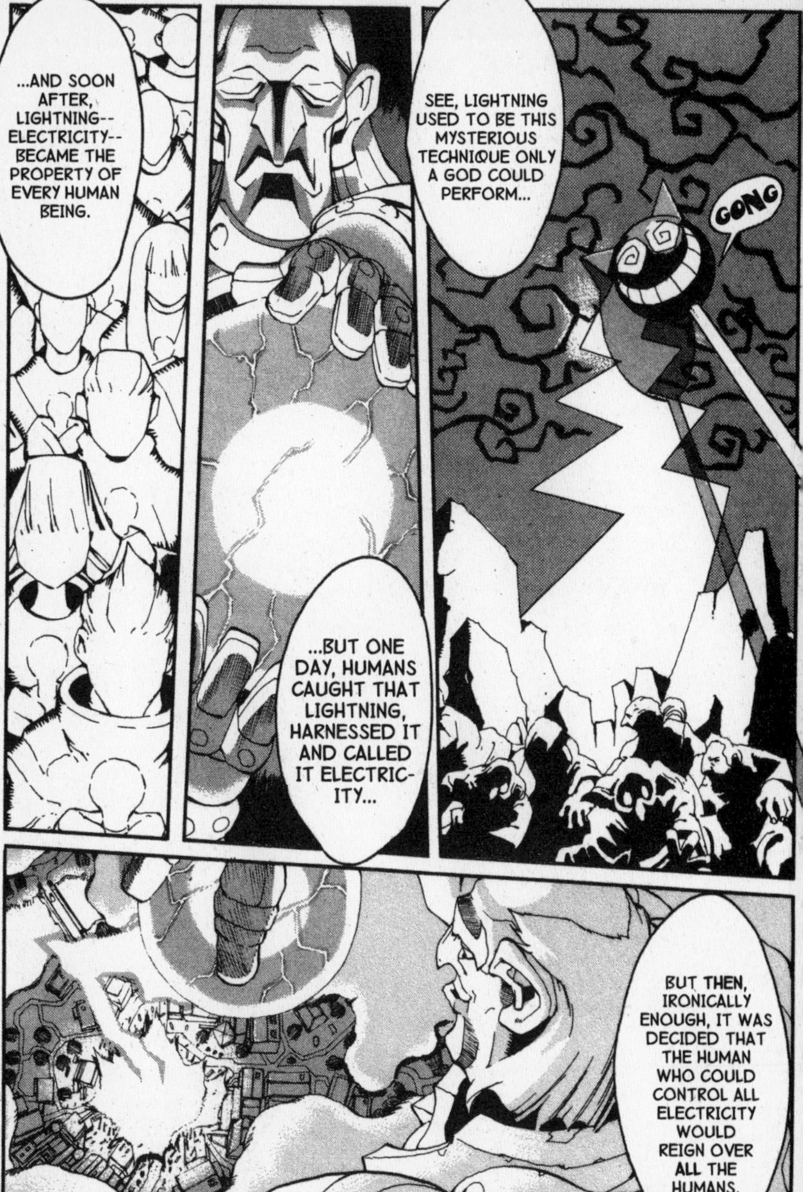
SEE, LIGHTNING USED TO BE THIS MYSTERIOUS TECHNIQUE ONLY A GOD COULD PERFORM...
GONG
...BUT ONE DAY, HUMANS CAUGHT THAT LIGHTNING, HARNESSED IT AND CALLED IT ELECTRIC-ITY...
...AND SOON AFTER, LIGHTNING--ELECTRICITY--BECAME THE PROPERTY OF EVERY HUMAN BEING.
BUT THEN, IRONICALLY ENOUGH, IT WAS DECIDED THAT THE HUMAN WHO COULD CONTROL ALL ELECTRICITY WOULD REIGN OVER ALL THE HUMANS.

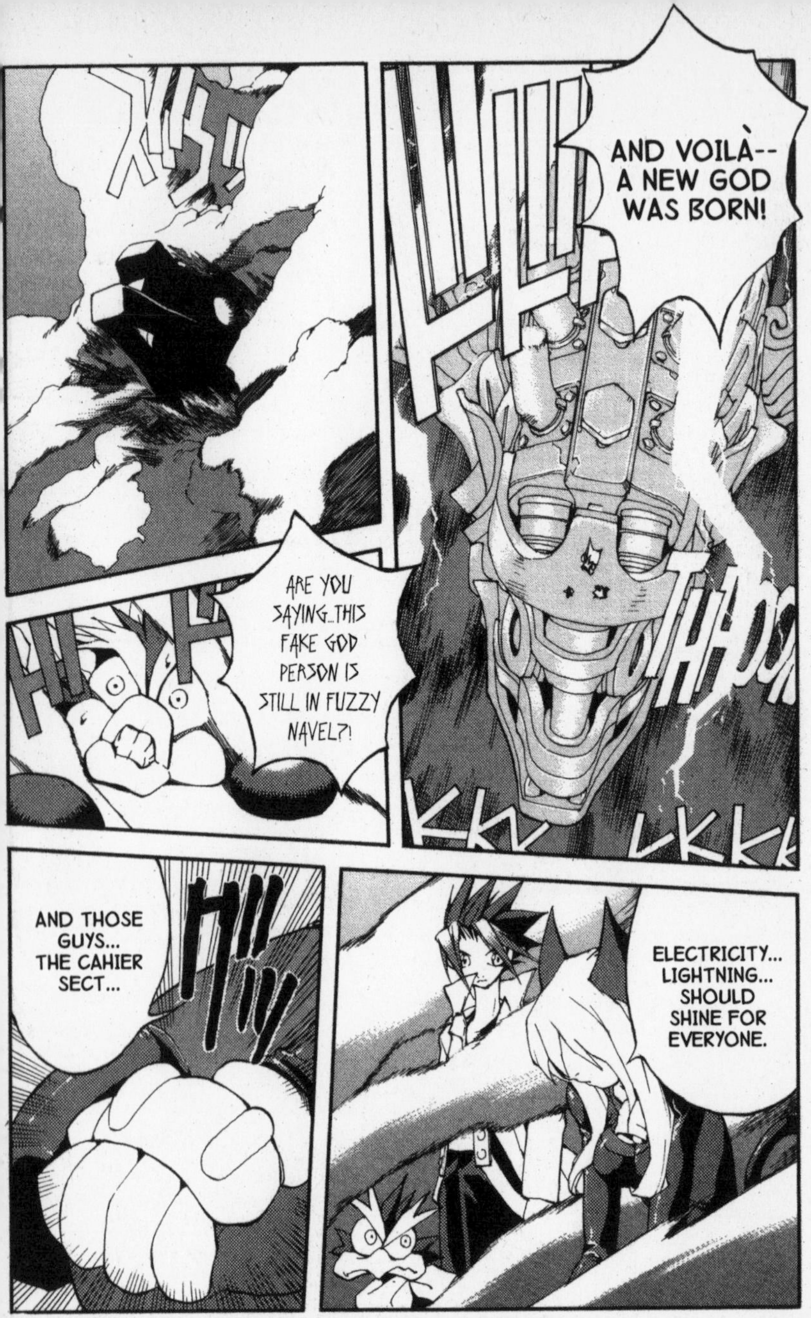
AND VOILÀ-- A NEW GOD WAS BORN!
ARE YOU SAYING...THIS FAKE GOD PERSON IS STILL IN FUZZY NAVEL?!
ELECTRICITY... LIGHTNING... SHOULD SHINE FOR EVERYONE.
AND THOSE GUYS... THE CAHIER SECT...

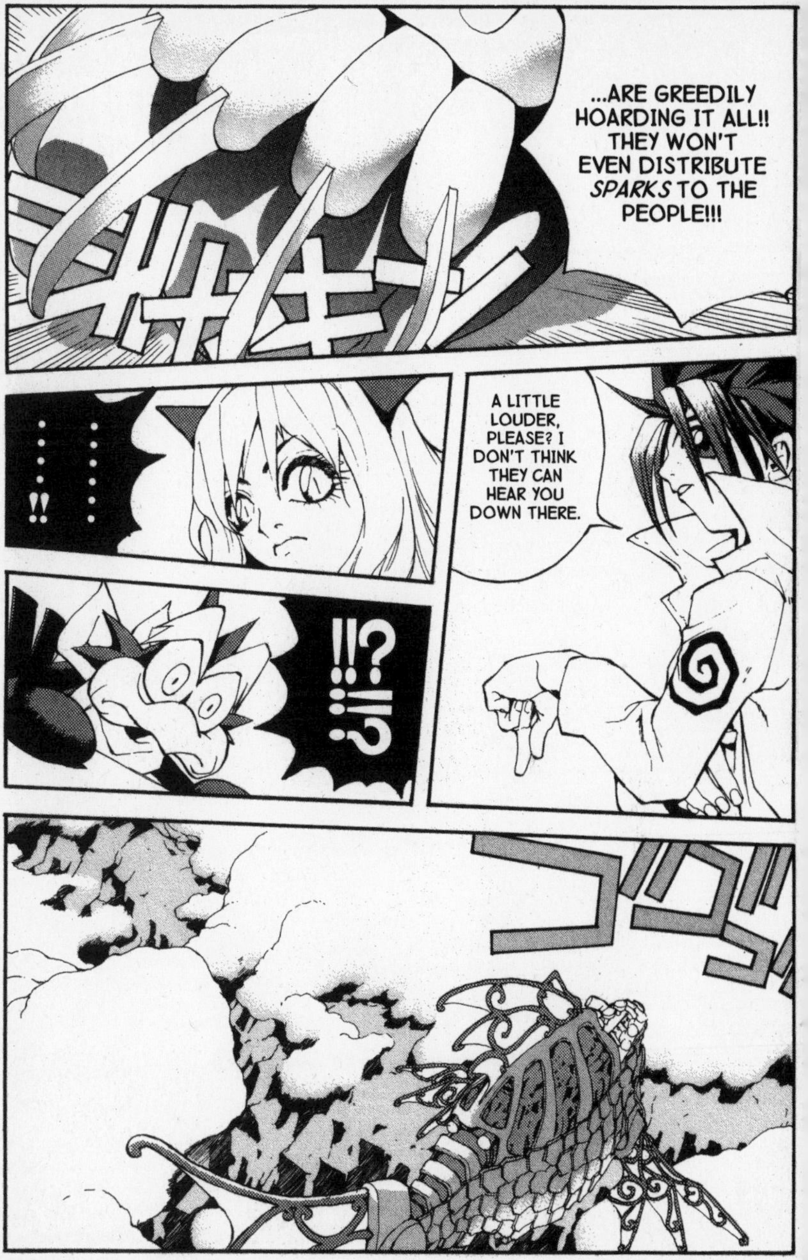
...ARE GREEDILY HOARDING IT ALL!! THEY WON'T EVEN DISTRIBUTE *SPARKS* TO THE PEOPLE!!!
A LITTLE LOUDER, PLEASE? I DON'T THINK THEY CAN HEAR YOU DOWN THERE.
......!!
!!?!!?

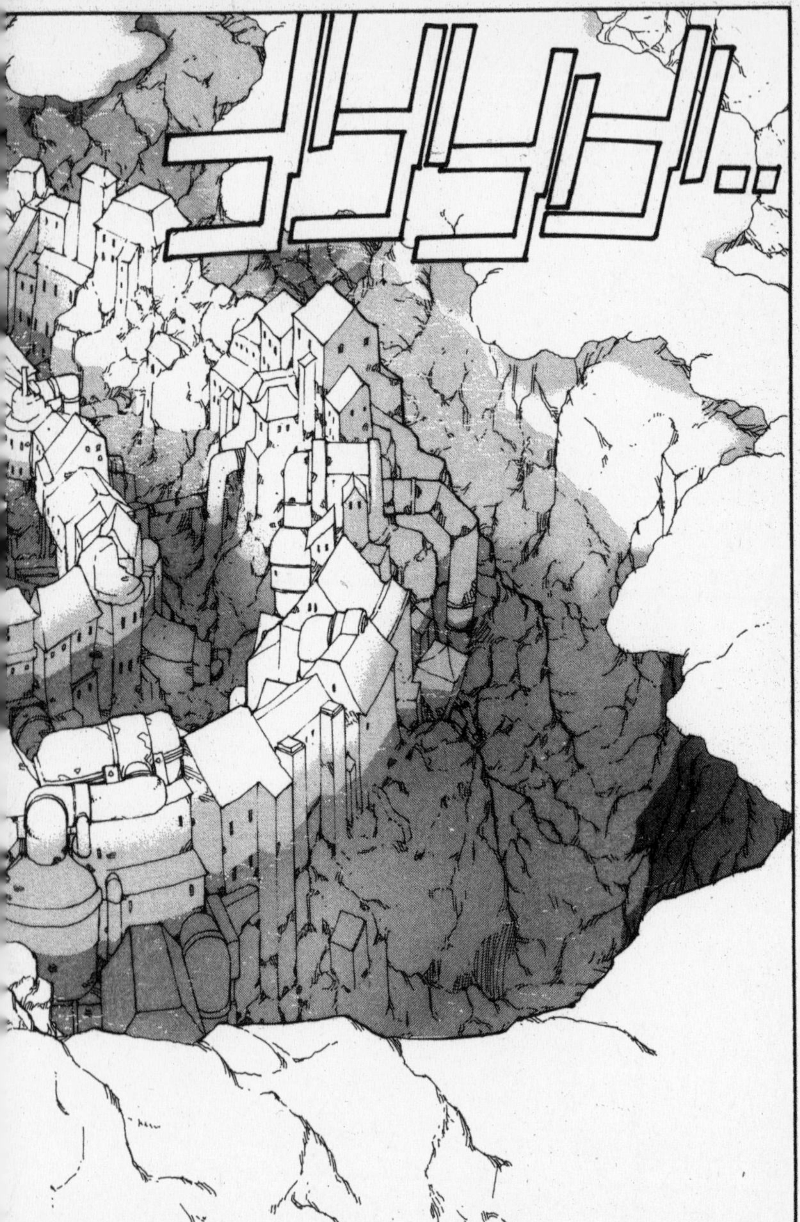
ゴゴゴゴ..

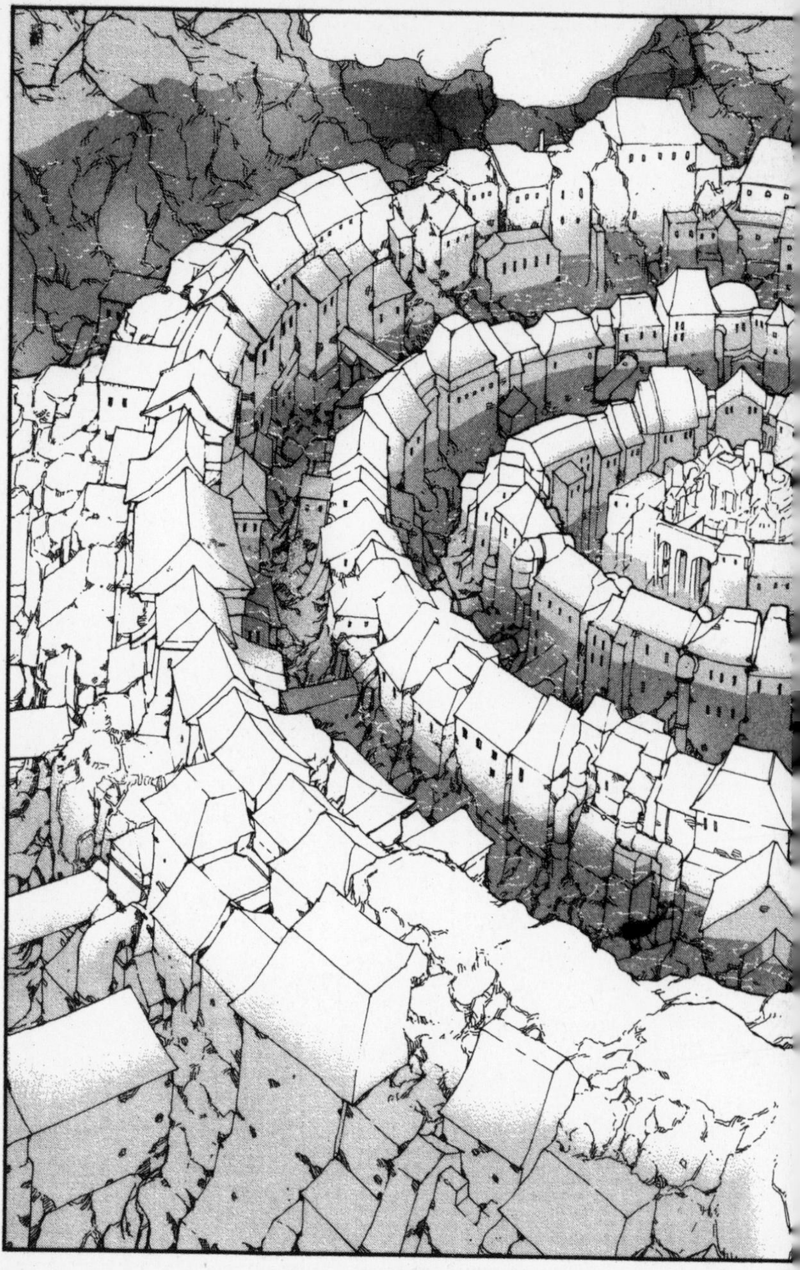

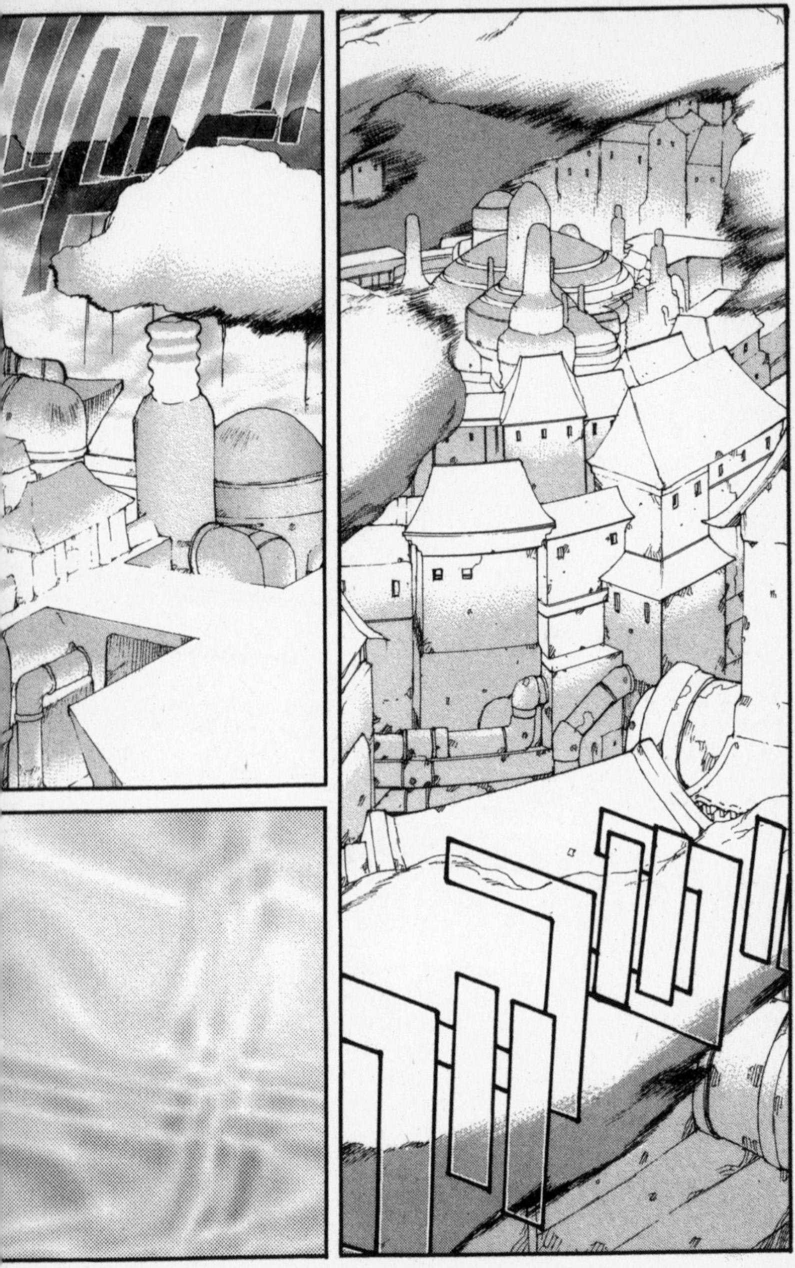

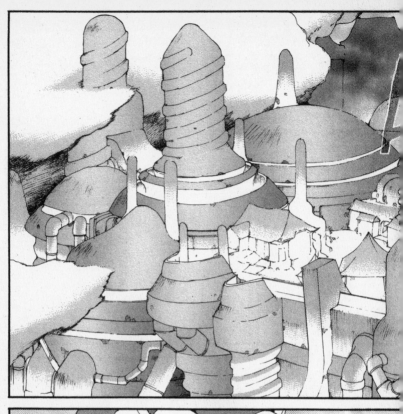

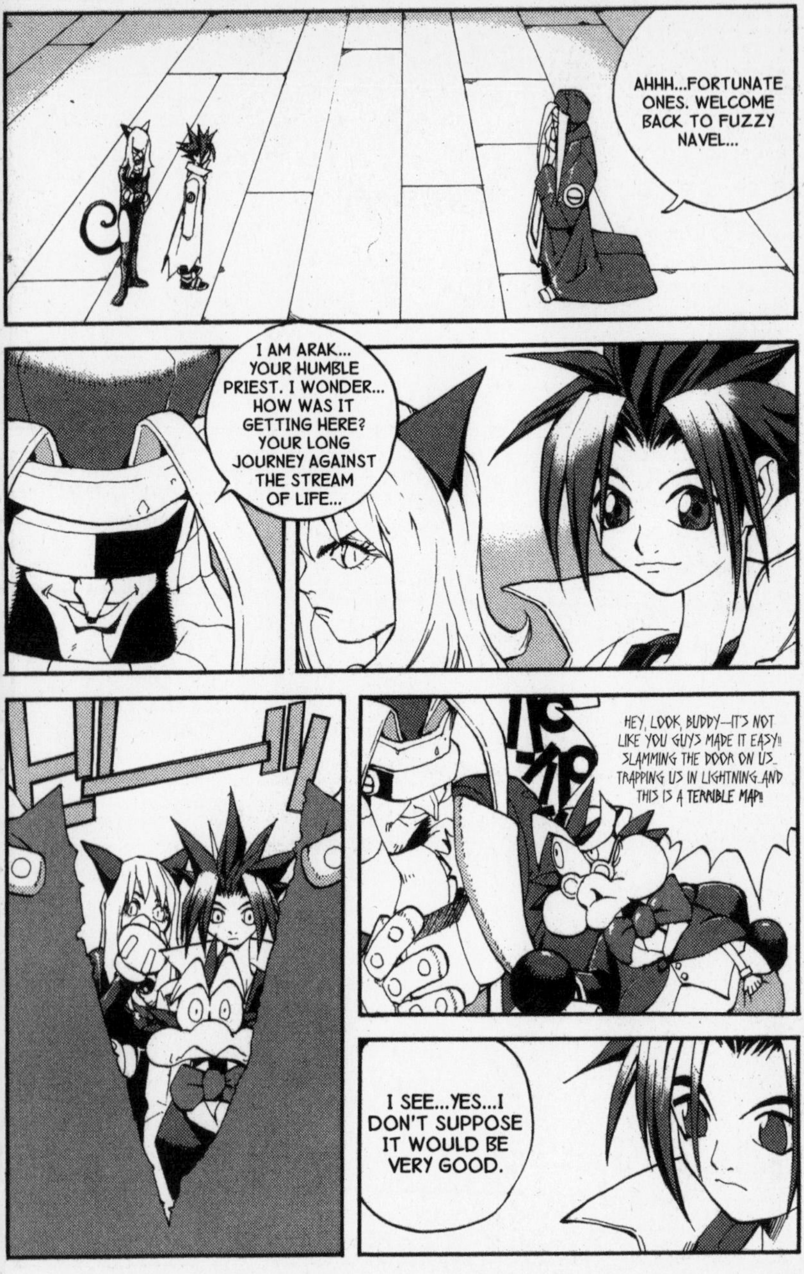
AHHH...FORTUNATE ONES. WELCOME BACK TO FUZZY NAVEL...
I AM ARAK... YOUR HUMBLE PRIEST. I WONDER... HOW WAS IT GETTING HERE? YOUR LONG JOURNEY AGAINST THE STREAM OF LIFE...
HEY, LOOK, BUDDY—IT'S NOT LIKE YOU GUYS MADE IT EASY!! SLAMMING THE DOOR ON US.. TRAPPING US IN LIGHTNING..AND THIS IS A TERRIBLE MAP!!
I SEE...YES...I DON'T SUPPOSE IT WOULD BE VERY GOOD.

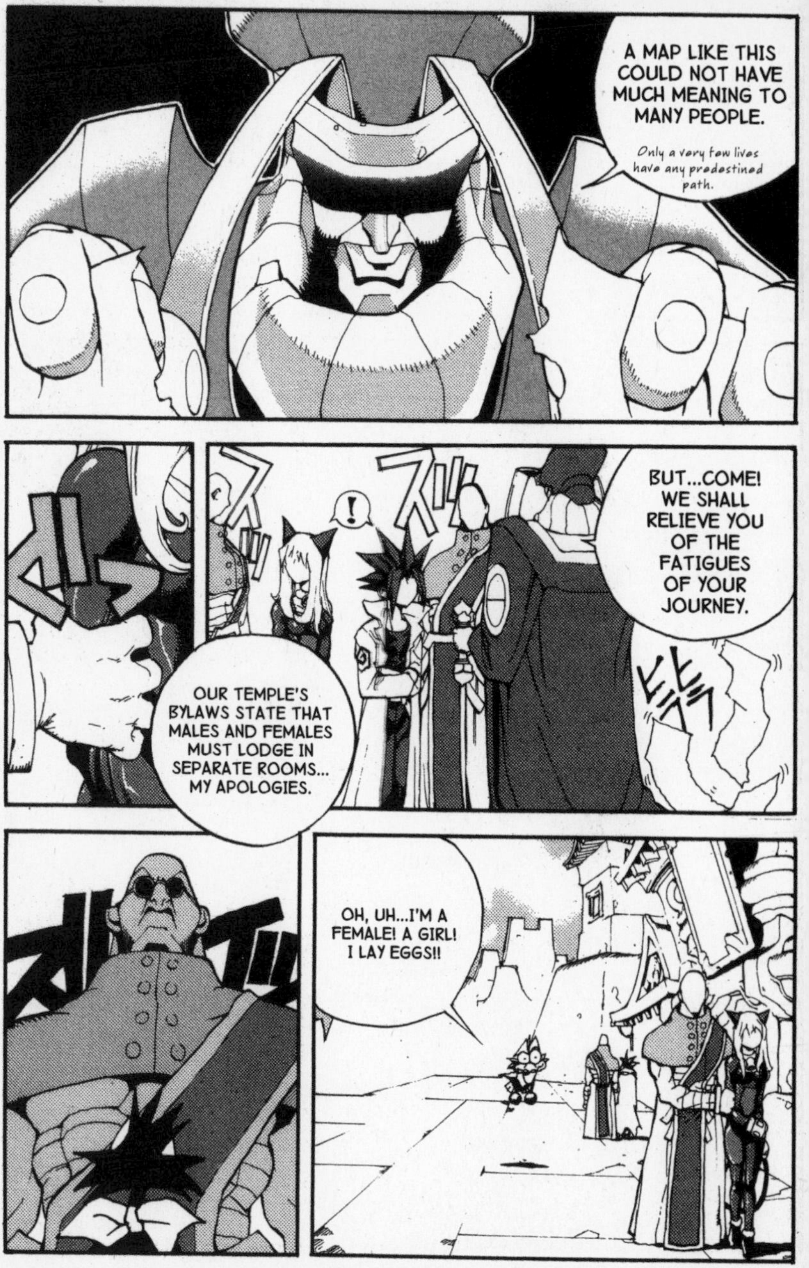
A MAP LIKE THIS COULD NOT HAVE MUCH MEANING TO MANY PEOPLE.
Only a very few lives have any predestined path.
BUT...COME! WE SHALL RELIEVE YOU OF THE FATIGUES OF YOUR JOURNEY.
!
OUR TEMPLE'S BYLAWS STATE THAT MALES AND FEMALES MUST LODGE IN SEPARATE ROOMS... MY APOLOGIES.
OH, UH...I'M A FEMALE! A GIRL! I LAY EGGS!!

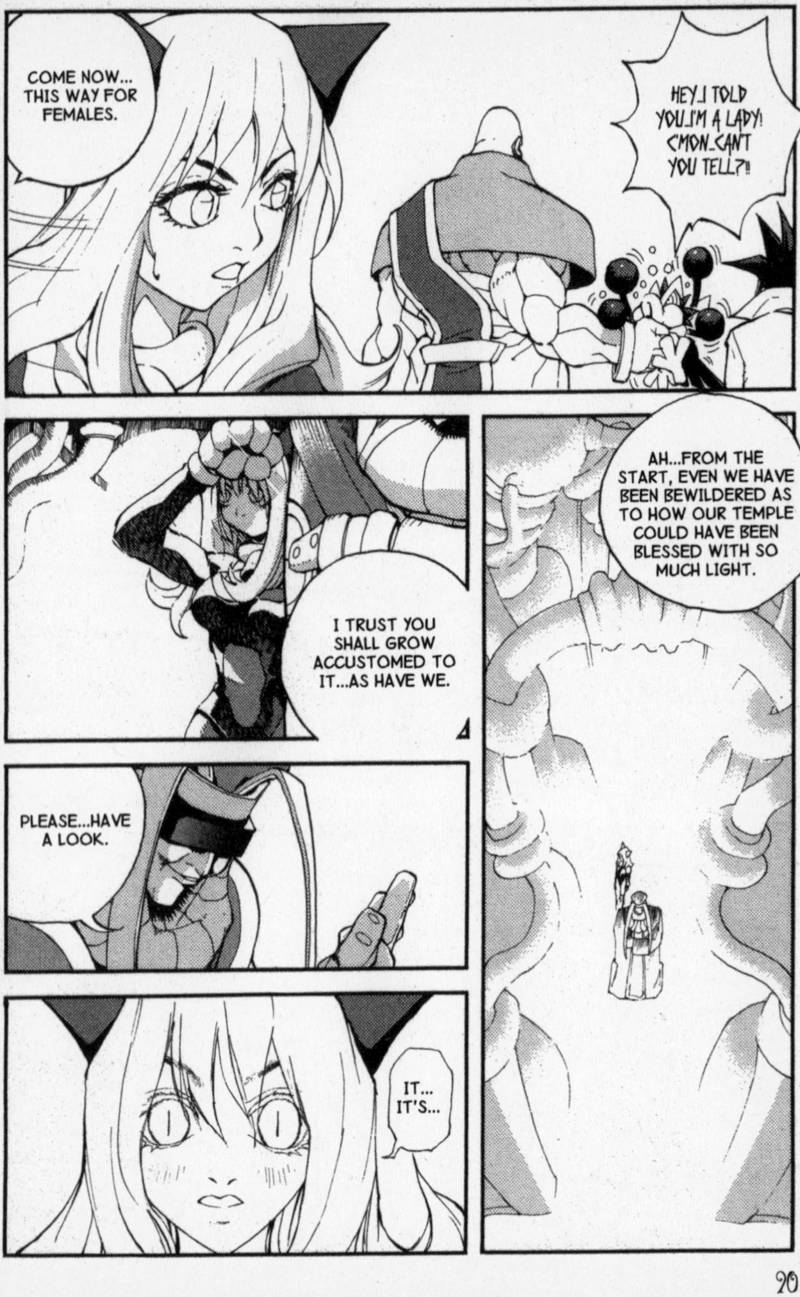
HEY...I TOLD YOU...I'M A LADY! C'MON...CAN'T YOU TELL?!!
COME NOW... THIS WAY FOR FEMALES.
AH...FROM THE START, EVEN WE HAVE BEEN BEWILDERED AS TO HOW OUR TEMPLE COULD HAVE BEEN BLESSED WITH SO MUCH LIGHT.
I TRUST YOU SHALL GROW ACCUSTOMED TO IT...AS HAVE WE.
PLEASE...HAVE A LOOK.
IT... IT'S...

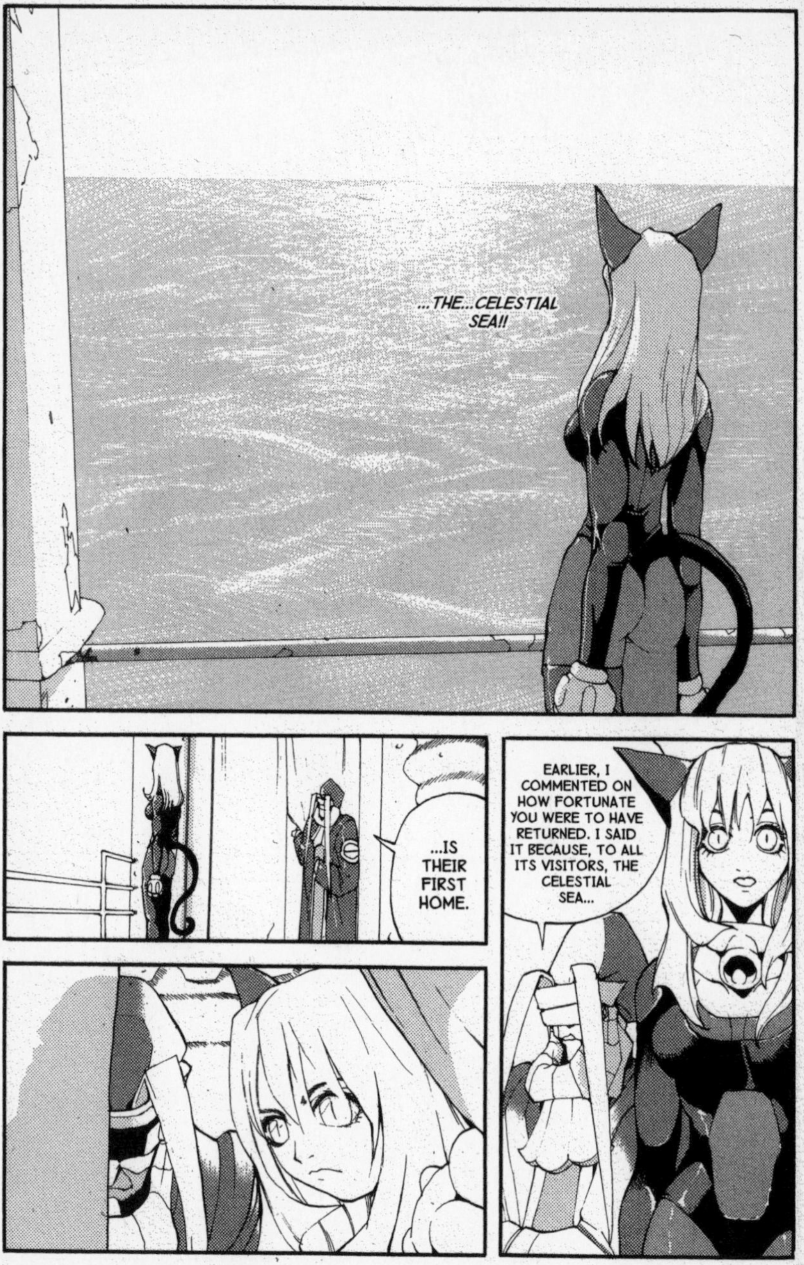
...THE...CELESTIAL SEA!!
EARLIER, I COMMENTED ON HOW FORTUNATE YOU WERE TO HAVE RETURNED. I SAID IT BECAUSE, TO ALL ITS VISITORS, THE CELESTIAL SEA...
...IS THEIR FIRST HOME.

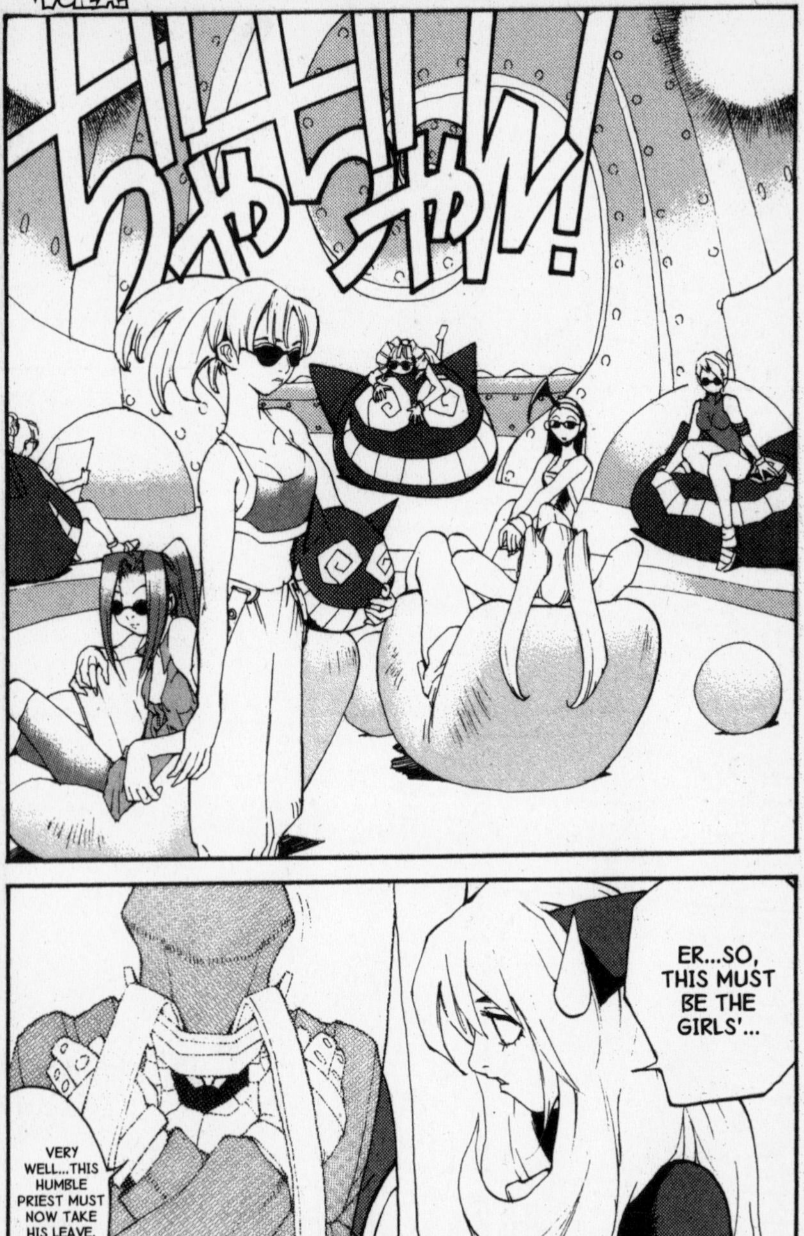
*VOILÀ!
ちゃららら〜ん!
ER...SO, THIS MUST BE THE GIRLS'...
VERY WELL...THIS HUMBLE PRIEST MUST NOW TAKE HIS LEAVE.

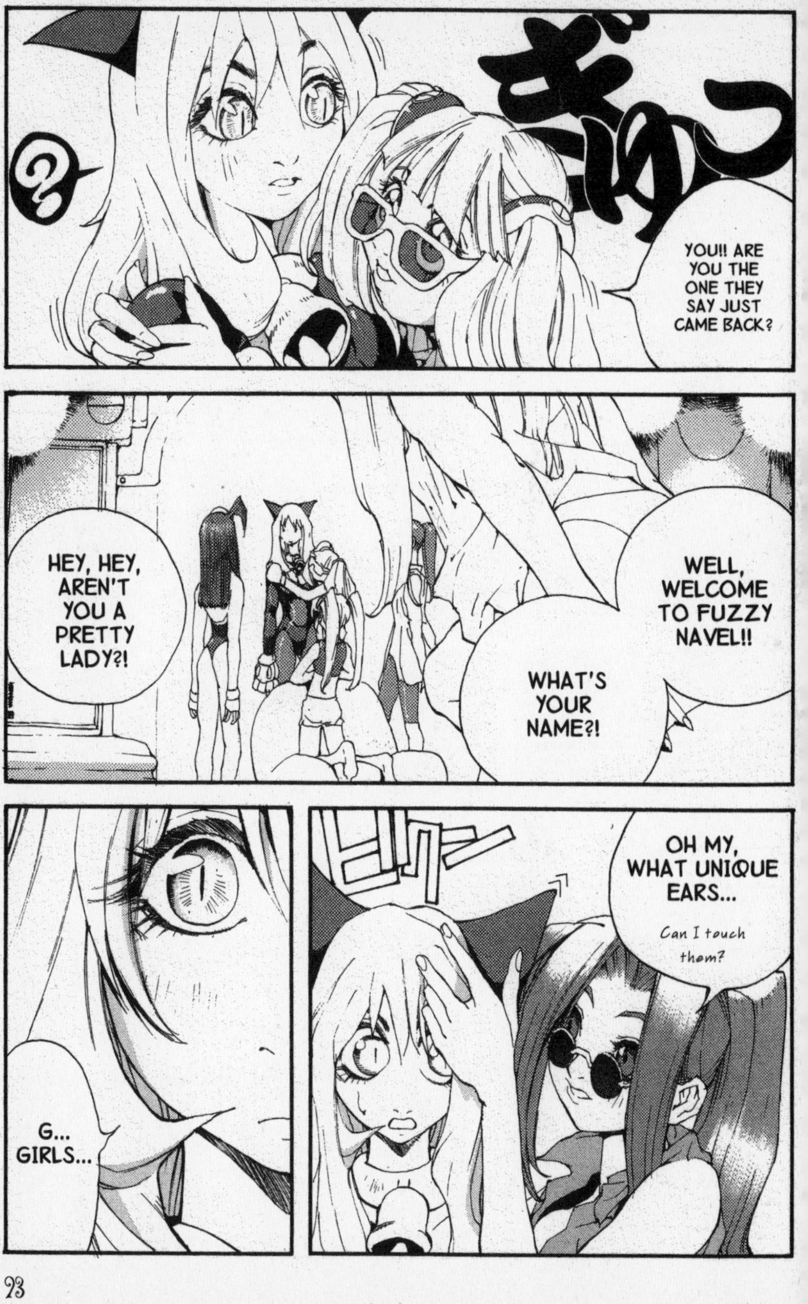
?
YOU!! ARE YOU THE ONE THEY SAY JUST CAME BACK?
WELL, WELCOME TO FUZZY NAVEL!!
WHAT'S YOUR NAME?!
HEY, HEY, AREN'T YOU A PRETTY LADY?!
OH MY, WHAT UNIQUE EARS...
Can I touch them?
G... GIRLS...

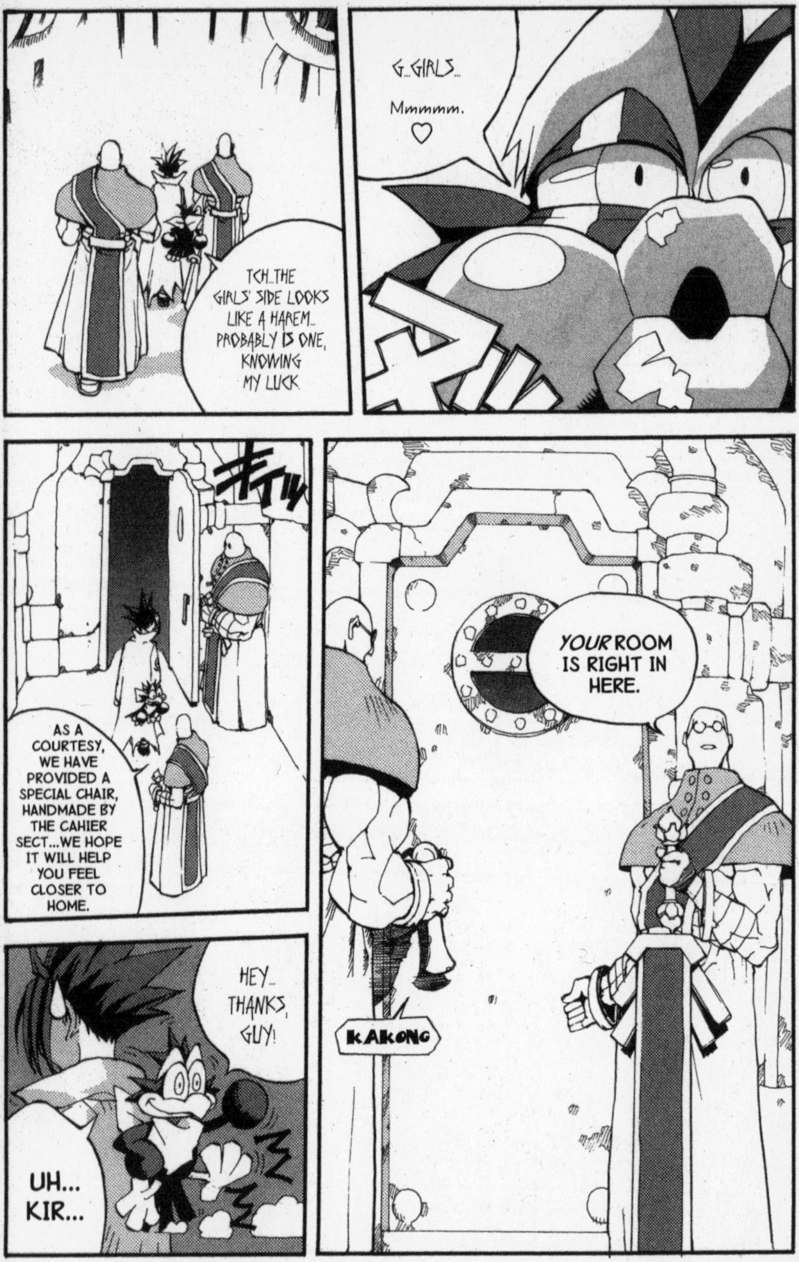
G...GIRLS...
Mmmmm. ♡
TCH...THE GIRLS' SIDE LOOKS LIKE A HAREM... PROBABLY IS ONE, KNOWING MY LUCK.
YOUR ROOM IS RIGHT IN HERE.
KAKONG
AS A COURTESY, WE HAVE PROVIDED A SPECIAL CHAIR, HANDMADE BY THE CAHIER SECT...WE HOPE IT WILL HELP YOU FEEL CLOSER TO HOME.
HEY... THANKS, GUY!
UH... KIR...

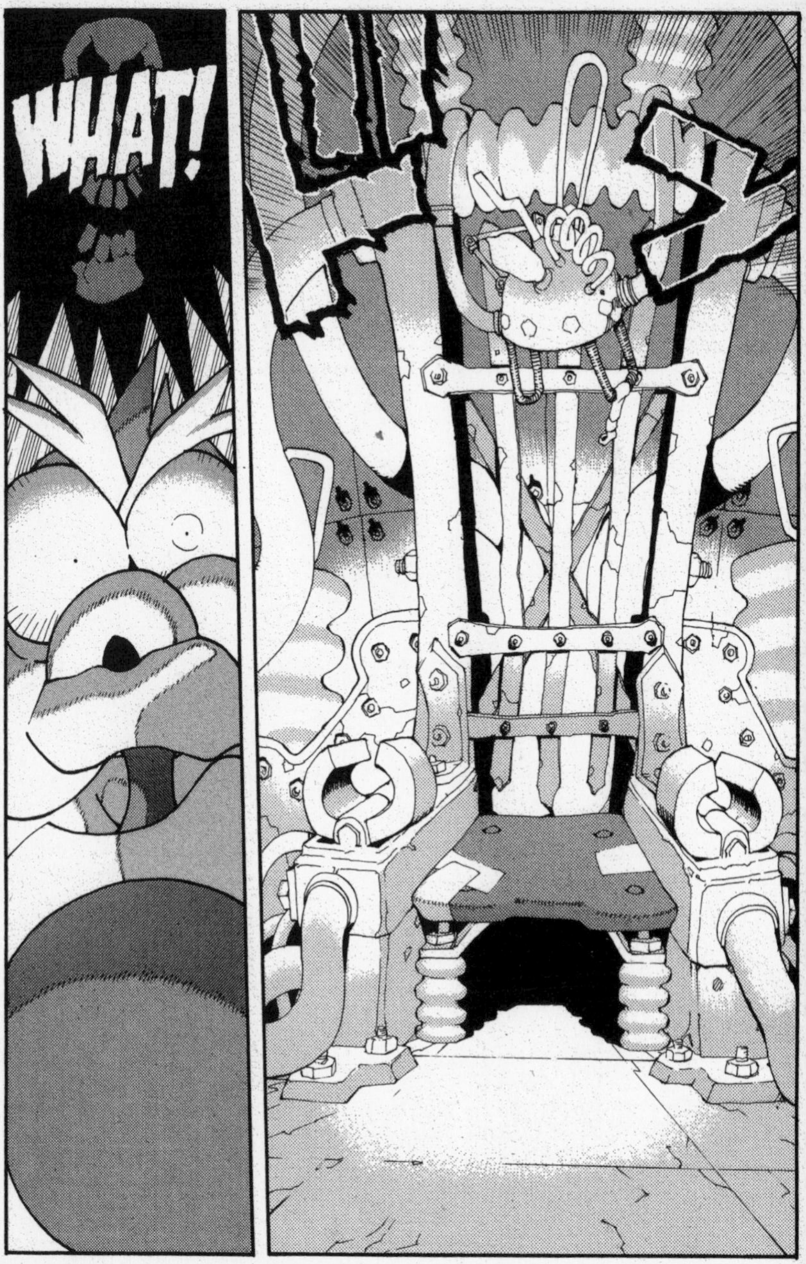
WHAT!

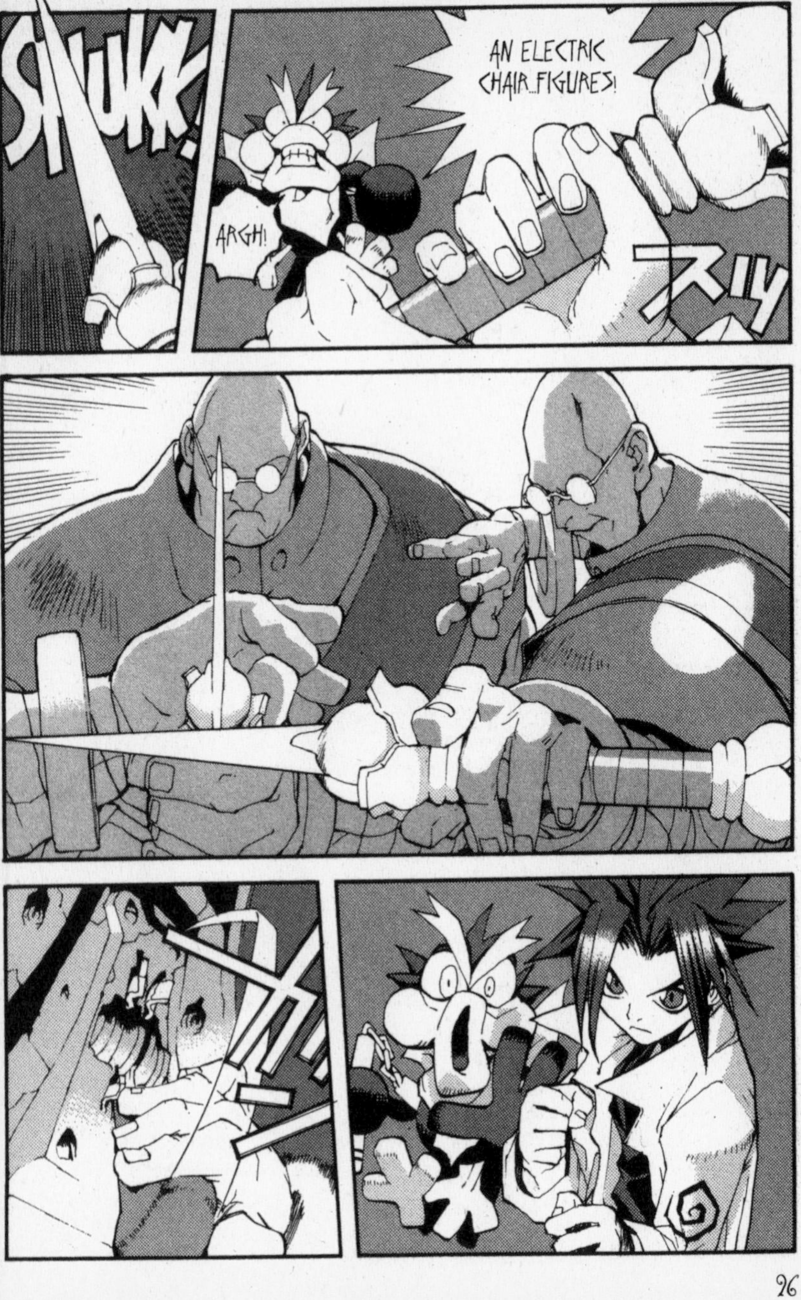
AN ELECTRIC CHAIR...FIGURES!
ARGH!
スッ
SHUKK!

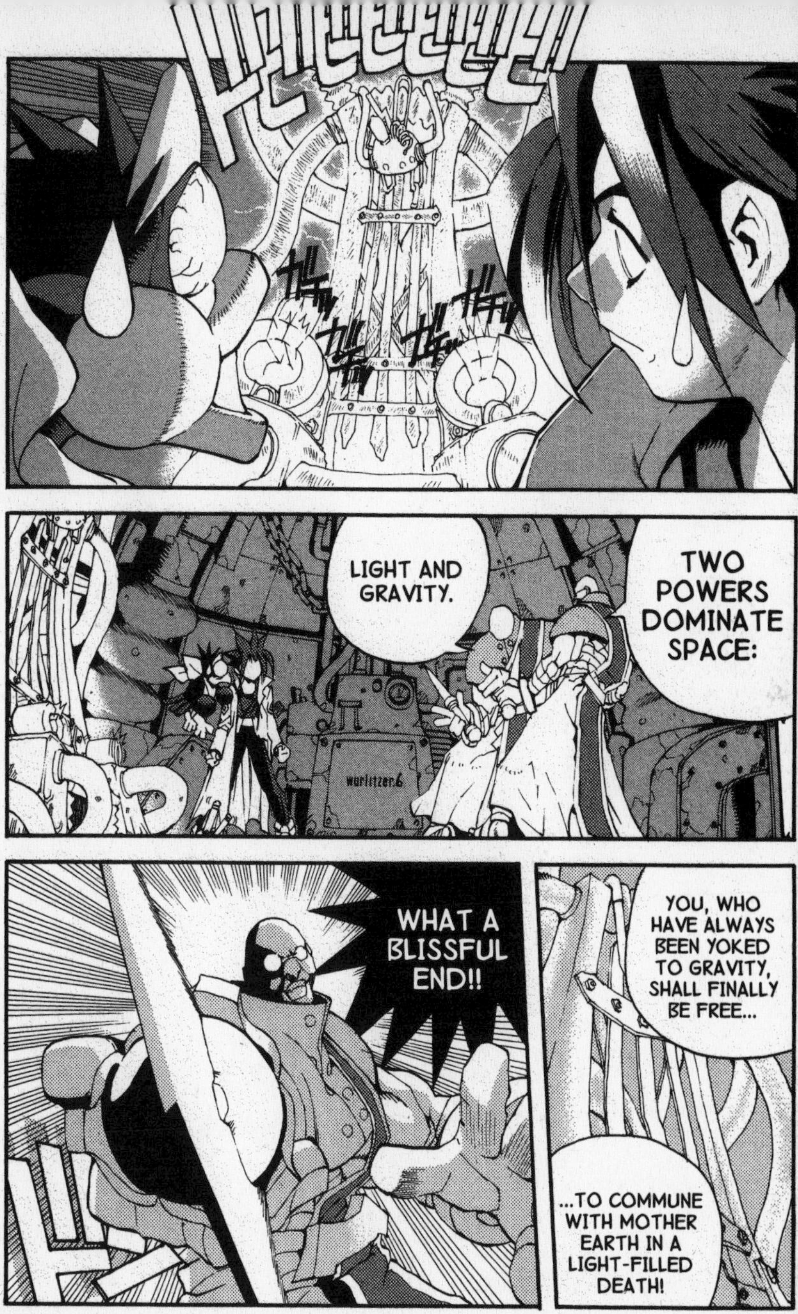
TWO POWERS DOMINATE SPACE:
LIGHT AND GRAVITY.
wurlitzer.6
YOU, WHO HAVE ALWAYS BEEN YOKED TO GRAVITY, SHALL FINALLY BE FREE...
...TO COMMUNE WITH MOTHER EARTH IN A LIGHT-FILLED DEATH!
WHAT A BLISSFUL END!!

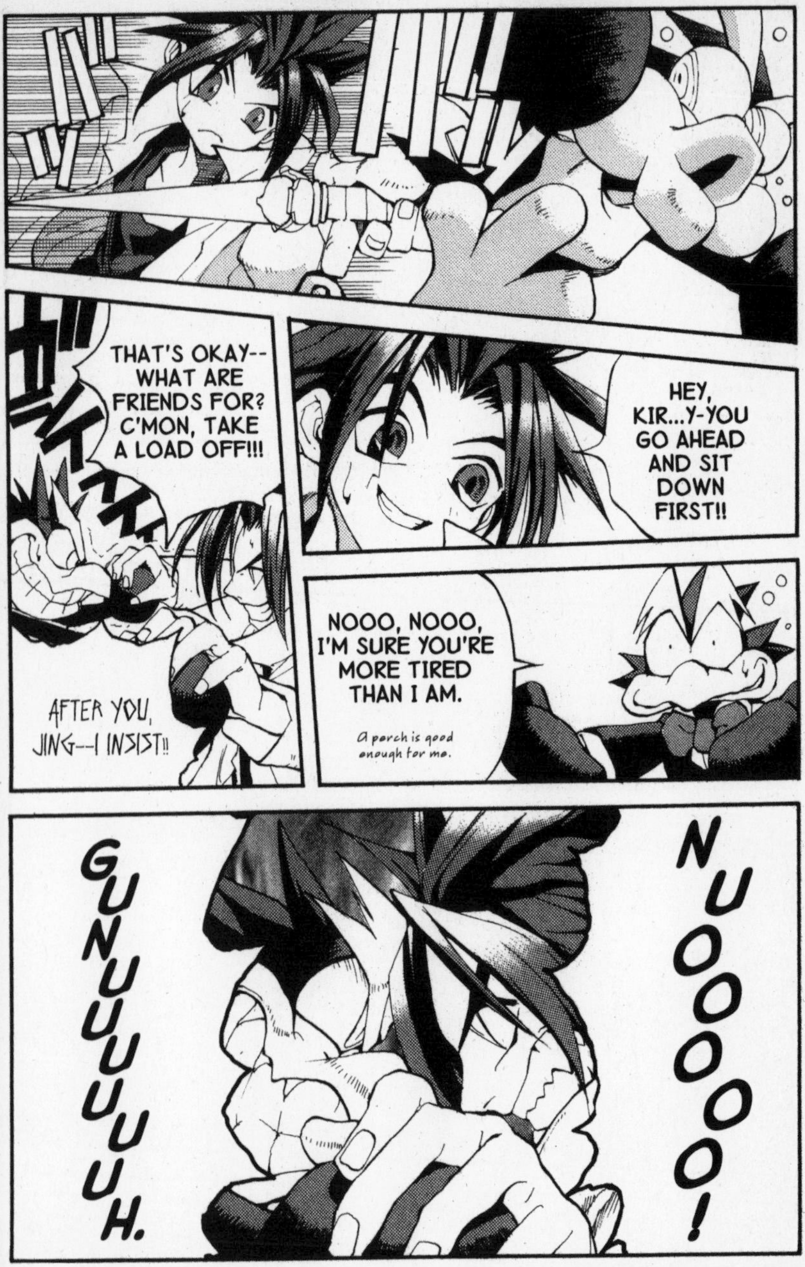
HEY, KIR...Y-YOU GO AHEAD AND SIT DOWN FIRST!!
NOOO, NOOO, I'M SURE YOU'RE MORE TIRED THAN I AM.
A perch is good enough for me.
THAT'S OKAY-- WHAT ARE FRIENDS FOR? C'MON, TAKE A LOAD OFF!!!
AFTER YOU, JING--I INSIST!!
NUOOOOOO!
GUNUUUUUH.

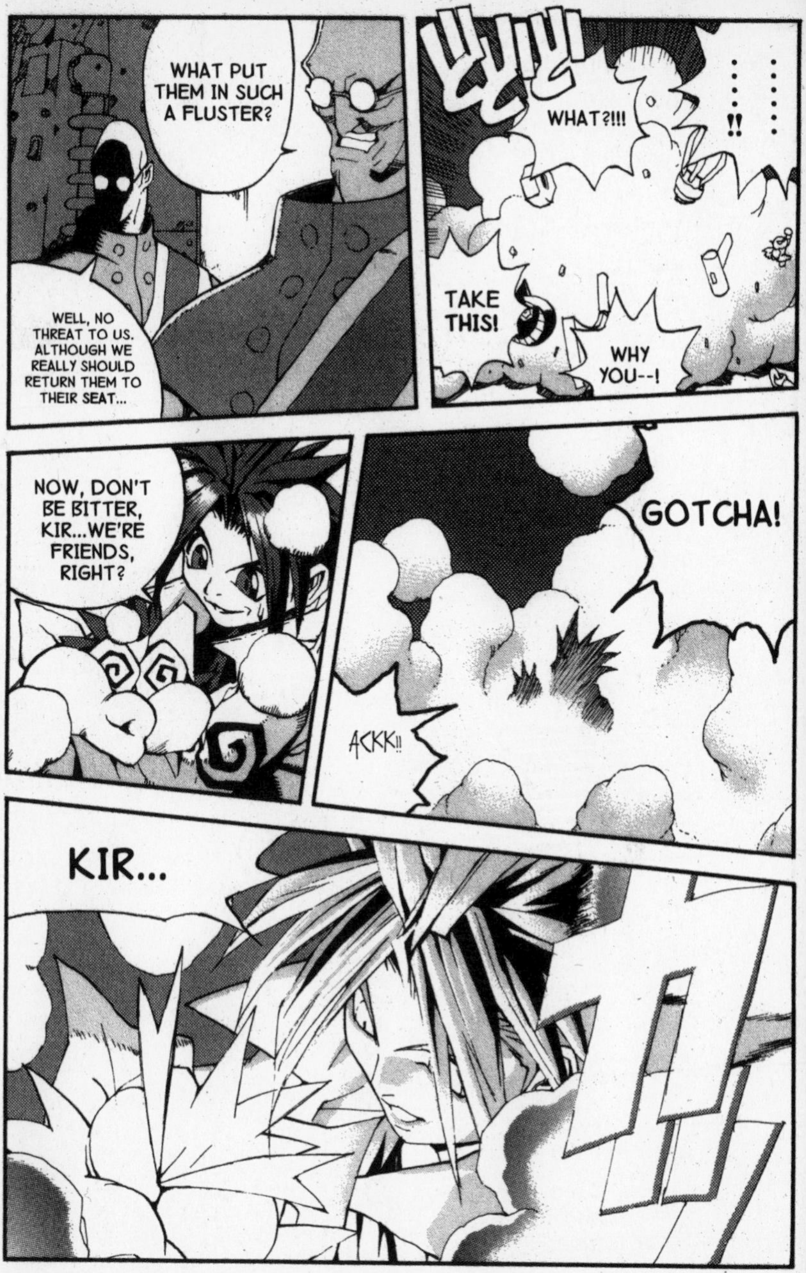

......!!
WHAT?!!!
TAKE THIS!
WHY YOU--!
WHAT PUT THEM IN SUCH A FLUSTER?
WELL, NO THREAT TO US. ALTHOUGH WE REALLY SHOULD RETURN THEM TO THEIR SEAT...
GOTCHA!
ACKK!!
NOW, DON'T BE BITTER, KIR...WE'RE FRIENDS, RIGHT?
KIR...

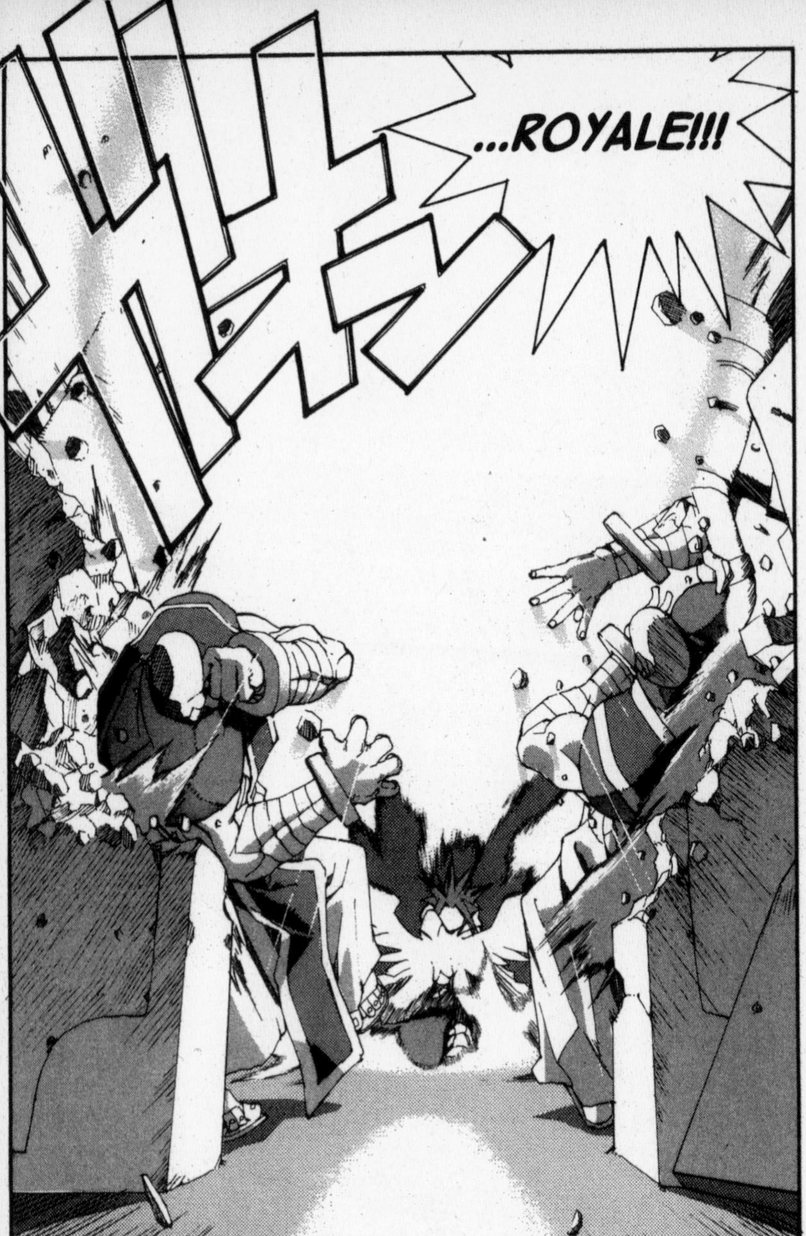
...ROYALE!!!

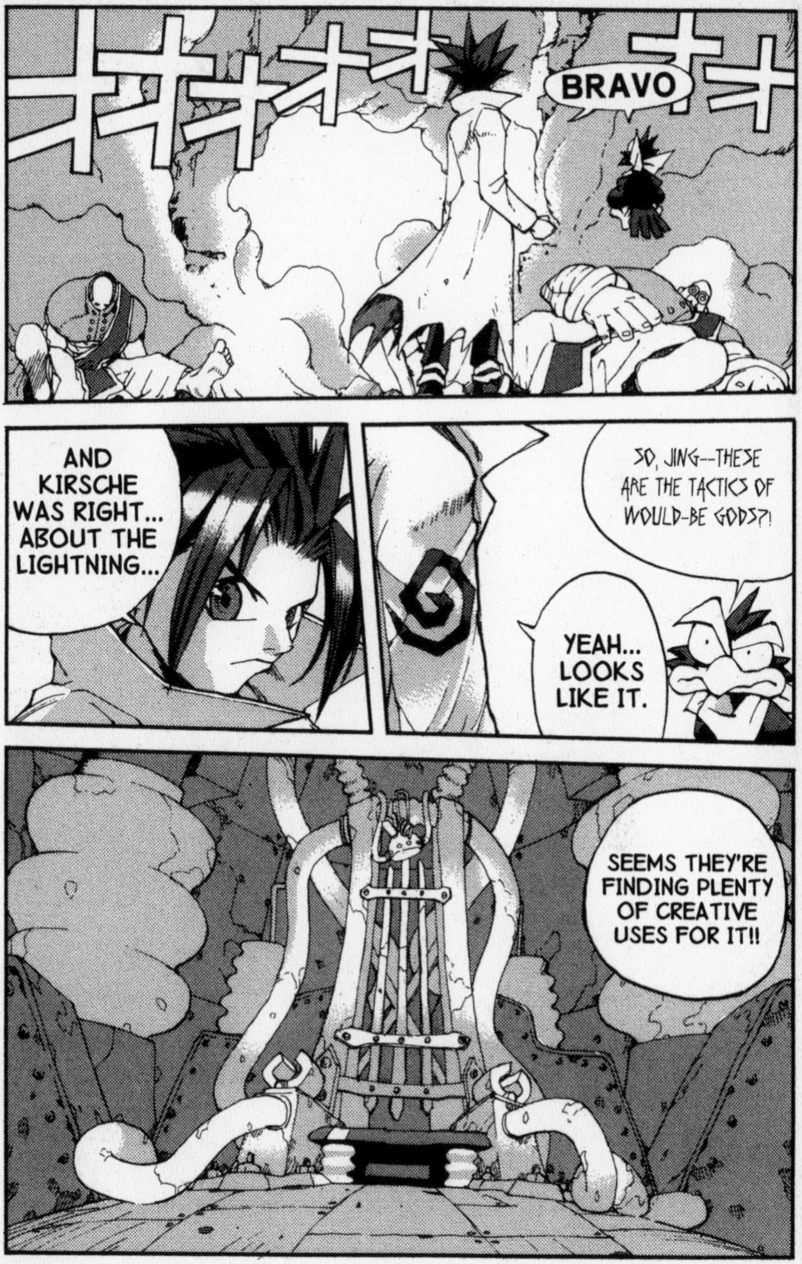
BRAVO
SO, JING--THESE ARE THE TACTICS OF WOULD-BE GODS?!
YEAH... LOOKS LIKE IT.
AND KIRSCHE WAS RIGHT... ABOUT THE LIGHTNING...
SEEMS THEY'RE FINDING PLENTY OF CREATIVE USES FOR IT!!

THE NIGHTTIME DEEPENS SILENTLY
AS DARKNESS CREEPS IN STEADILY
FROM AN UNKNOWN GARDEN IN THE SKY...

...IN A TOWN LIT ONLY DURING THE DAY...

...THE ELECTRICAL MISCHIEF OF GOD'S DEVICE
SHOWS NO SIGN OF ENDING SOON...

(EXCERPTS FROM THE DIARY OF ARAK,
A BELIEVER OF THE CAHIER SECT)

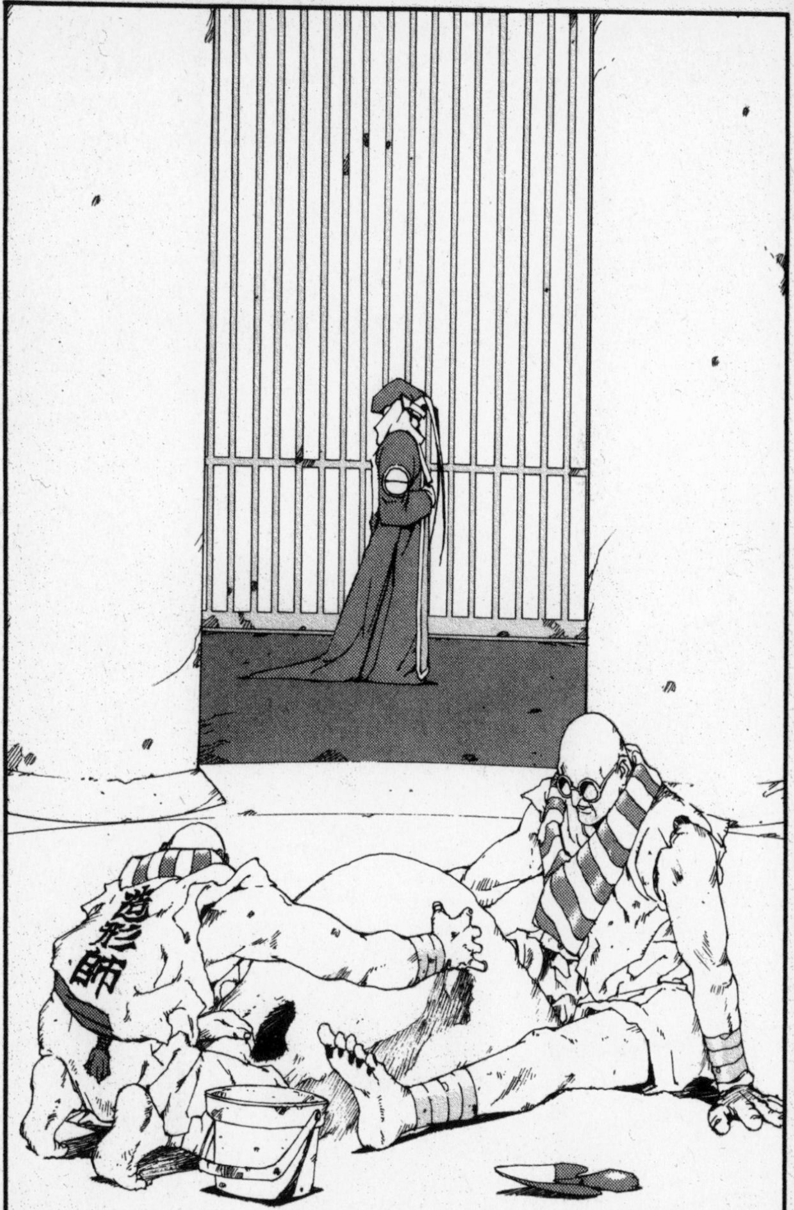
造形師

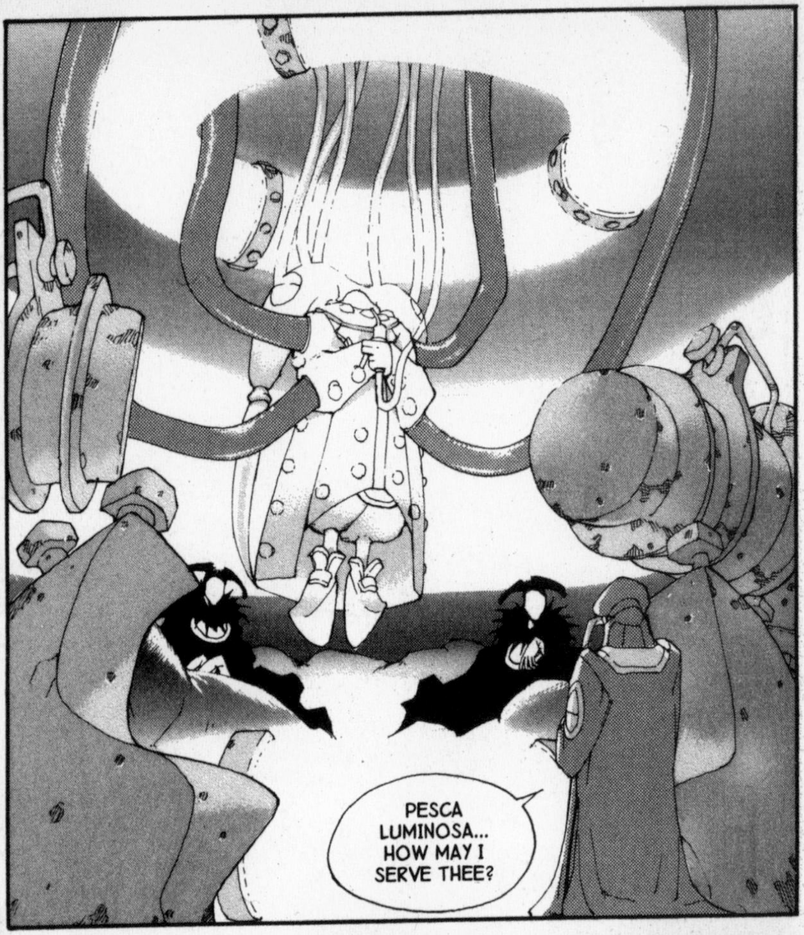
PESCA LUMINOSA... HOW MAY I SERVE THEE?

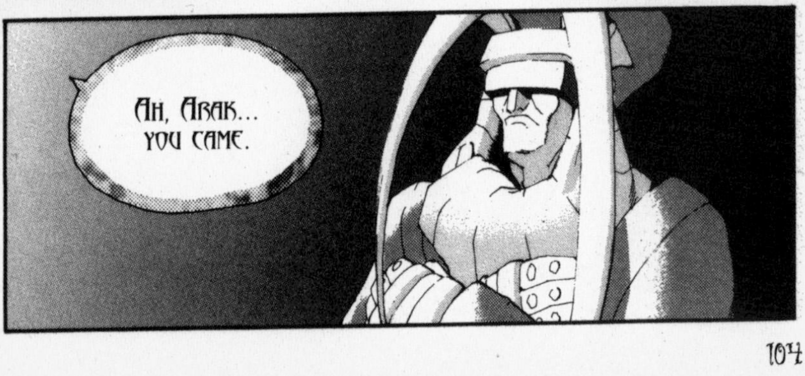
AH, ARAK... YOU CAME.

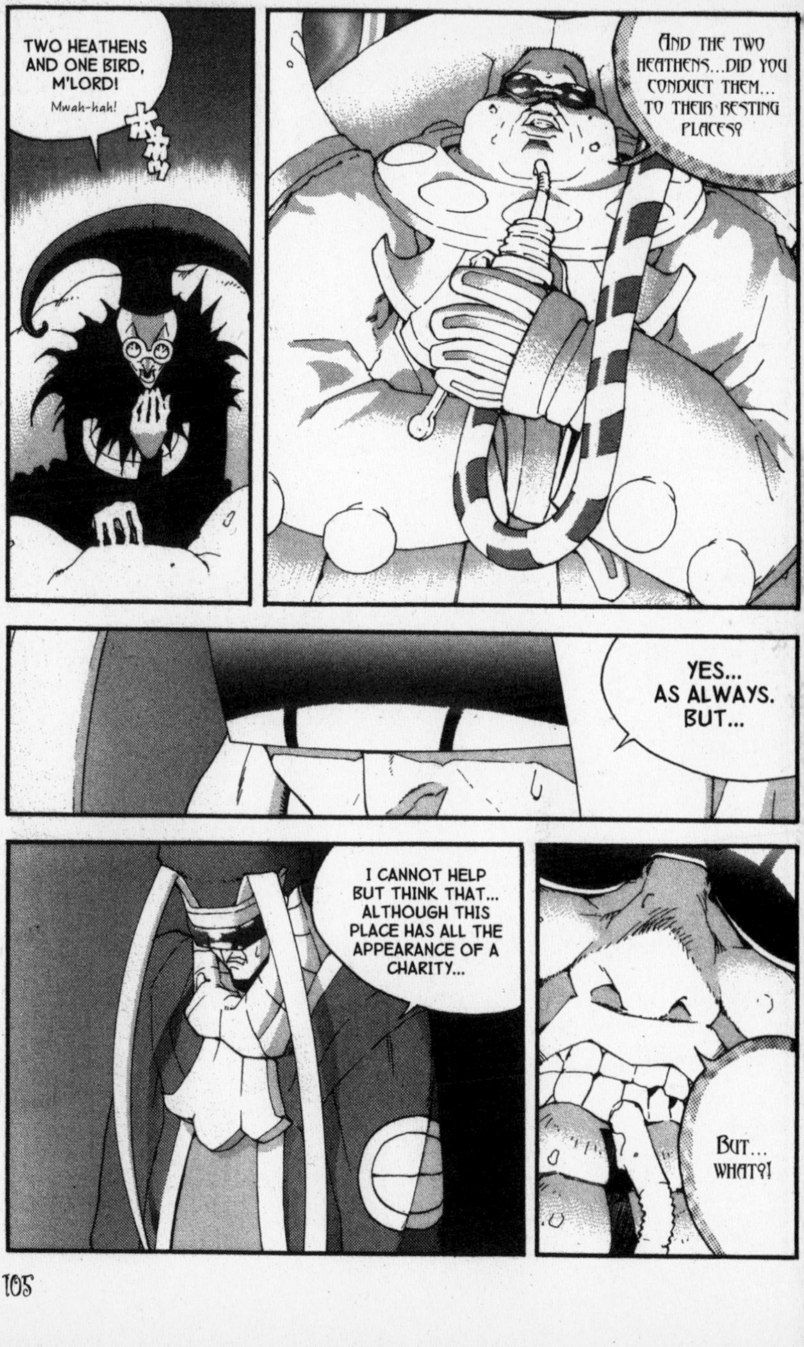

AND THE TWO HEATHENS...DID YOU CONDUCT THEM... TO THEIR RESTING PLACES?
TWO HEATHENS AND ONE BIRD, M'LORD!
Mwah-hah!
YES... AS ALWAYS. BUT...
BUT... WHAT?!
I CANNOT HELP BUT THINK THAT... ALTHOUGH THIS PLACE HAS ALL THE APPEARANCE OF A CHARITY...

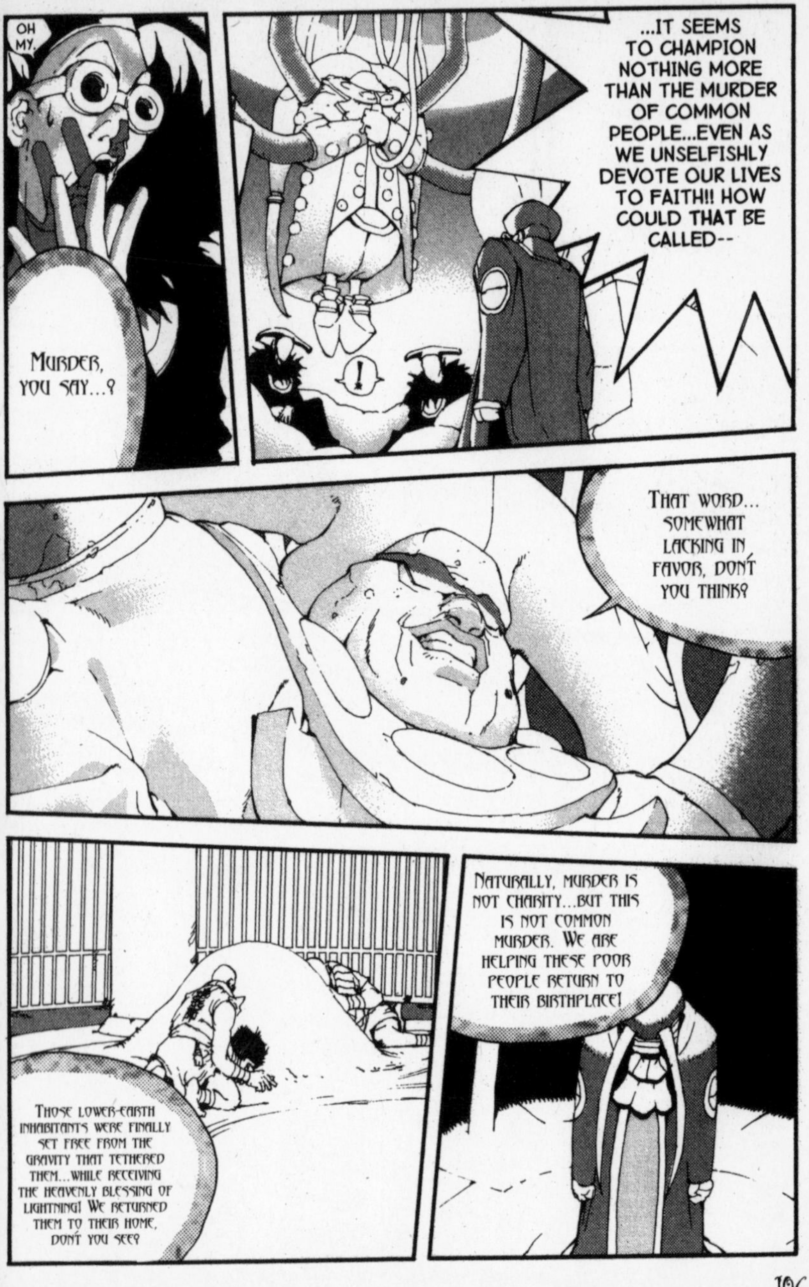
...IT SEEMS TO CHAMPION NOTHING MORE THAN THE MURDER OF COMMON PEOPLE...EVEN AS WE UNSELFISHLY DEVOTE OUR LIVES TO FAITH!! HOW COULD THAT BE CALLED--
!
OH MY.
MURDER, YOU SAY...?
THAT WORD... SOMEWHAT LACKING IN FAVOR, DON'T YOU THINK?
NATURALLY, MURDER IS NOT CHARITY...BUT THIS IS NOT COMMON MURDER. WE ARE HELPING THESE POOR PEOPLE RETURN TO THEIR BIRTHPLACE!
THOSE LOWER-EARTH INHABITANTS WERE FINALLY SET FREE FROM THE GRAVITY THAT TETHERED THEM...WHILE RECEIVING THE HEAVENLY BLESSING OF LIGHTNING! WE RETURNED THEM TO THEIR HOME, DON'T YOU SEE?

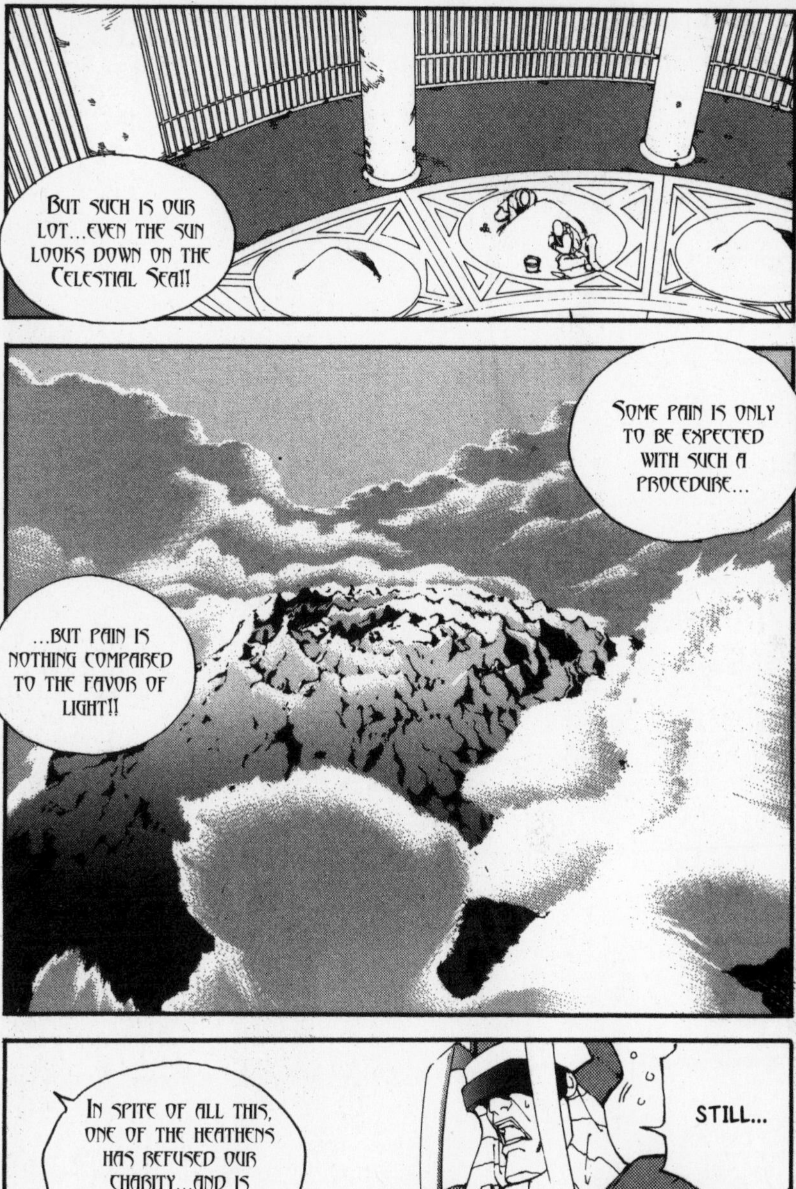
But such is our lot...even the sun looks down on the Celestial Sea!!
Some pain is only to be expected with such a procedure...
...but pain is nothing compared to the favor of light!!
STILL...
In spite of all this, one of the heathens has refused our charity...and is currently roaming our temple.

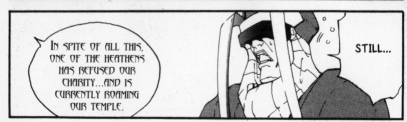

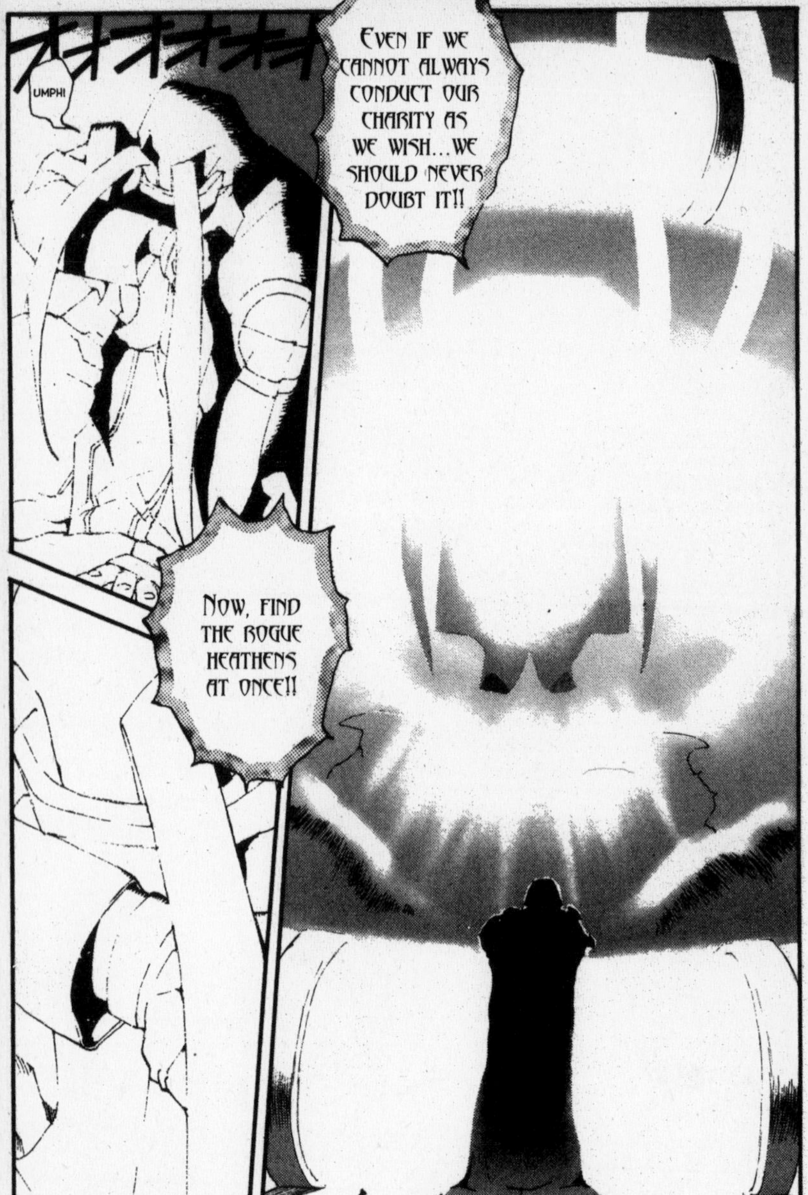

Even if we cannot always conduct our charity as we wish...we should never doubt it!!
Now, find the rogue heathens at once!!
オオオオオオ
UMPH!

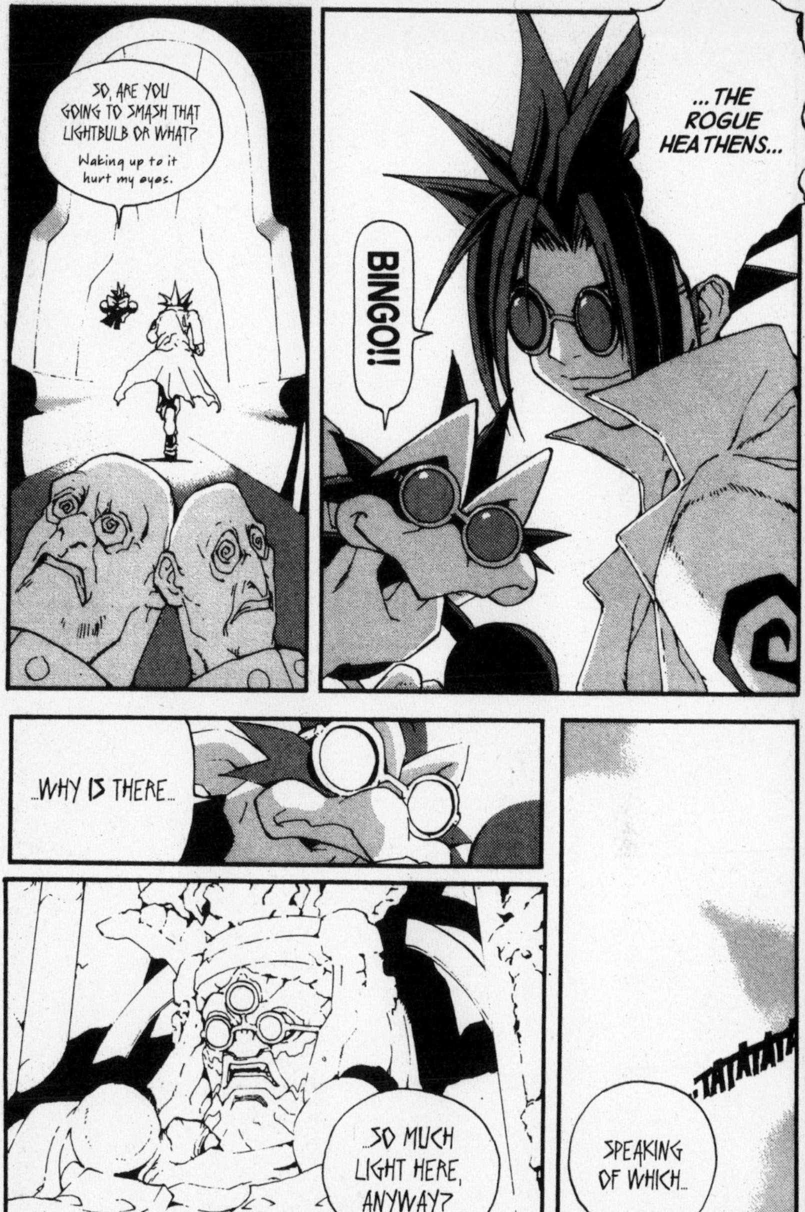
...THE ROGUE HEATHENS...
BINGO!!
SO, ARE YOU GOING TO SMASH THAT LIGHTBULB OR WHAT?
Waking up to it hurt my eyes.
...WHY IS THERE...
...SO MUCH LIGHT HERE, ANYWAY?
SPEAKING OF WHICH...
TATATATA

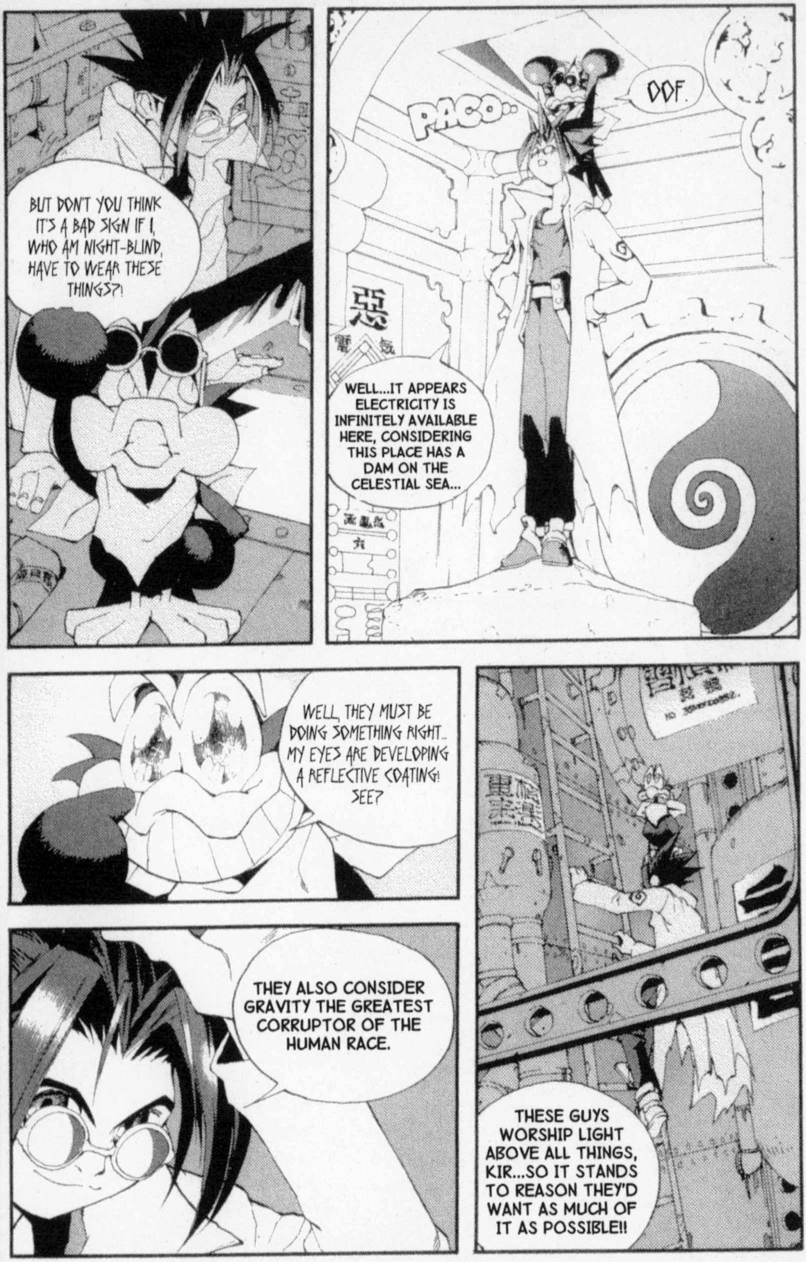
OOF.
PACO..
WELL...IT APPEARS ELECTRICITY IS INFINITELY AVAILABLE HERE, CONSIDERING THIS PLACE HAS A DAM ON THE CELESTIAL SEA...
BUT DON'T YOU THINK IT'S A BAD SIGN IF I, WHO AM NIGHT-BLIND, HAVE TO WEAR THESE THINGS?!
THESE GUYS WORSHIP LIGHT ABOVE ALL THINGS, KIR...SO IT STANDS TO REASON THEY'D WANT AS MUCH OF IT AS POSSIBLE!!
WELL, THEY MUST BE DOING SOMETHING RIGHT.. MY EYES ARE DEVELOPING A REFLECTIVE COATING! SEE?
THEY ALSO CONSIDER GRAVITY THE GREATEST CORRUPTOR OF THE HUMAN RACE.

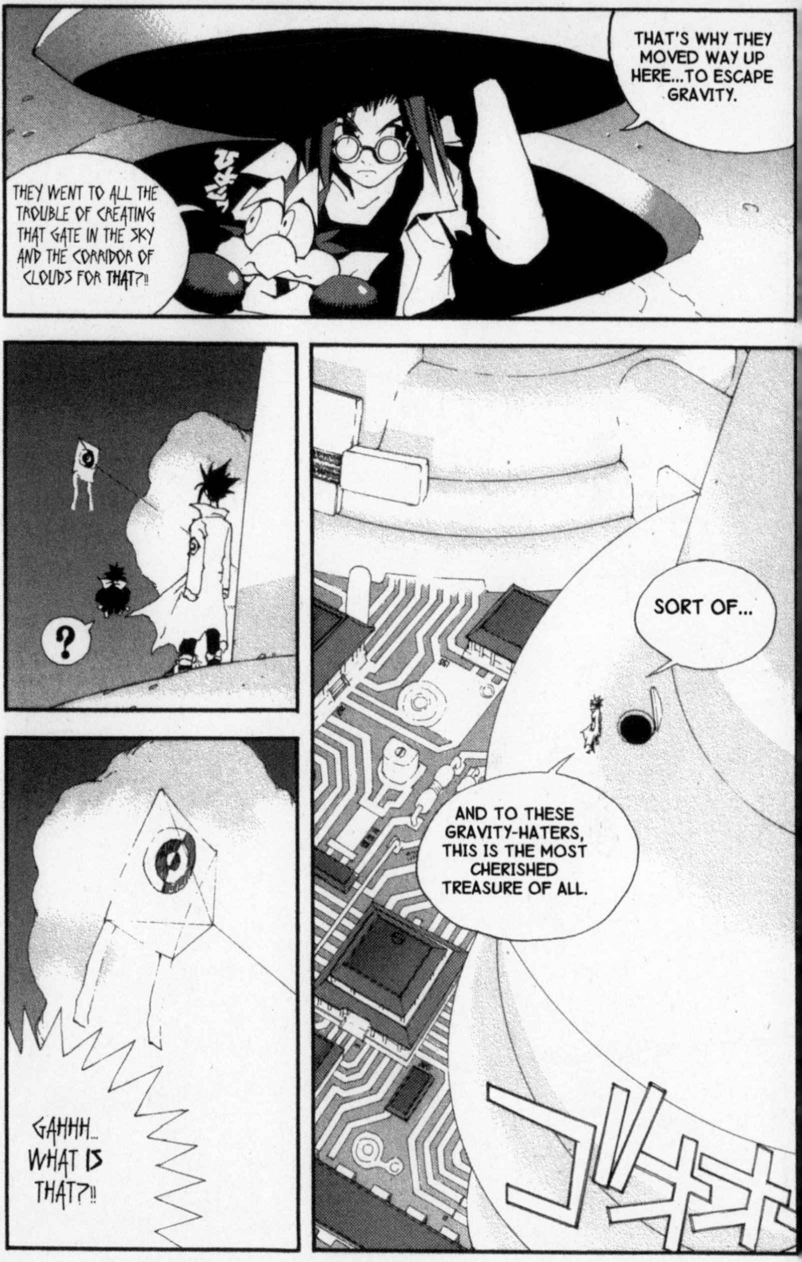
THAT'S WHY THEY MOVED WAY UP HERE...TO ESCAPE GRAVITY.
THEY WENT TO ALL THE TROUBLE OF CREATING THAT GATE IN THE SKY AND THE CORRIDOR OF CLOUDS FOR THAT?!!
SORT OF...
AND TO THESE GRAVITY-HATERS, THIS IS THE MOST CHERISHED TREASURE OF ALL.
?
GAHHH... WHAT IS THAT?!!

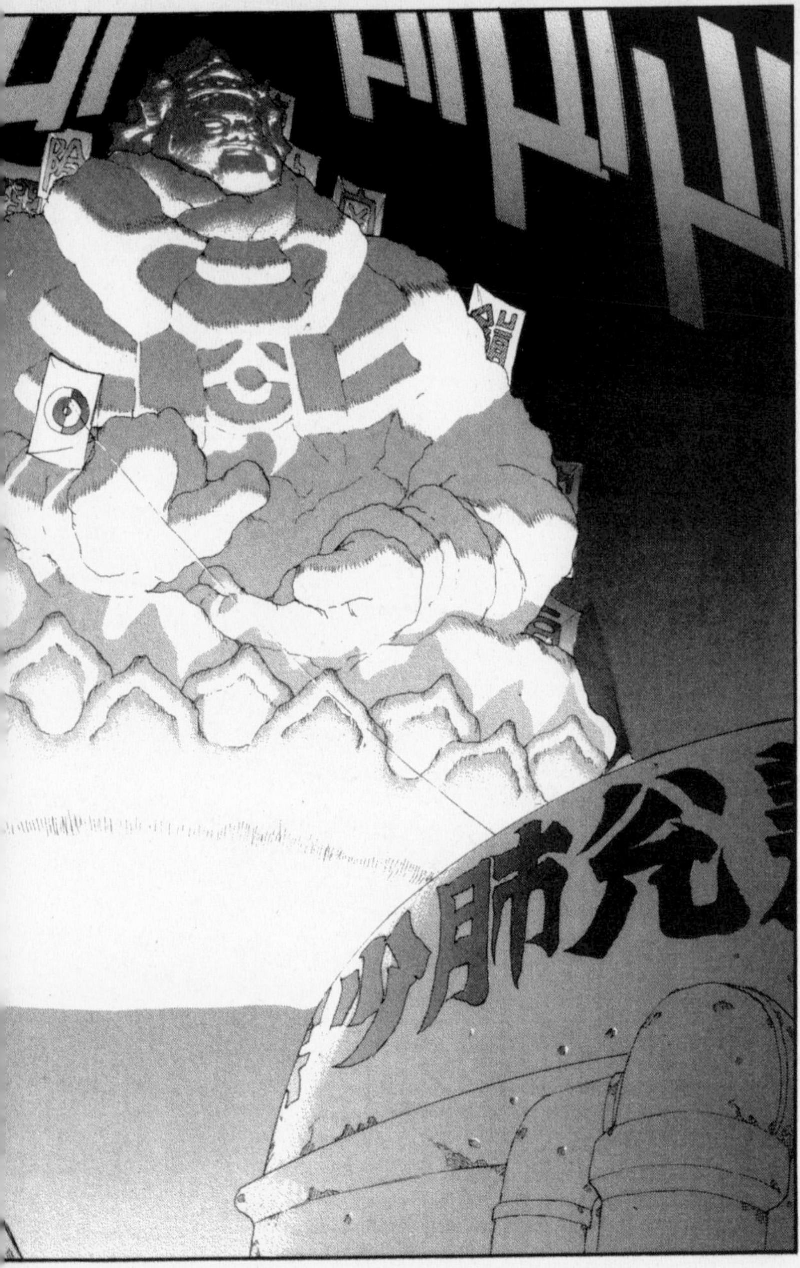

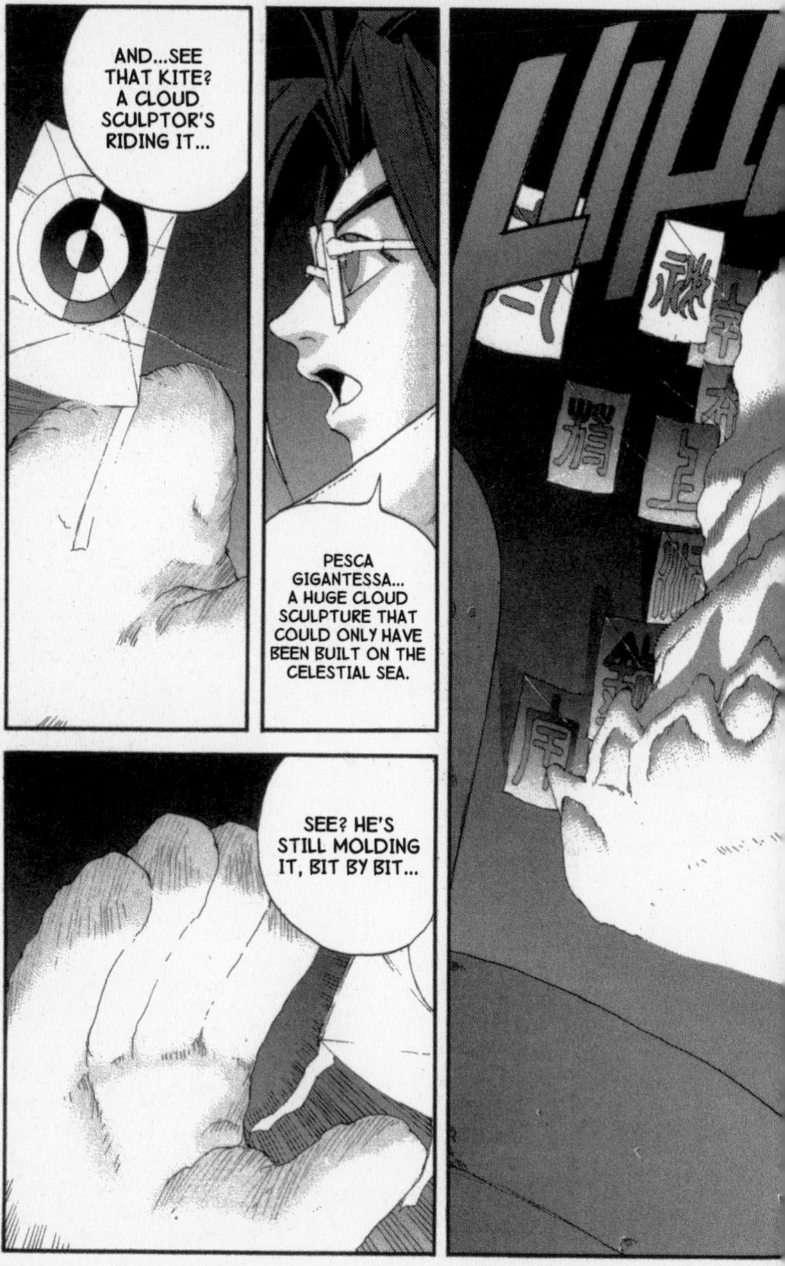
PESCA GIGANTESSA... A HUGE CLOUD SCULPTURE THAT COULD ONLY HAVE BEEN BUILT ON THE CELESTIAL SEA.
AND...SEE THAT KITE? A CLOUD SCULPTOR'S RIDING IT...
SEE? HE'S STILL MOLDING IT, BIT BY BIT...

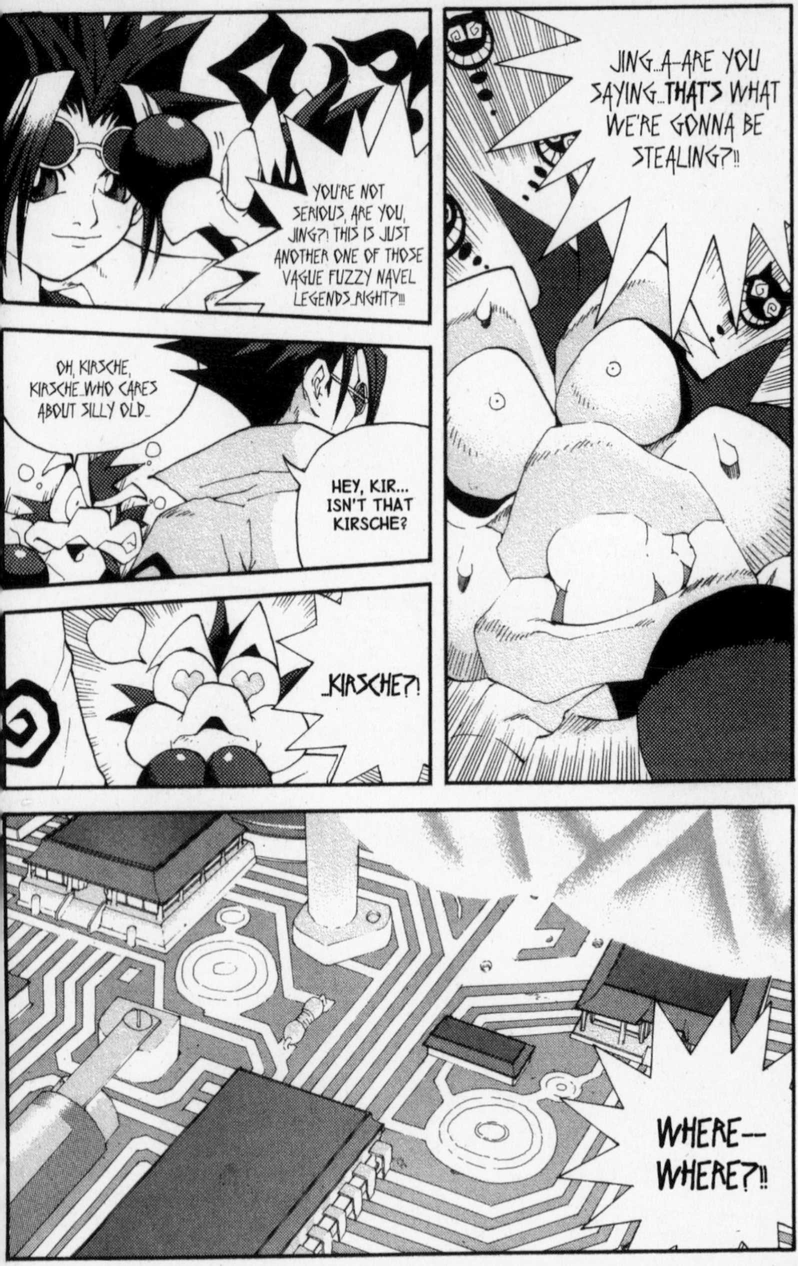
JING...A-ARE YOU SAYING...THAT'S WHAT WE'RE GONNA BE STEALING?!!
YOU'RE NOT SERIOUS, ARE YOU, JING?! THIS IS JUST ANOTHER ONE OF THOSE VAGUE FUZZY NAVEL LEGENDS...RIGHT?!!
HEY, KIR... ISN'T THAT KIRSCHE?
OH, KIRSCHE, KIRSCHE...WHO CARES ABOUT SILLY OLD...
...KIRSCHE?!
WHERE--WHERE?!!

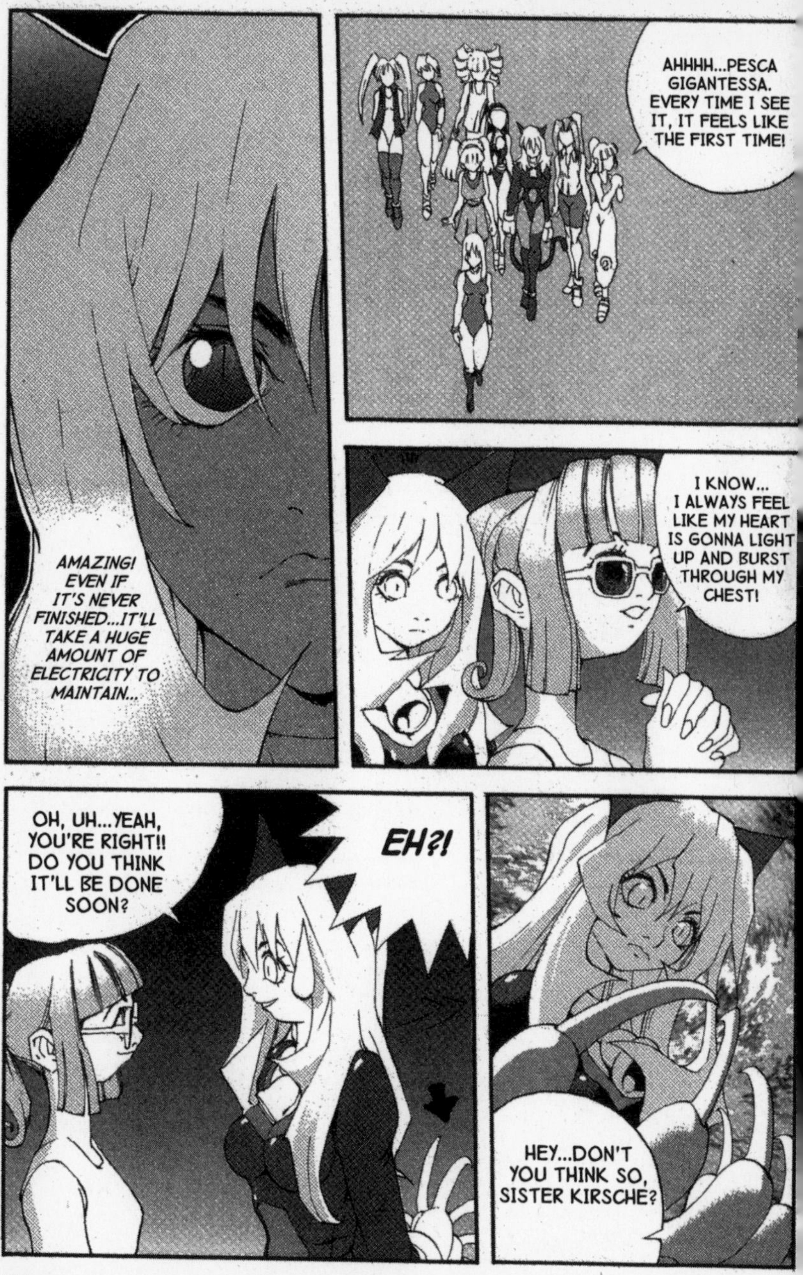
AHHHH...PESCA GIGANTESSA. EVERY TIME I SEE IT, IT FEELS LIKE THE FIRST TIME!
I KNOW... I ALWAYS FEEL LIKE MY HEART IS GONNA LIGHT UP AND BURST THROUGH MY CHEST!
AMAZING! EVEN IF IT'S NEVER FINISHED...IT'LL TAKE A HUGE AMOUNT OF ELECTRICITY TO MAINTAIN...
HEY...DON'T YOU THINK SO, SISTER KIRSCHE?
EH?!
OH, UH...YEAH, YOU'RE RIGHT!! DO YOU THINK IT'LL BE DONE SOON?

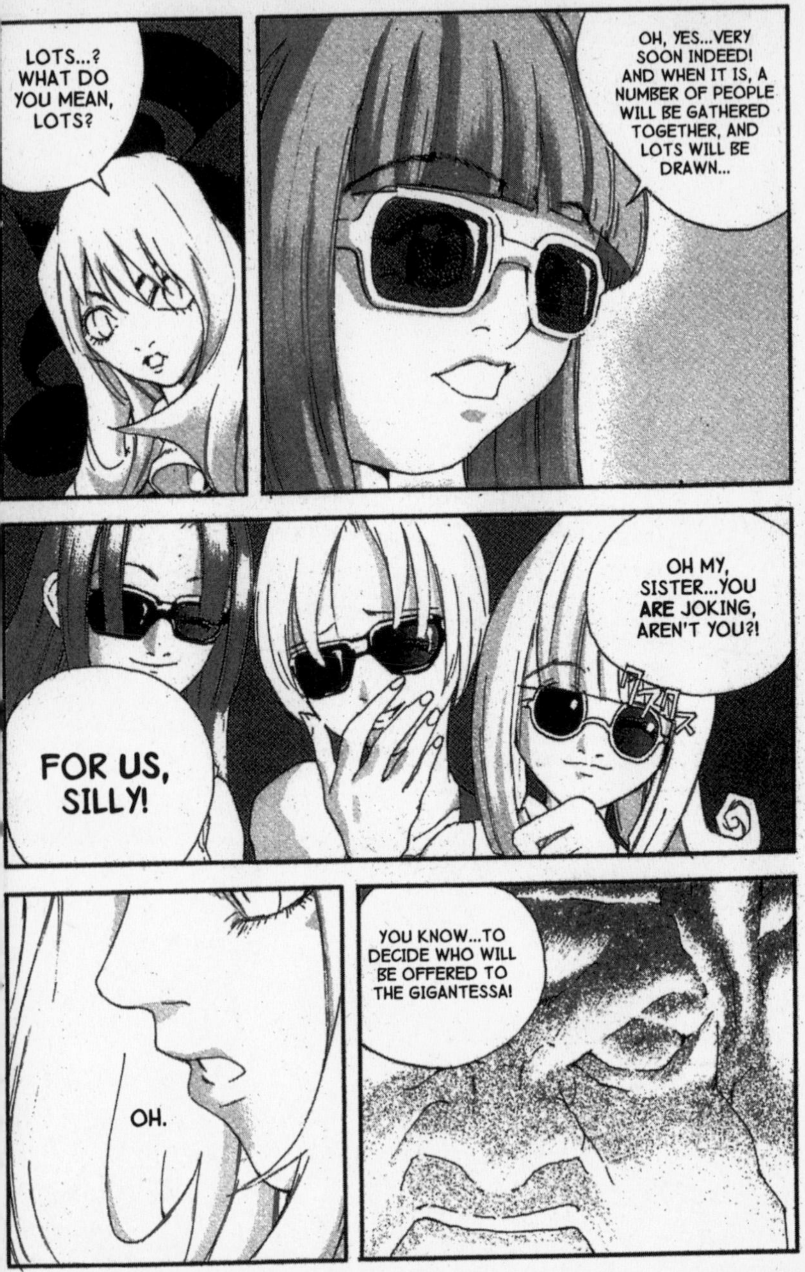
OH, YES...VERY SOON INDEED! AND WHEN IT IS, A NUMBER OF PEOPLE WILL BE GATHERED TOGETHER, AND LOTS WILL BE DRAWN...
LOTS...? WHAT DO YOU MEAN, LOTS?
OH MY, SISTER...YOU **ARE** JOKING, AREN'T YOU?!
FOR US, SILLY!
YOU KNOW...TO DECIDE WHO WILL BE OFFERED TO THE GIGANTESSA!
OH.

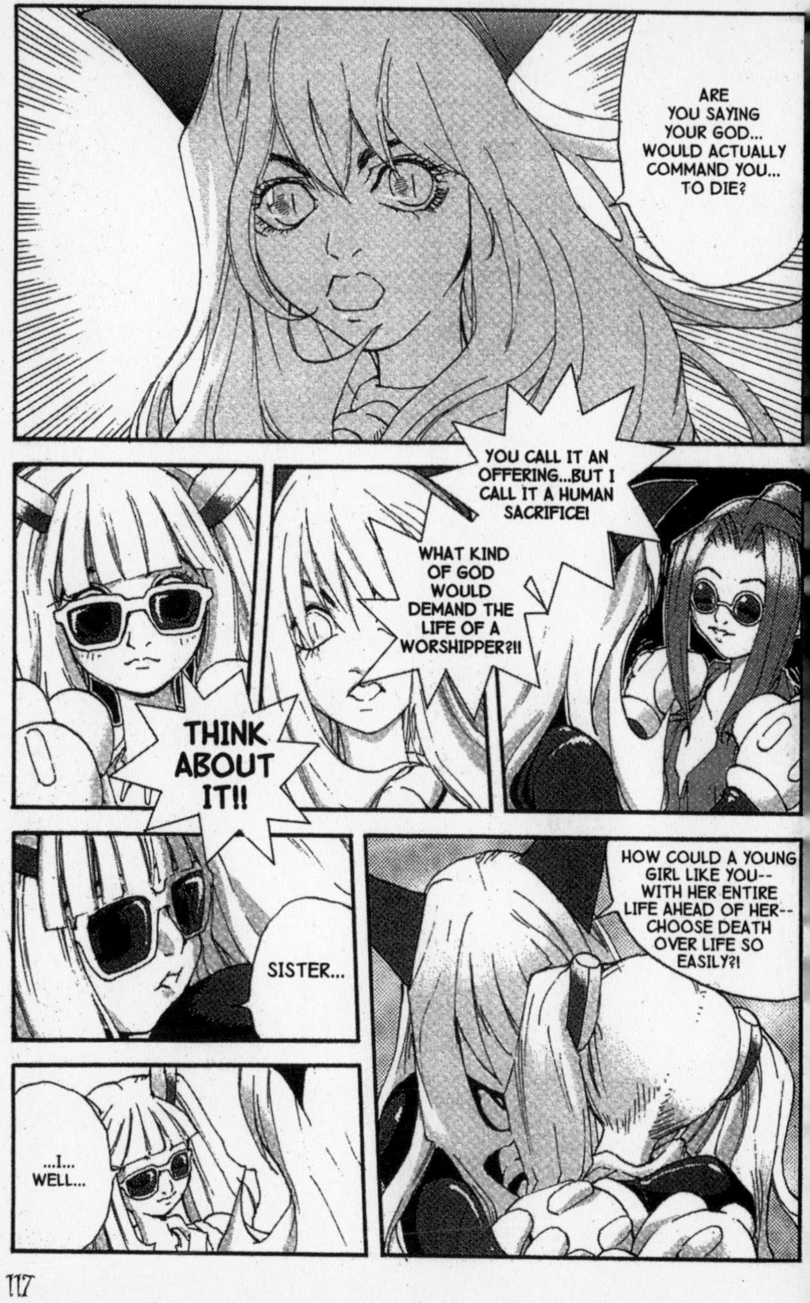
ARE YOU SAYING YOUR GOD... WOULD ACTUALLY COMMAND YOU... TO DIE?
YOU CALL IT AN OFFERING...BUT I CALL IT A HUMAN SACRIFICE!
WHAT KIND OF GOD WOULD DEMAND THE LIFE OF A WORSHIPPER?!!
THINK ABOUT IT!!
HOW COULD A YOUNG GIRL LIKE YOU--WITH HER ENTIRE LIFE AHEAD OF HER--CHOOSE DEATH OVER LIFE SO EASILY?!
SISTER...
...I... WELL...

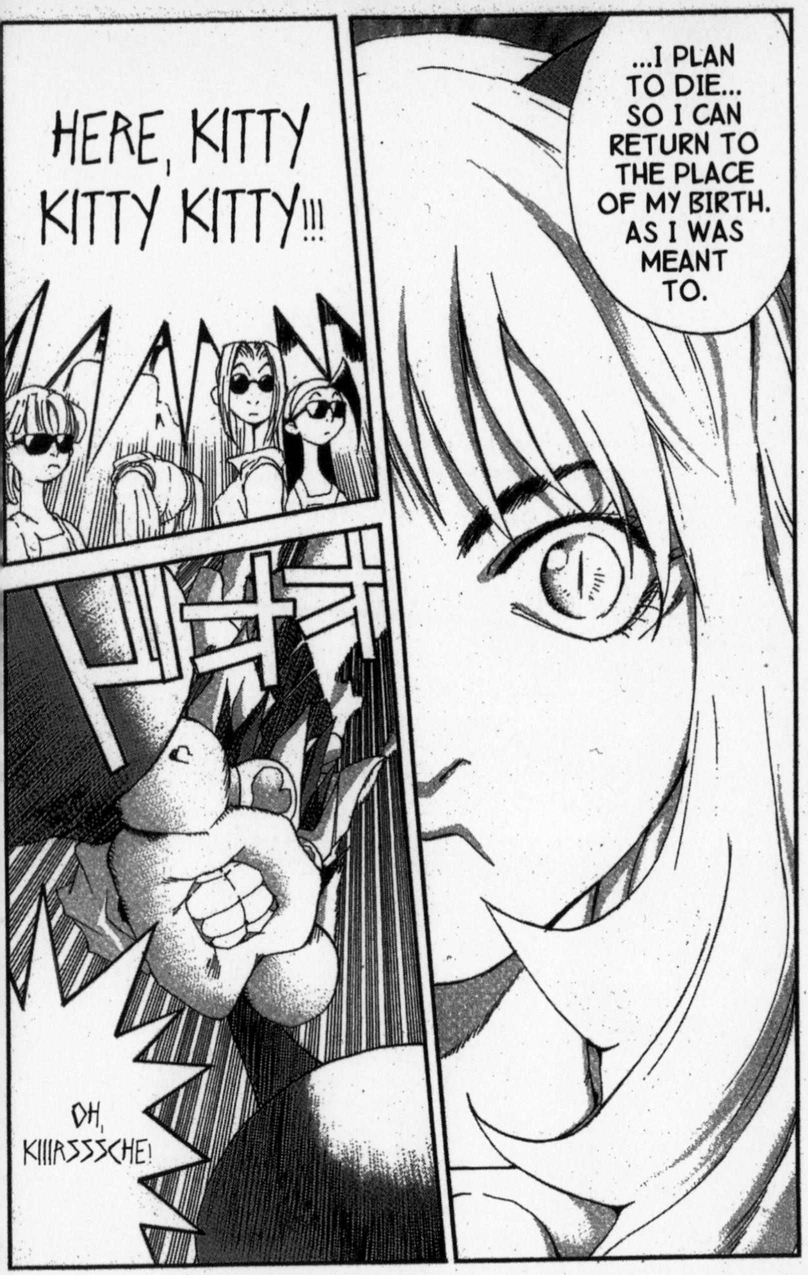
...I PLAN TO DIE... SO I CAN RETURN TO THE PLACE OF MY BIRTH. AS I WAS MEANT TO.
HERE, KITTY KITTY KITTY!!!
OH, KIIIRSSSCHE!

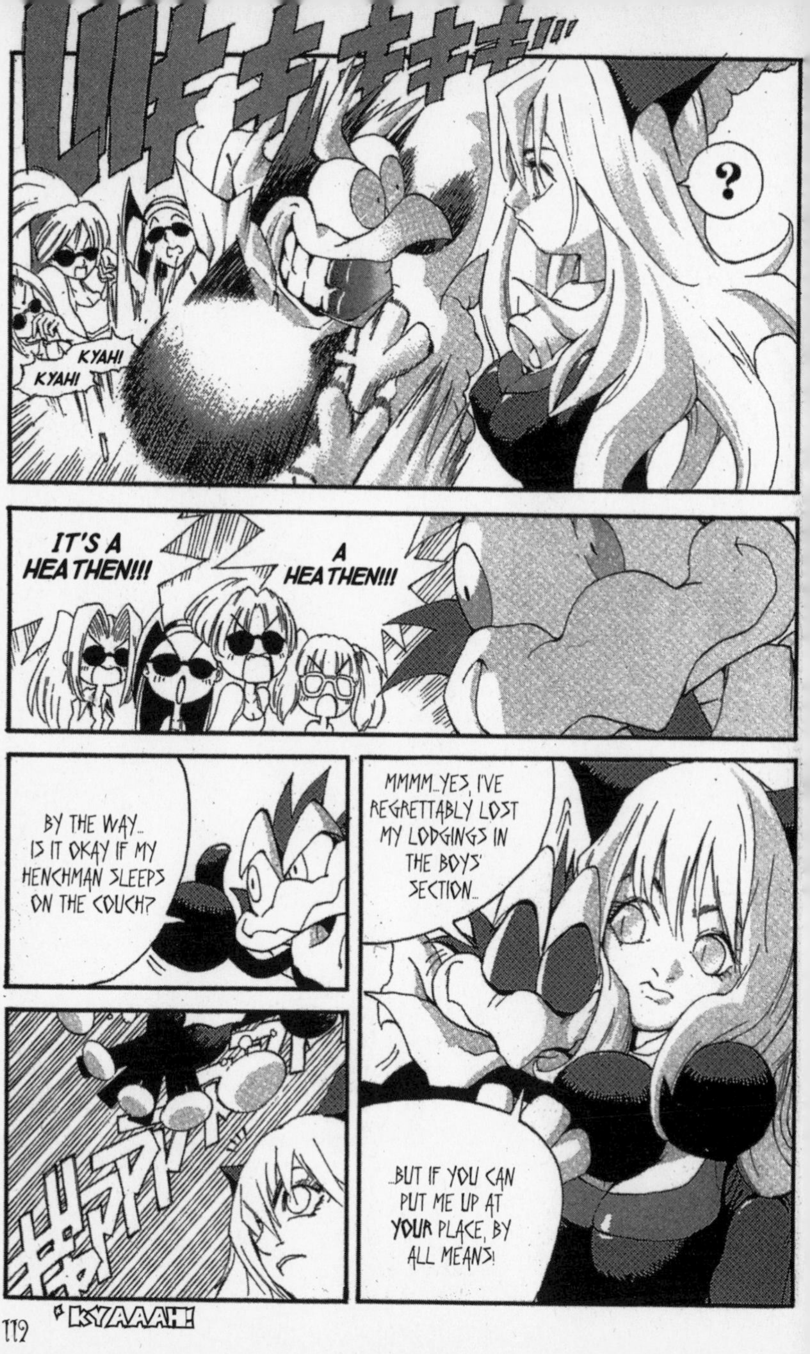
?
KYAH!
KYAH!
A HEATHEN!!!
IT'S A HEATHEN!!!
MMMM...YES, I'VE REGRETTABLY LOST MY LODGINGS IN THE BOYS' SECTION...
...BUT IF YOU CAN PUT ME UP AT YOUR PLACE, BY ALL MEANS!
BY THE WAY... IS IT OKAY IF MY HENCHMAN SLEEPS ON THE COUCH?

*KYAAAH!

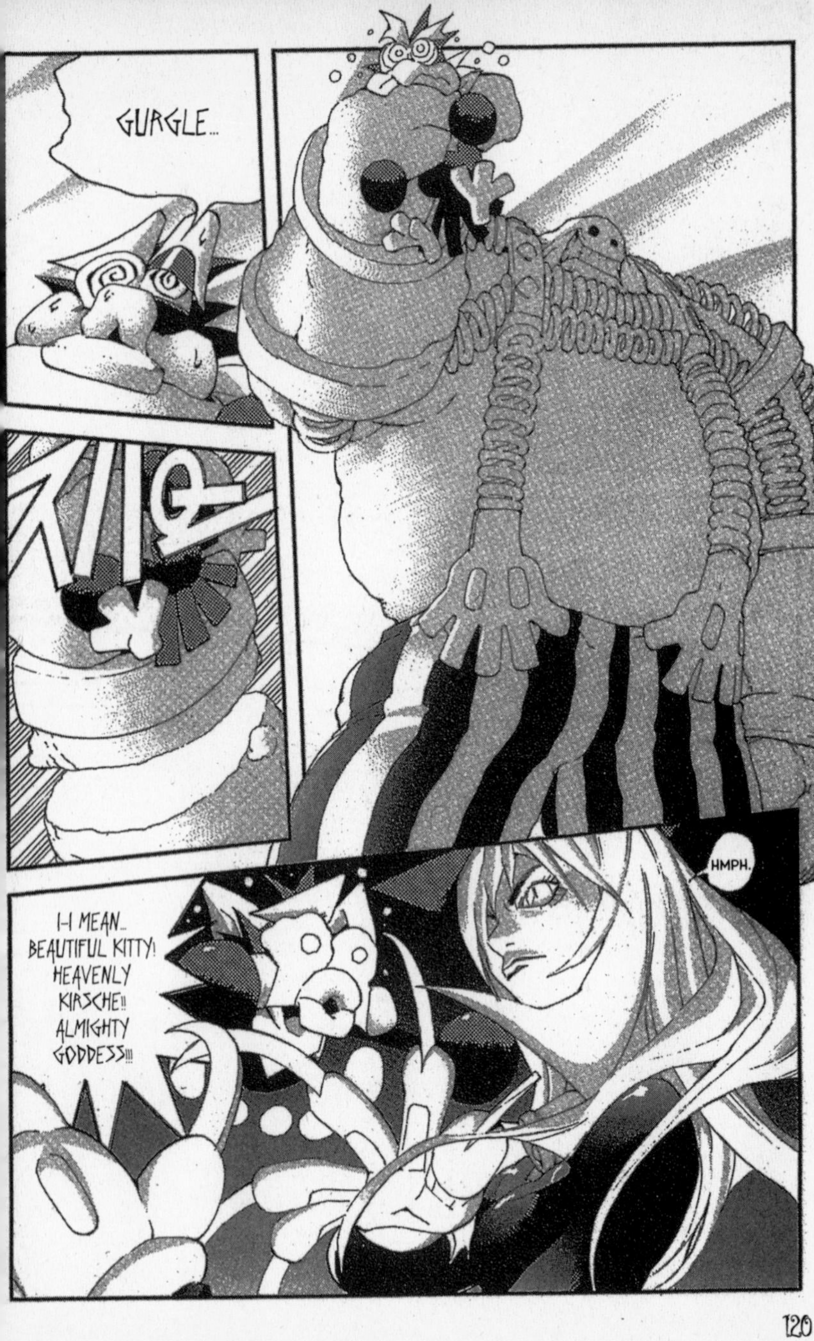
GURGLE...
HMPH.
I-I MEAN... BEAUTIFUL KITTY! HEAVENLY KIRSCHE!! ALMIGHTY GODDESS!!!

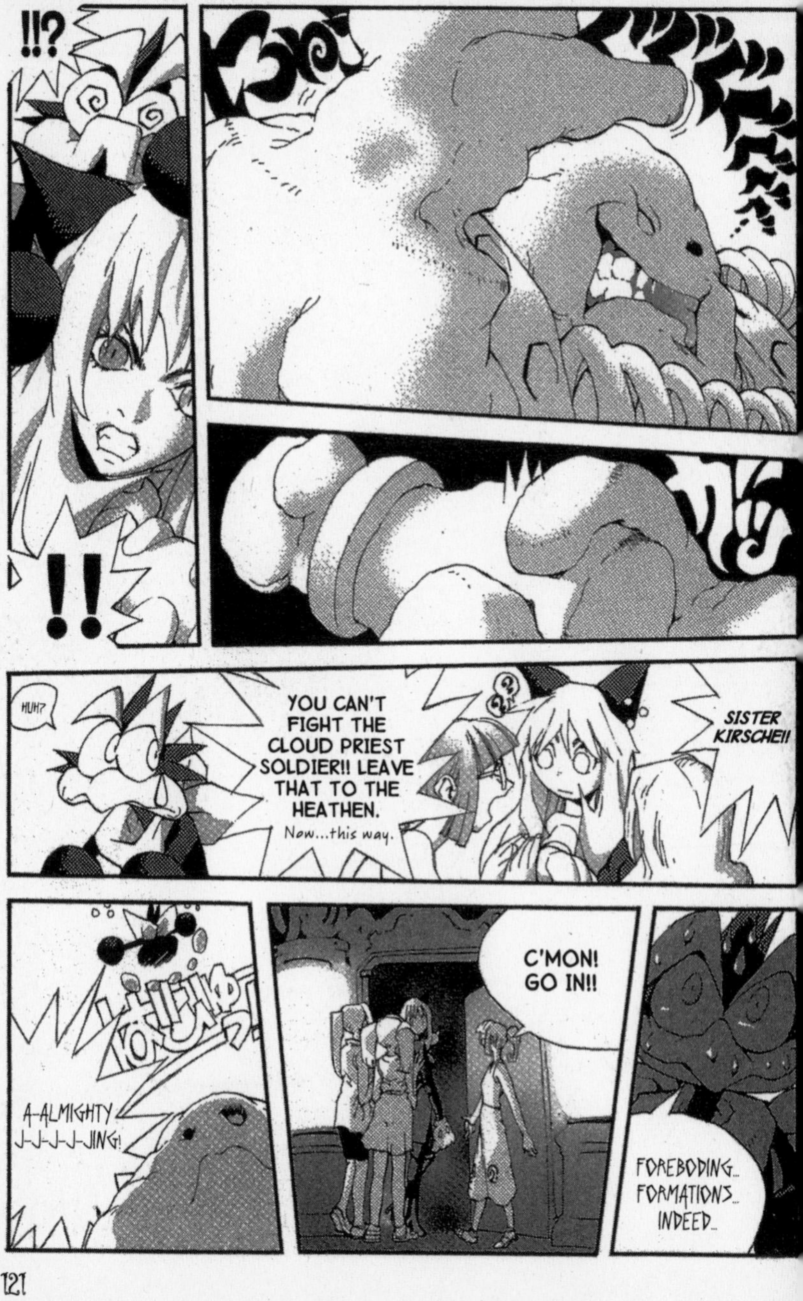
!!?
!!
SISTER KIRSCHE!!
YOU CAN'T FIGHT THE CLOUD PRIEST SOLDIER!! LEAVE THAT TO THE HEATHEN.
Now...this way.
HUH?
FOREBODING... FORMATIONS... INDEED...
C'MON! GO IN!!
A-ALMIGHTY J-J-J-J-JING!

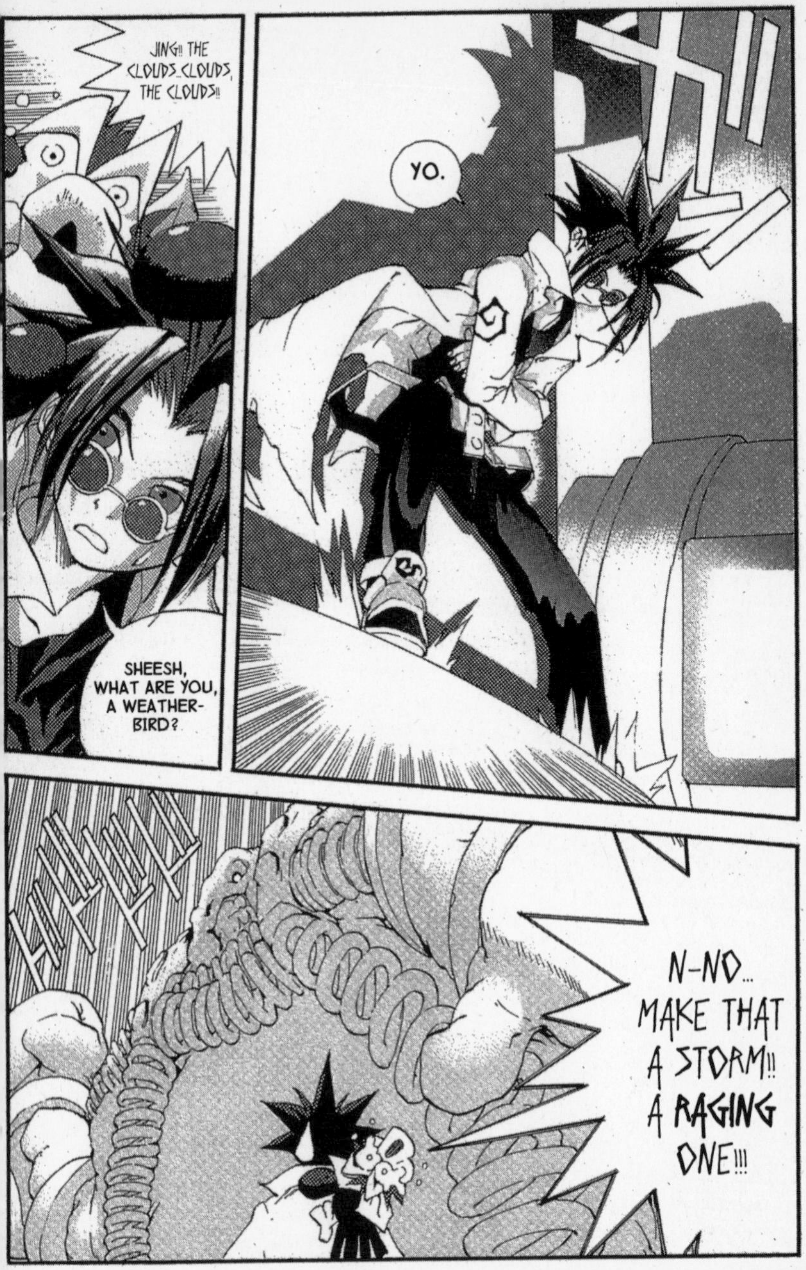
YO.
JING!! THE CLOUDS...CLOUDS, THE CLOUDS!!
SHEESH, WHAT ARE YOU, A WEATHER-BIRD?
N-NO... MAKE THAT A STORM!! A RAGING ONE!!!

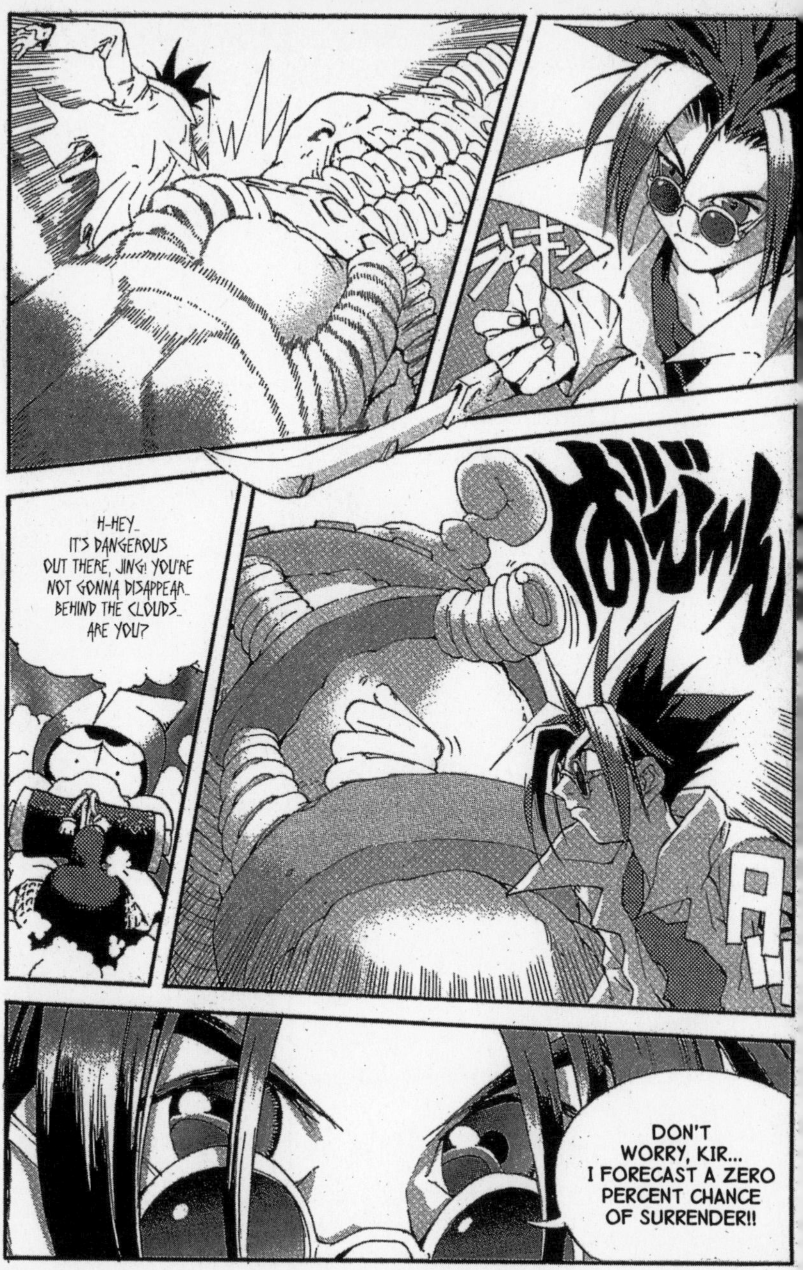
H-HEY... IT'S DANGEROUS OUT THERE, JING! YOU'RE NOT GONNA DISAPPEAR... BEHIND THE CLOUDS... ARE YOU?
DON'T WORRY, KIR... I FORECAST A ZERO PERCENT CHANCE OF SURRENDER!!

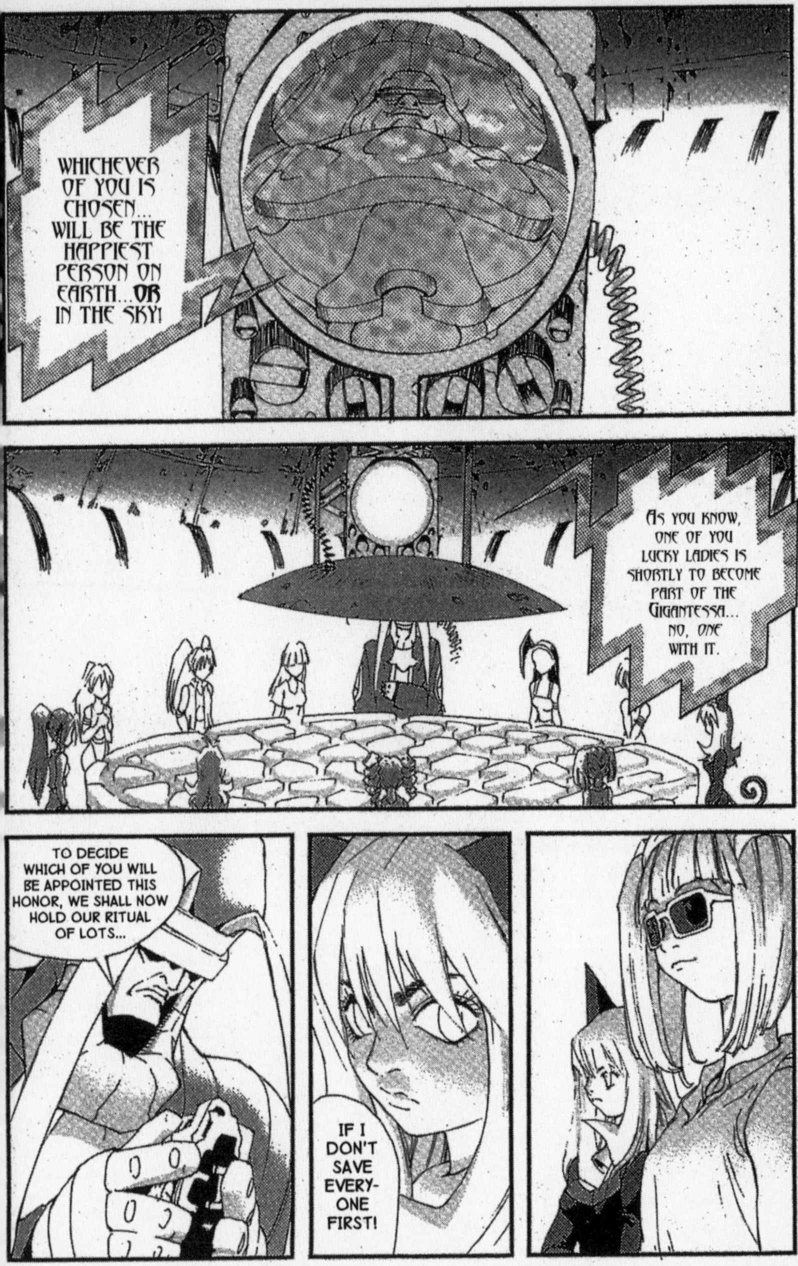
WHICHEVER OF YOU IS CHOSEN... WILL BE THE HAPPIEST PERSON ON EARTH...OR IN THE SKY!
AS YOU KNOW, ONE OF YOU LUCKY LADIES IS SHORTLY TO BECOME PART OF THE GIGANTESSA... NO, ONE WITH IT.
IF I DON'T SAVE EVERY-ONE FIRST!
TO DECIDE WHICH OF YOU WILL BE APPOINTED THIS HONOR, WE SHALL NOW HOLD OUR RITUAL OF LOTS...

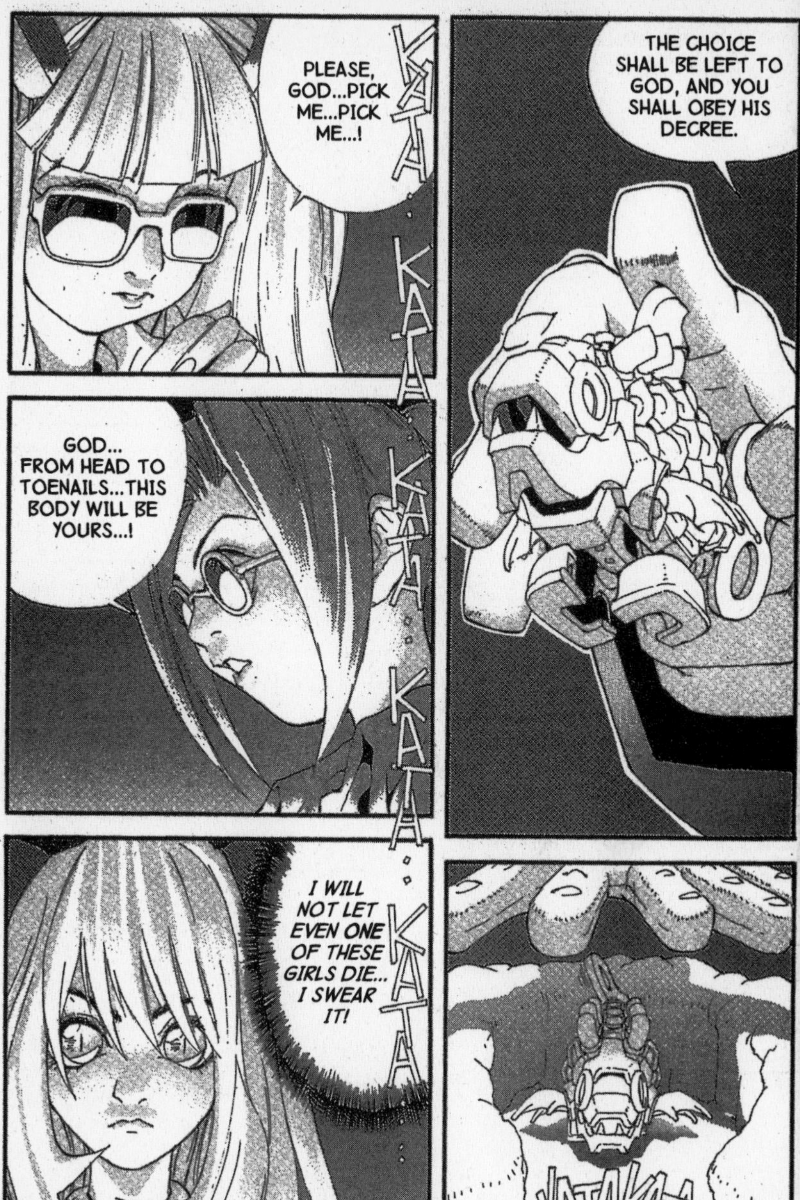
THE CHOICE SHALL BE LEFT TO GOD, AND YOU SHALL OBEY HIS DECREE.
PLEASE, GOD...PICK ME...PICK ME...!
KATA...
GOD... FROM HEAD TO TOENAILS...THIS BODY WILL BE YOURS...!
KATA KATA KATA...
KATAKATA...
I WILL NOT LET EVEN ONE OF THESE GIRLS DIE... I SWEAR IT!
KATA

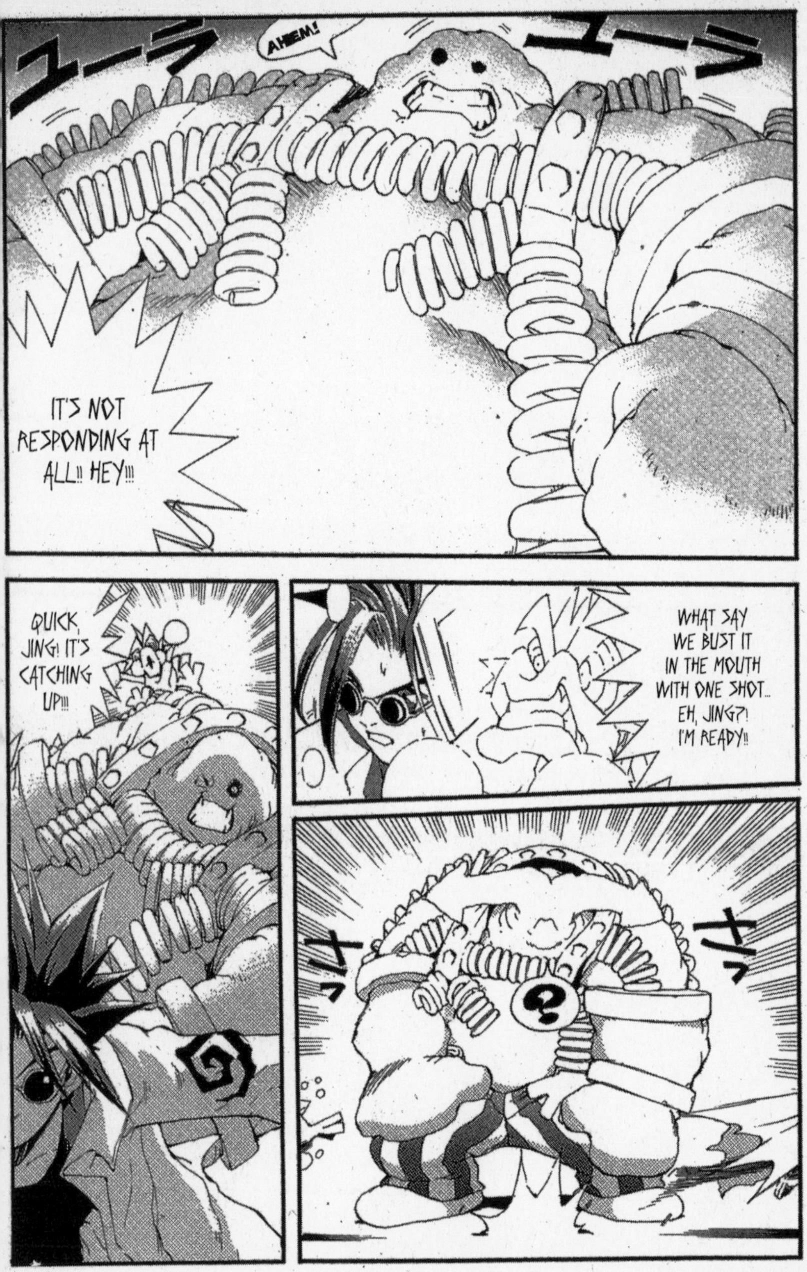
ユーラ
AHEM!
ユーラ
IT'S NOT RESPONDING AT ALL!! HEY!!!
WHAT SAY WE BUST IT IN THE MOUTH WITH ONE SHOT... EH, JING?! I'M READY!!
QUICK, JING! IT'S CATCHING UP!!!

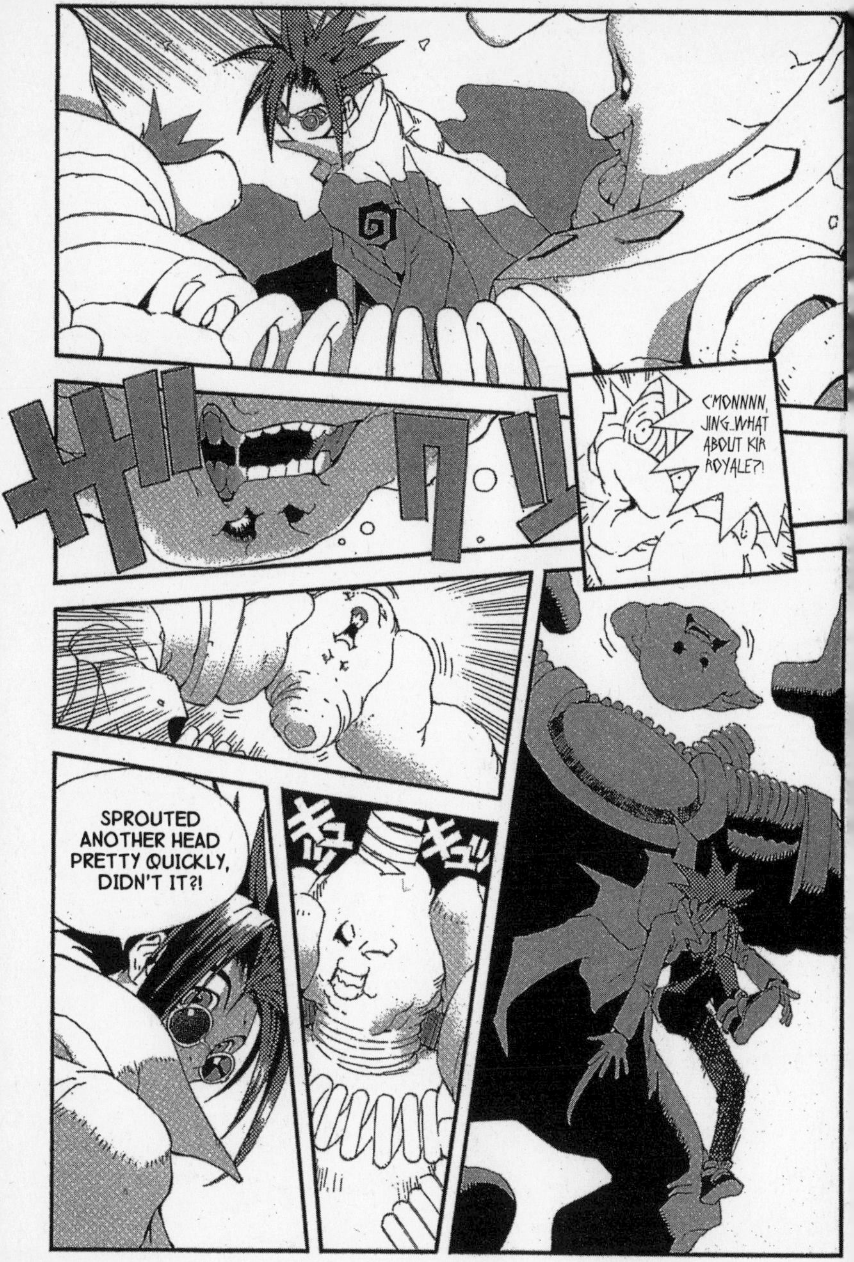
C'MONNNN, JING...WHAT ABOUT KIR ROYALE?!
キュッ
キュッ
SPROUTED ANOTHER HEAD PRETTY QUICKLY, DIDN'T IT?!

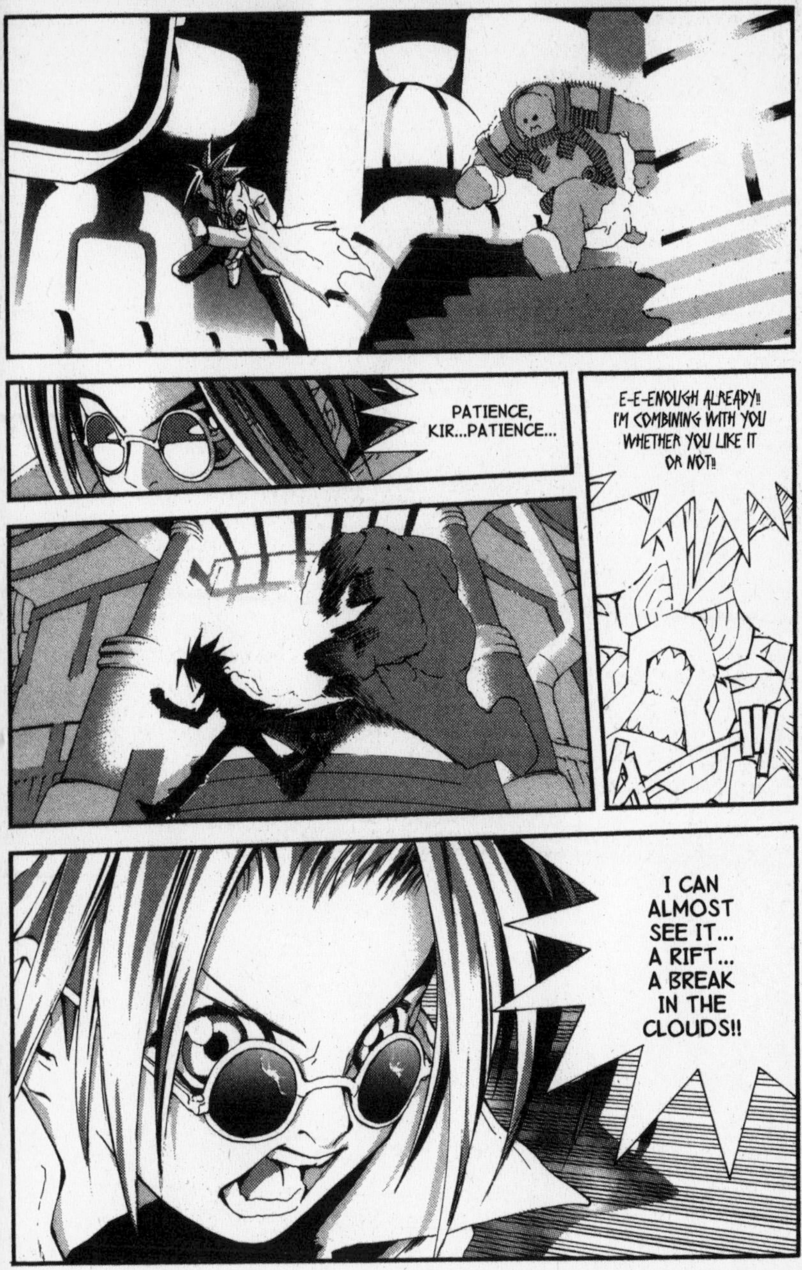
E-E-ENOUGH ALREADY!! I'M COMBINING WITH YOU WHETHER YOU LIKE IT OR NOT!!
PATIENCE, KIR...PATIENCE...
I CAN ALMOST SEE IT... A RIFT... A BREAK IN THE CLOUDS!!

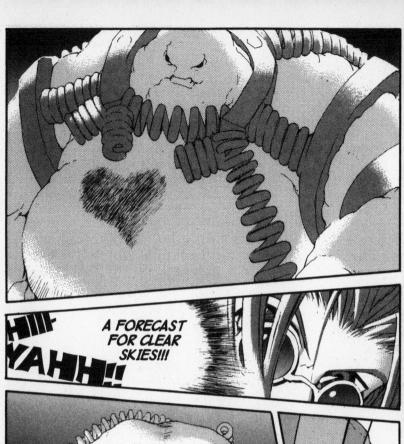

A FORECAST
FOR CLEAR
SKIES!!!

YAHH!!

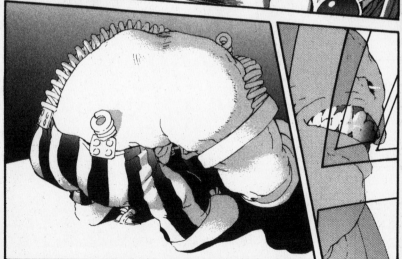

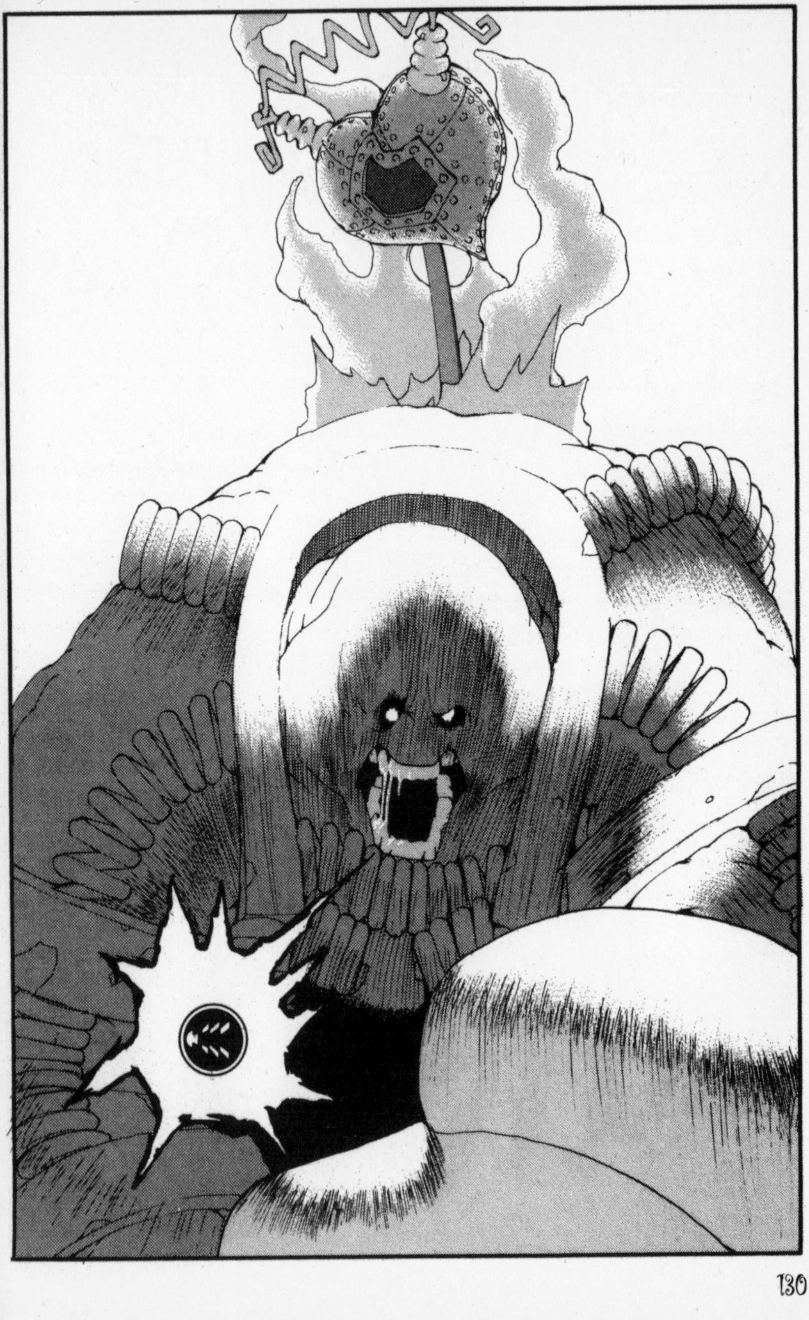

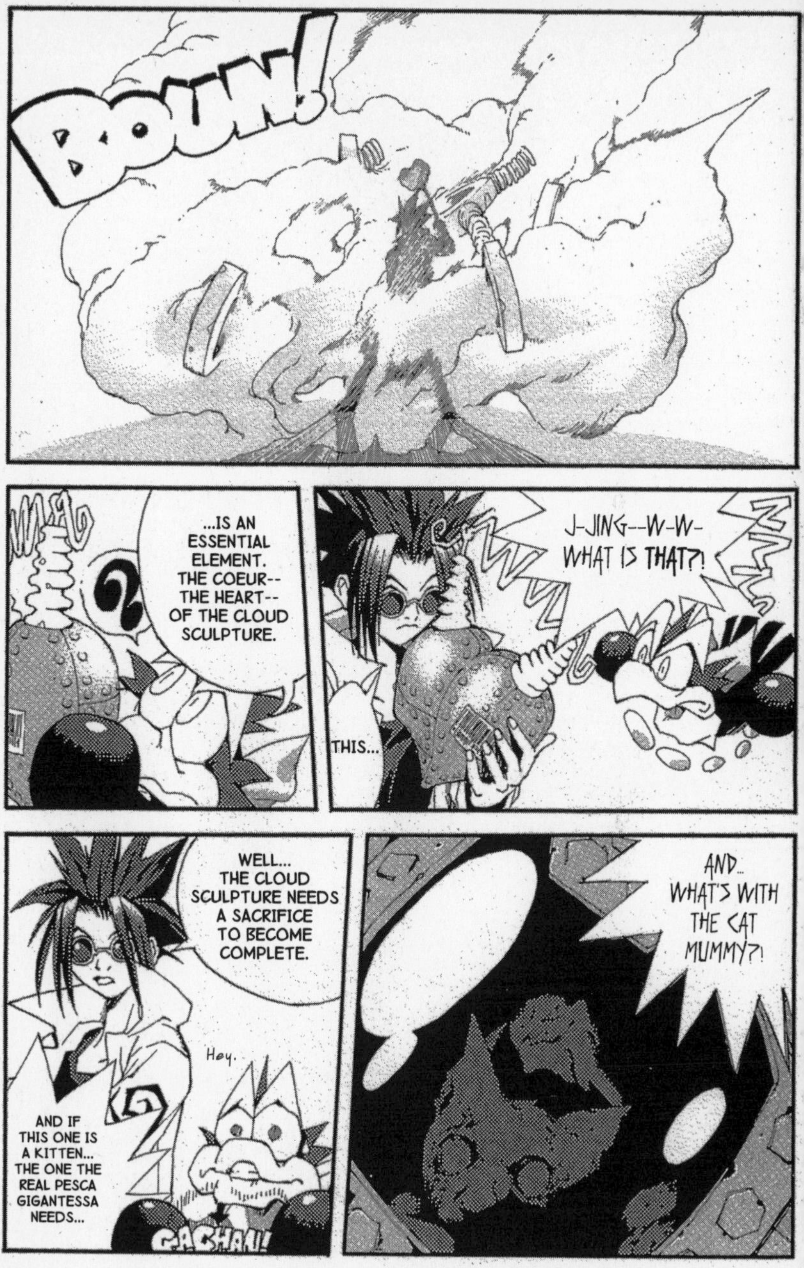
BOOM!
J-JING--W-W-WHAT IS THAT?!
THIS...
...IS AN ESSENTIAL ELEMENT. THE COEUR--THE HEART--OF THE CLOUD SCULPTURE.
AND... WHAT'S WITH THE CAT MUMMY?!
WELL... THE CLOUD SCULPTURE NEEDS A SACRIFICE TO BECOME COMPLETE.
Hey.
AND IF THIS ONE IS A KITTEN... THE ONE THE REAL PESCA GIGANTESSA NEEDS...
GACHAN!

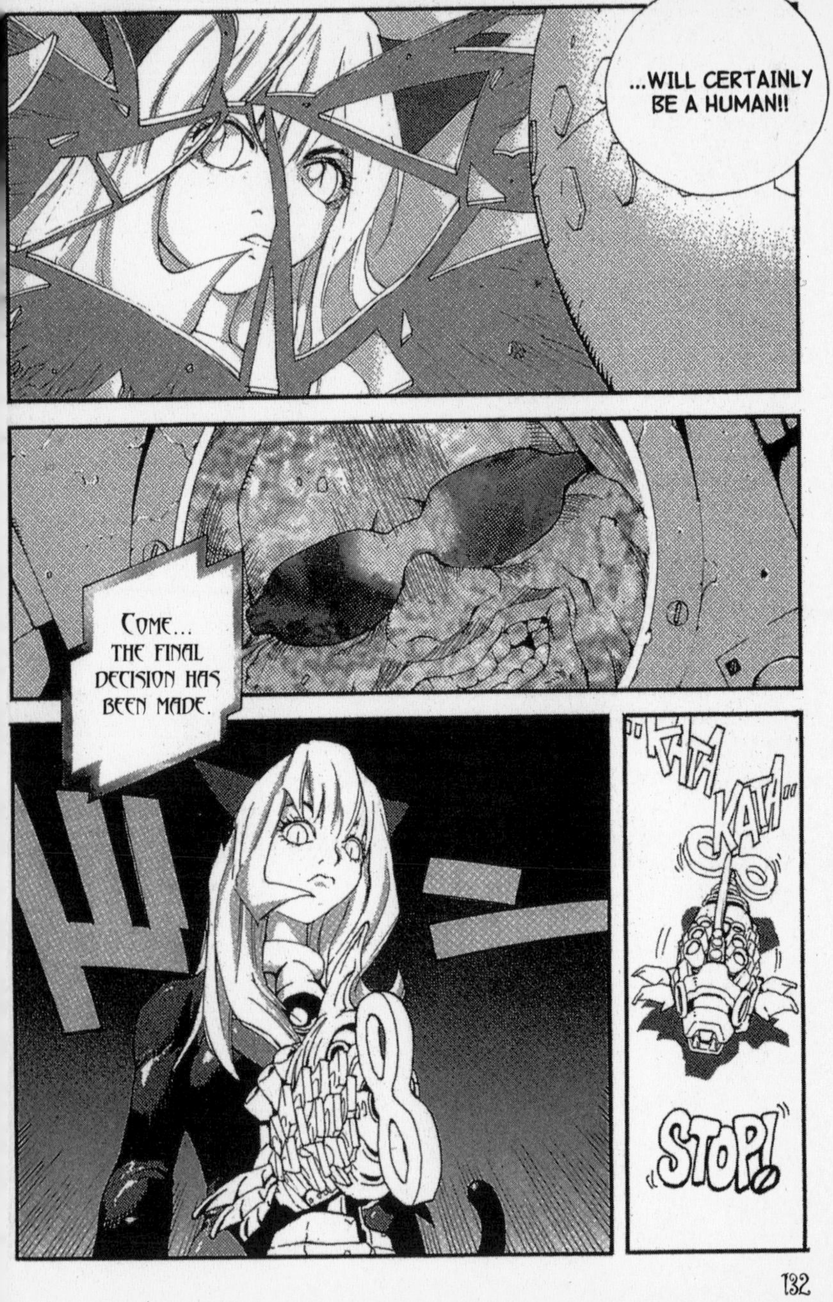
...WILL CERTAINLY BE A HUMAN!!
COME... THE FINAL DECISION HAS BEEN MADE.
KATA KATA
STOP!

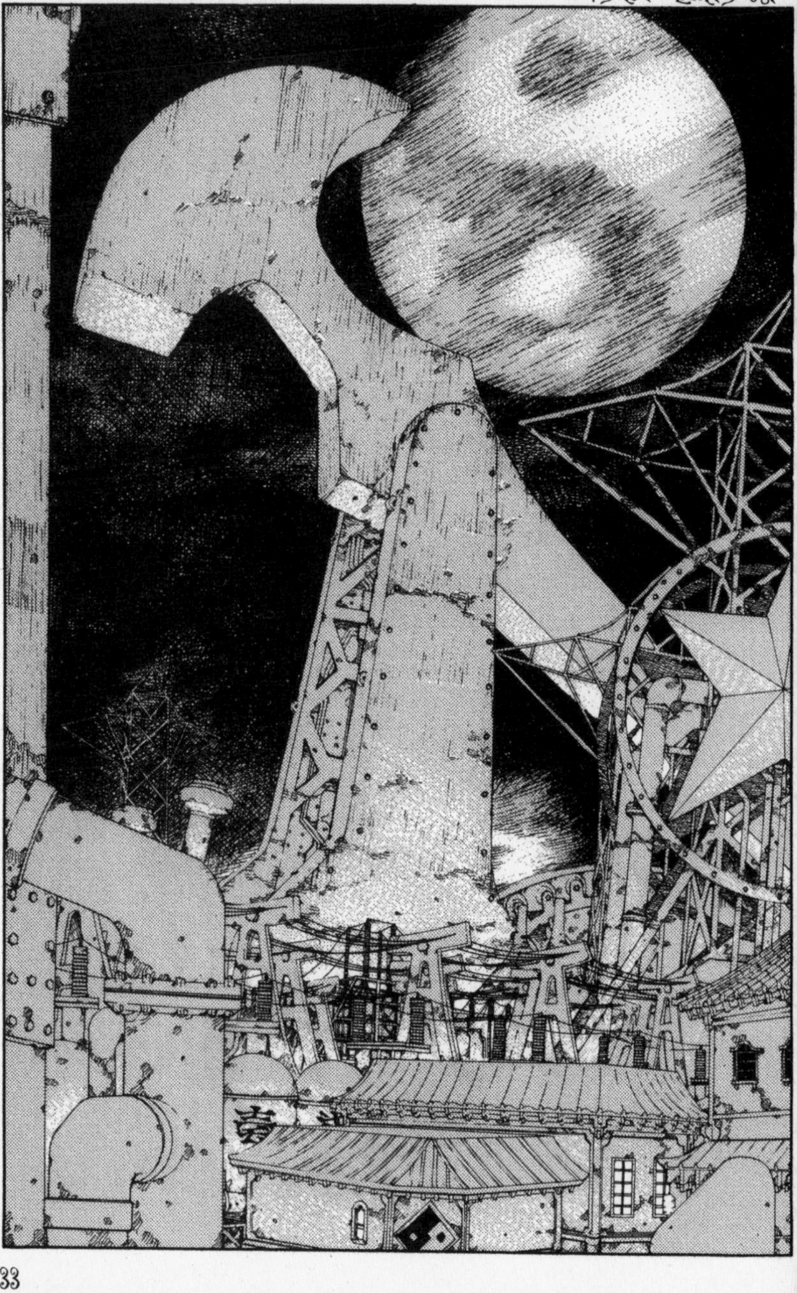

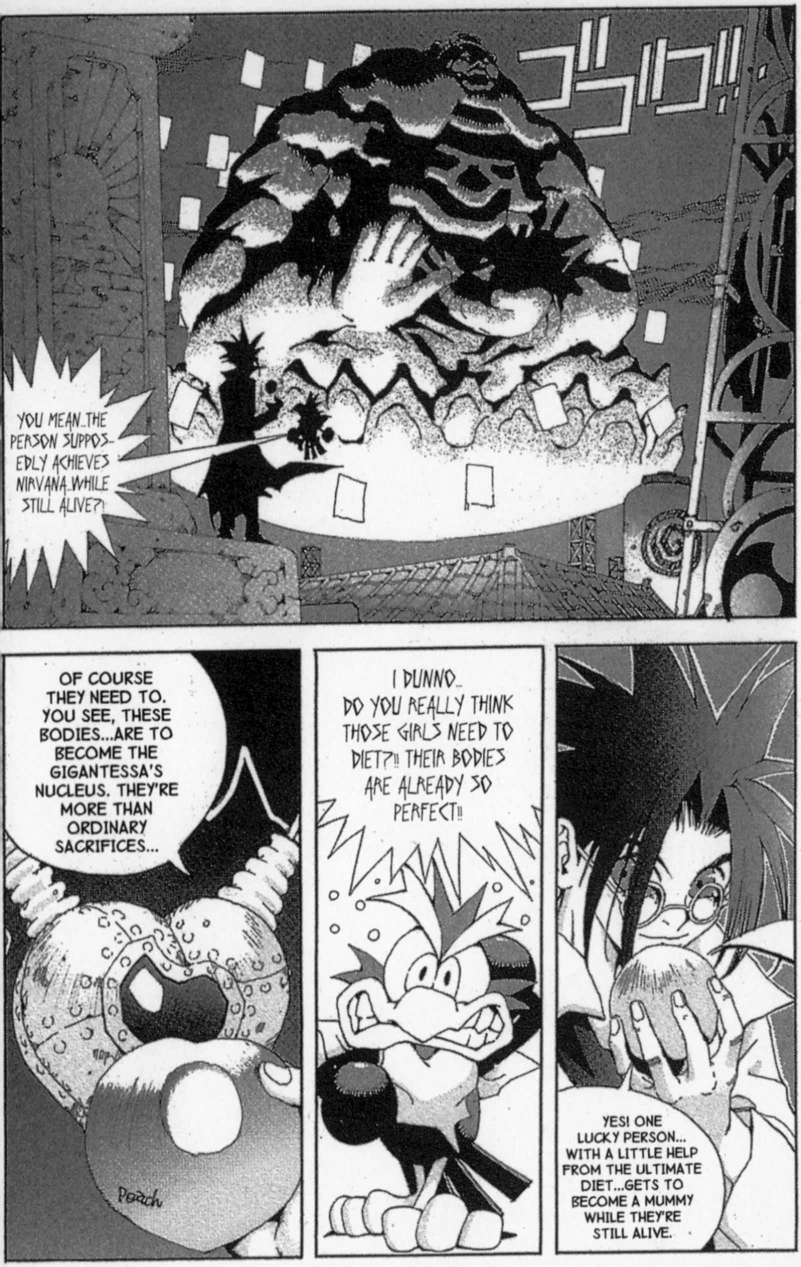
YOU MEAN...THE PERSON SUPPOSEDLY ACHIEVES NIRVANA...WHILE STILL ALIVE?!
YES! ONE LUCKY PERSON... WITH A LITTLE HELP FROM THE ULTIMATE DIET...GETS TO BECOME A MUMMY WHILE THEY'RE STILL ALIVE.
I DUNNO... DO YOU REALLY THINK THOSE GIRLS NEED TO DIET?!! THEIR BODIES ARE ALREADY SO PERFECT!!
OF COURSE THEY NEED TO. YOU SEE, THESE BODIES...ARE TO BECOME THE GIGANTESSA'S NUCLEUS. THEY'RE MORE THAN ORDINARY SACRIFICES...

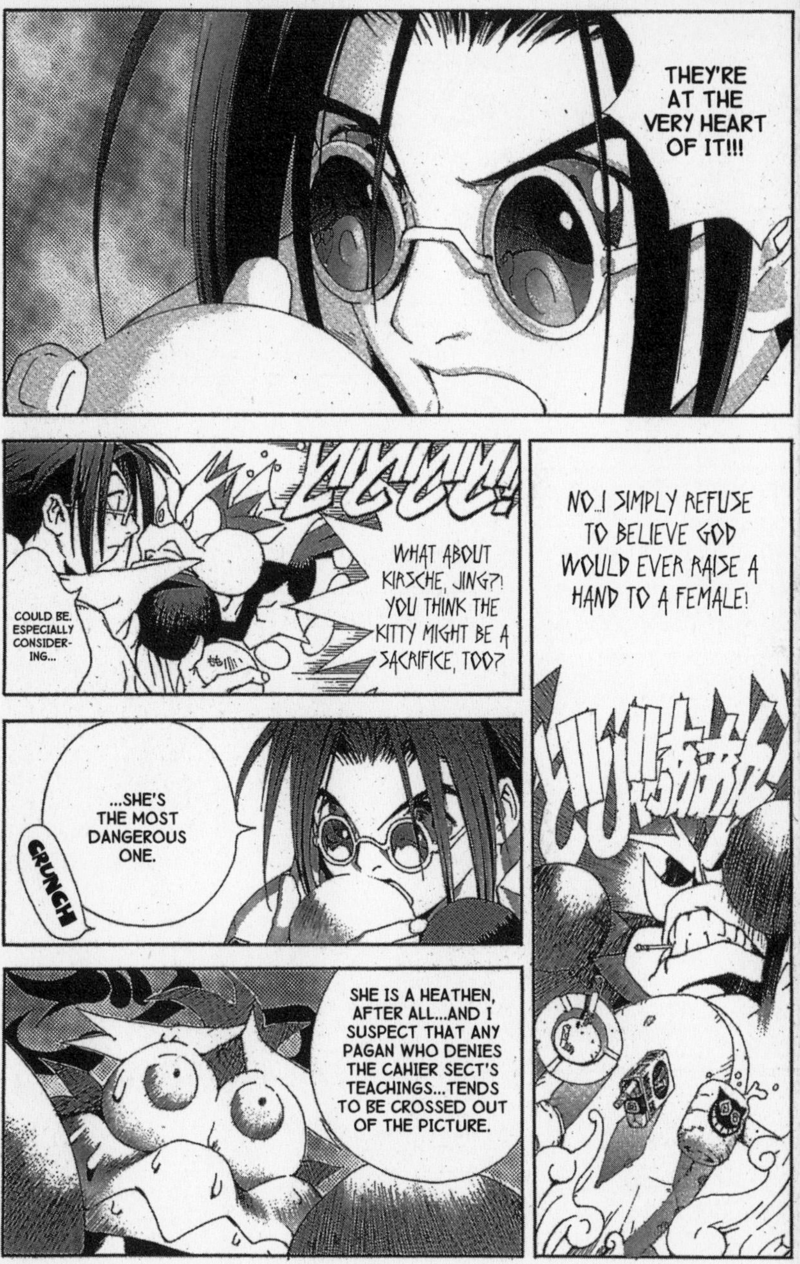
THEY'RE AT THE VERY HEART OF IT!!!
NO...I SIMPLY REFUSE TO BELIEVE GOD WOULD EVER RAISE A HAND TO A FEMALE!
WHAT ABOUT KIRSCHE, JING?! YOU THINK THE KITTY MIGHT BE A SACRIFICE, TOO?
COULD BE. ESPECIALLY CONSIDER-ING...
...SHE'S THE MOST DANGEROUS ONE.
CRUNCH
SHE IS A HEATHEN, AFTER ALL...AND I SUSPECT THAT ANY PAGAN WHO DENIES THE CAHIER SECT'S TEACHINGS...TENDS TO BE CROSSED OUT OF THE PICTURE.

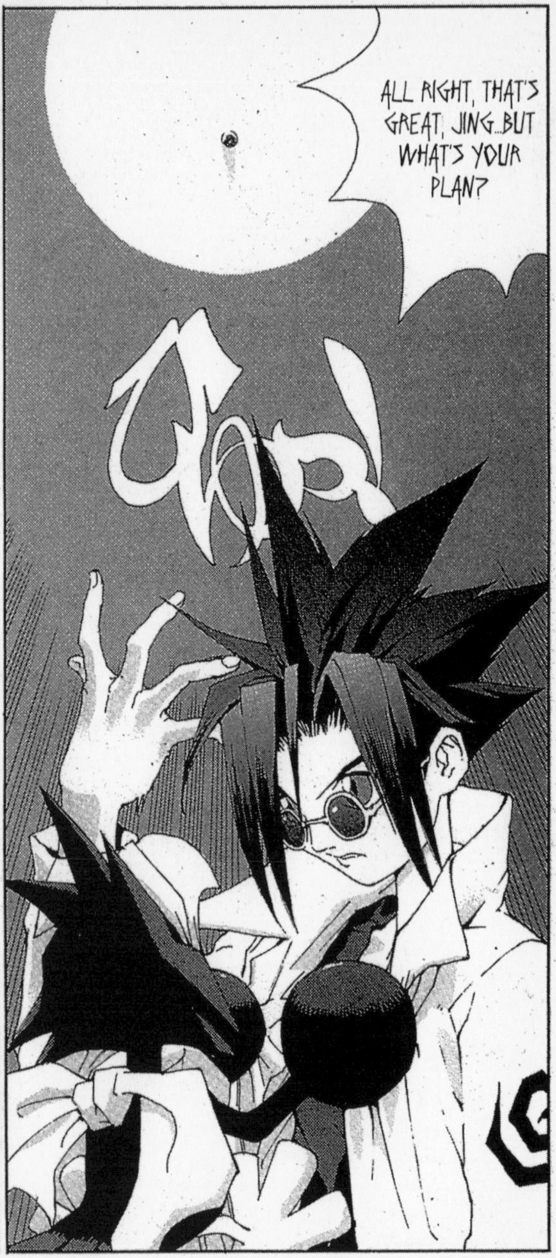
ALL RIGHT, THAT'S GREAT, JING...BUT WHAT'S YOUR PLAN?
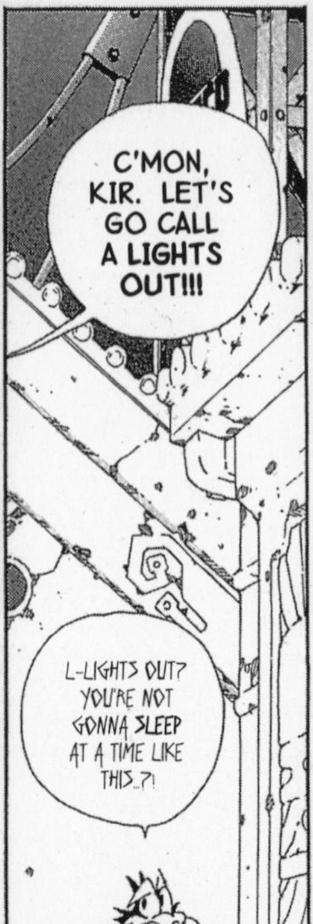
C'MON, KIR. LET'S GO CALL A LIGHTS OUT!!!
L-LIGHTS OUT? YOU'RE NOT GONNA SLEEP AT A TIME LIKE THIS...?!

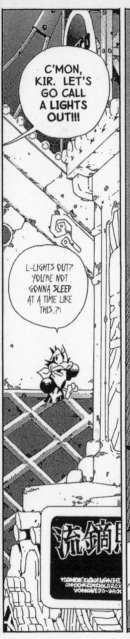

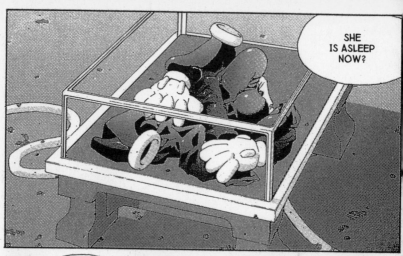

SHE IS ASLEEP NOW?

YES... AND IF WE PURIFY THE ABLUTIONS OF INSULATION TOMORROW MORNING, WE WILL BE ABLE TO DISCHARGE THE COEUR.

HO HO! SOMEHOW I HAD EXPECTED A LITTLE MORE... RESISTANCE... FROM HER AND HER PAGAN FOLLOWERS.

THAT GIRL MAY BE A HEATHEN...BUT SHE IS AS NOBLE AS THEY COME!

EVEN WHEN SHE WAS SELECTED...

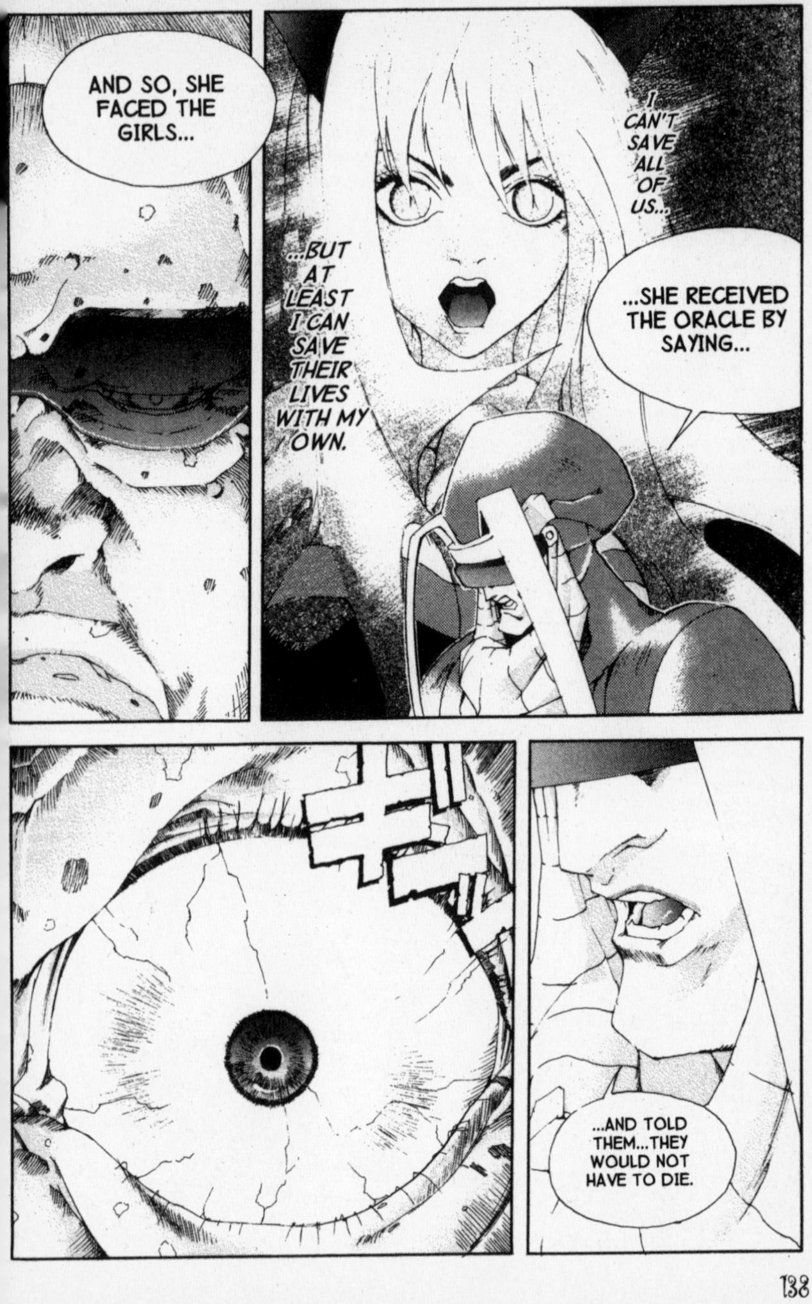
I CAN'T SAVE ALL OF US...
...BUT AT LEAST I CAN SAVE THEIR LIVES WITH MY OWN.
...SHE RECEIVED THE ORACLE BY SAYING...
AND SO, SHE FACED THE GIRLS...
...AND TOLD THEM...THEY WOULD NOT HAVE TO DIE.

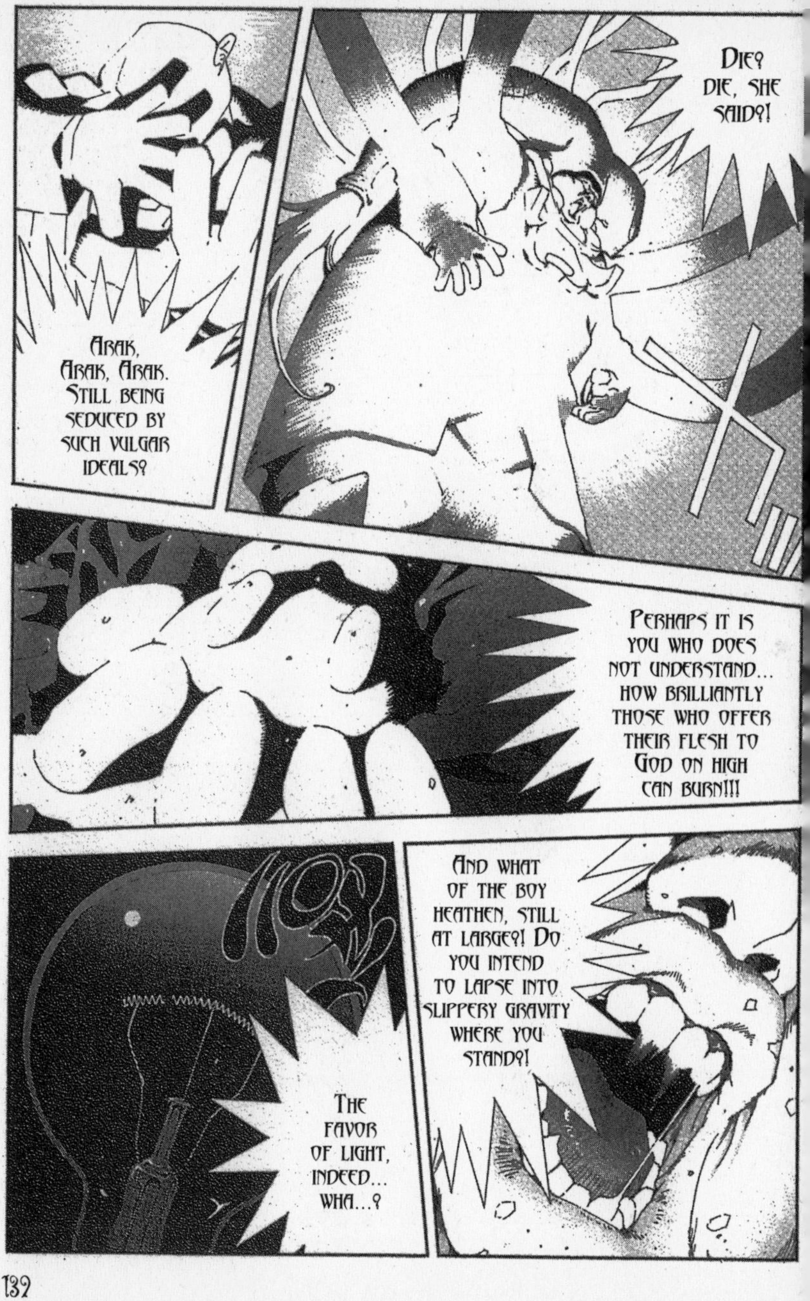
Die? Die, she said?!
Arak, Arak, Arak. Still being seduced by such vulgar ideals?
Perhaps it is you who does not understand... how brilliantly those who offer their flesh to God on high can burn!!!
And what of the boy heathen, still at large?! Do you intend to lapse into slippery gravity where you stand?!
The favor of light, indeed... wha...?

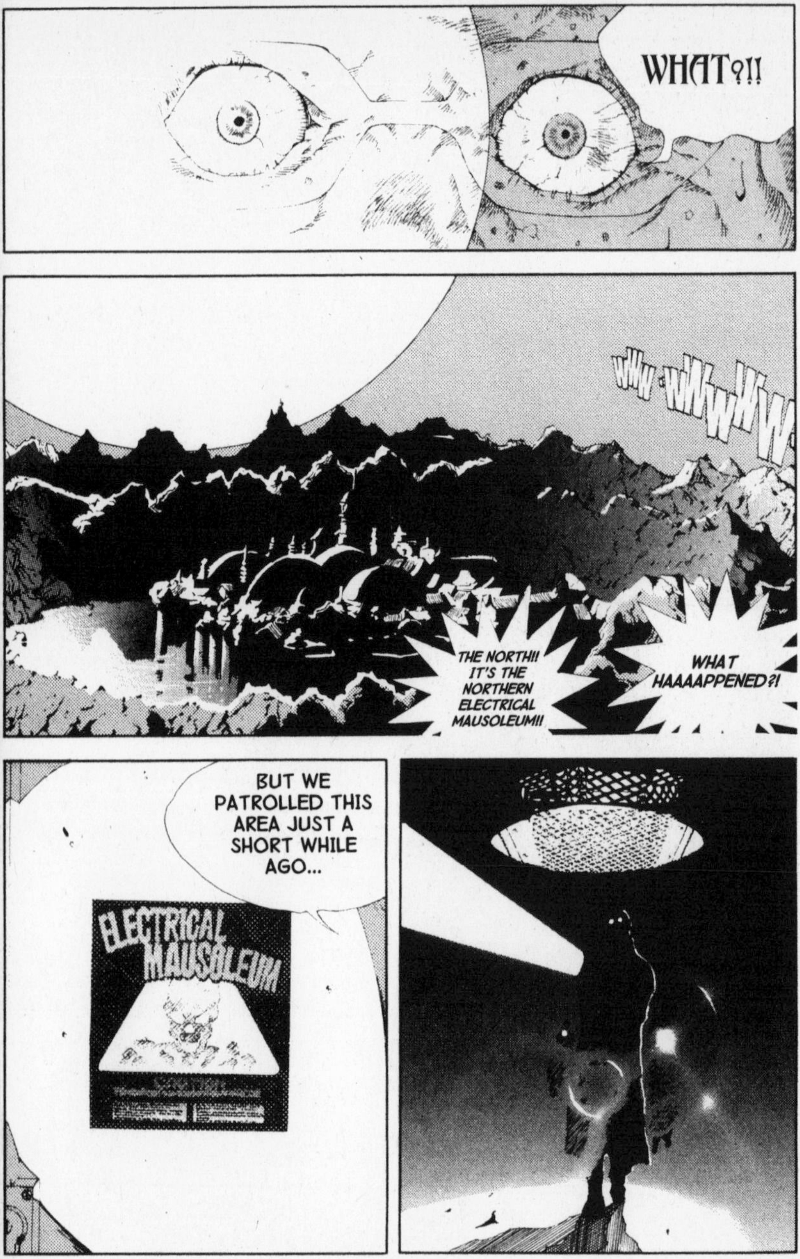
WHAT?!!
WHAT HAAAAPPENED?!
THE NORTH!! IT'S THE NORTHERN ELECTRICAL MAUSOLEUM!!
BUT WE PATROLLED THIS AREA JUST A SHORT WHILE AGO...
ELECTRICAL MAUSOLEUM

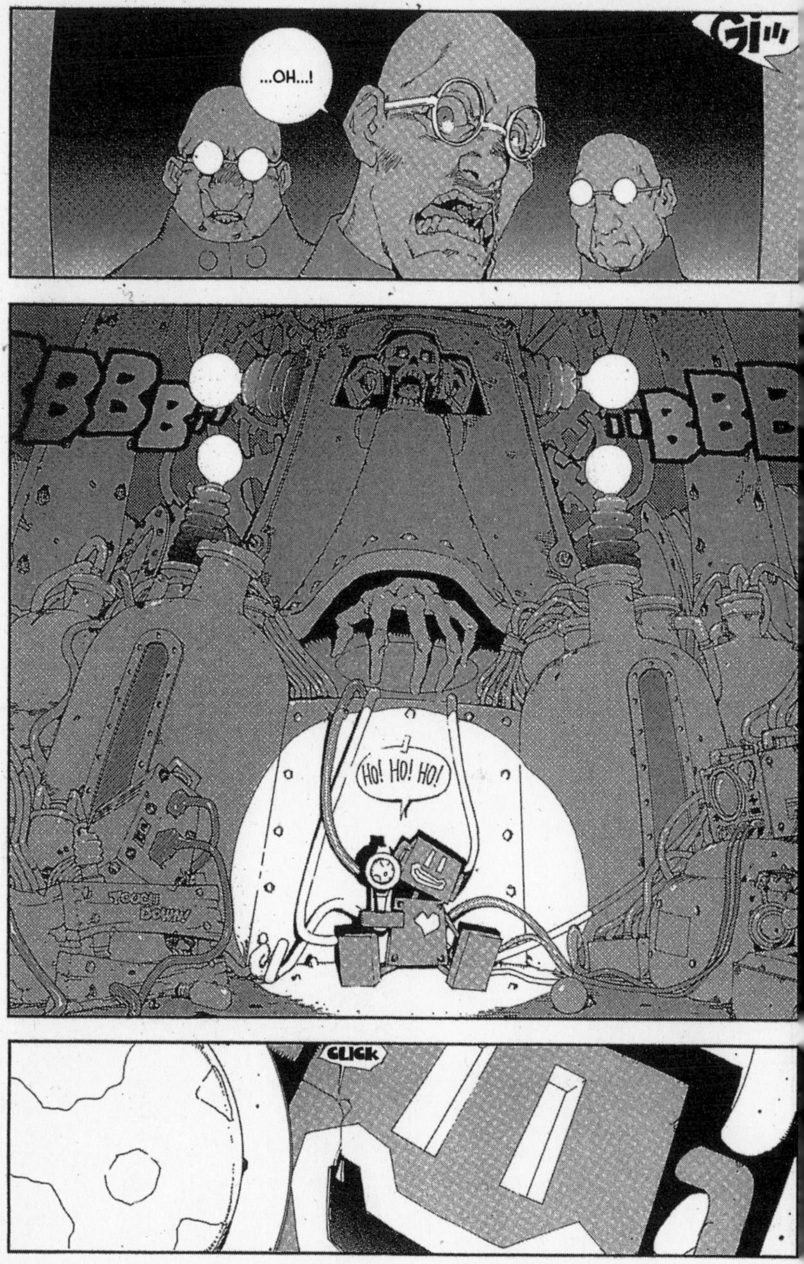
GI
...OH...!
BBB
BBB
HO! HO! HO!
CLICK

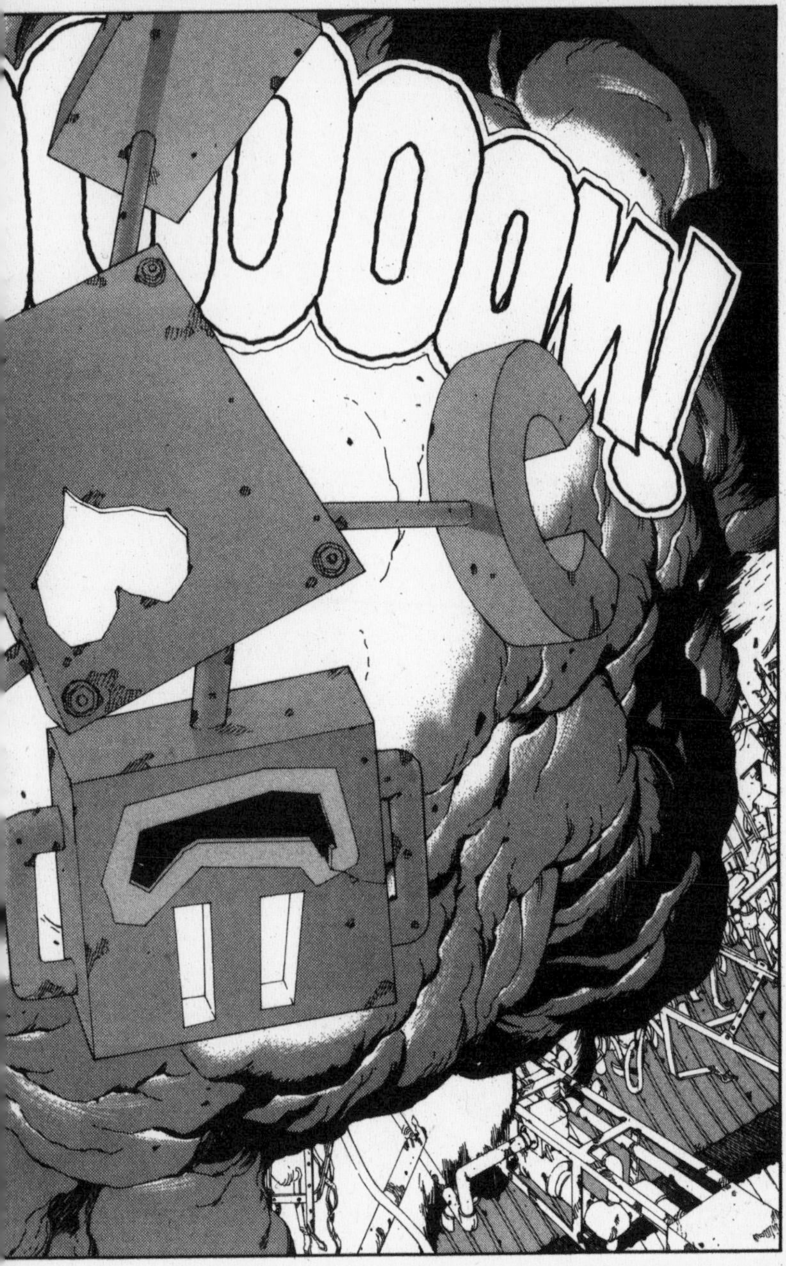
OOOOM!

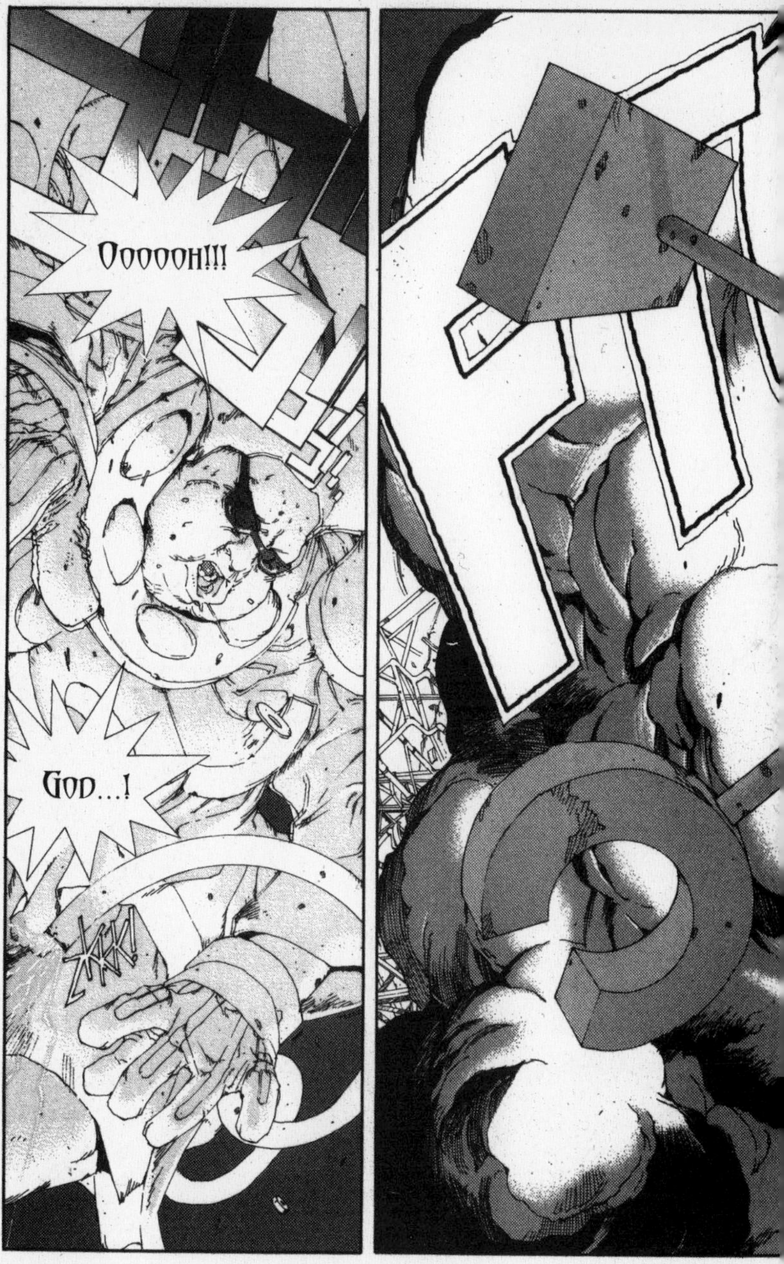
OOOOOH!!!
GOD...!
ZAK!

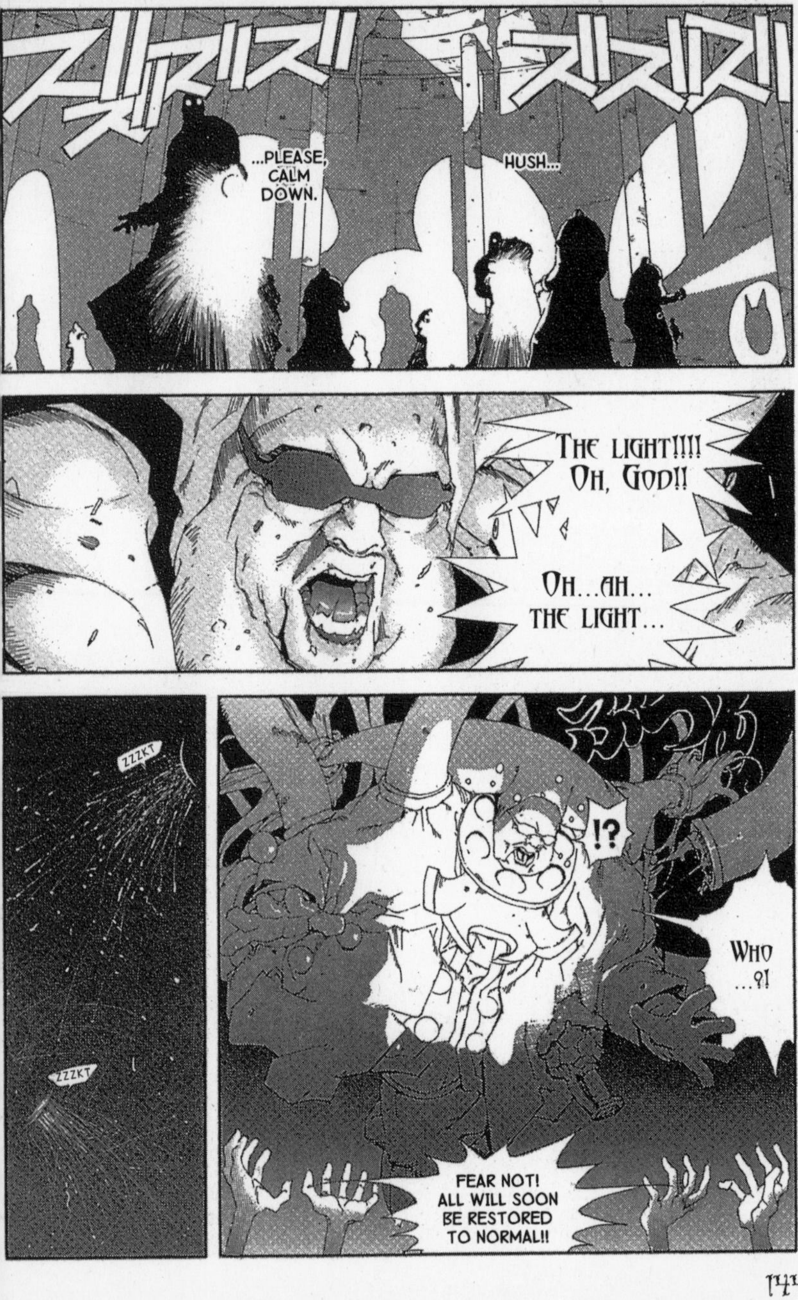
HUSH...
...PLEASE, CALM DOWN.
THE LIGHT!!!! OH, GOD!!
OH...AH... THE LIGHT...
!?
WHO ...?!
FEAR NOT! ALL WILL SOON BE RESTORED TO NORMAL!!
ZZZKT
ZZZKT

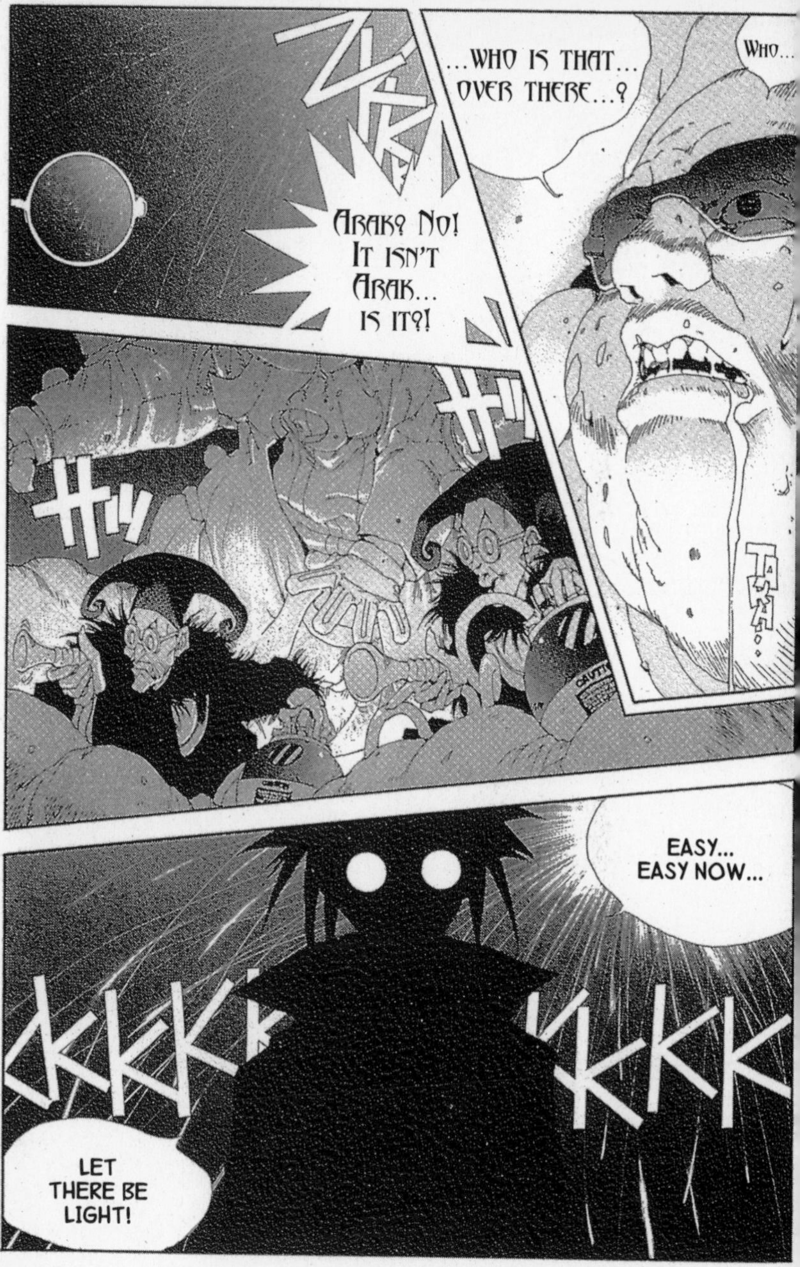
WHO...
...WHO IS THAT... OVER THERE...?
ARAK? NO! IT ISN'T ARAK... IS IT?!
EASY... EASY NOW...
LET THERE BE LIGHT!

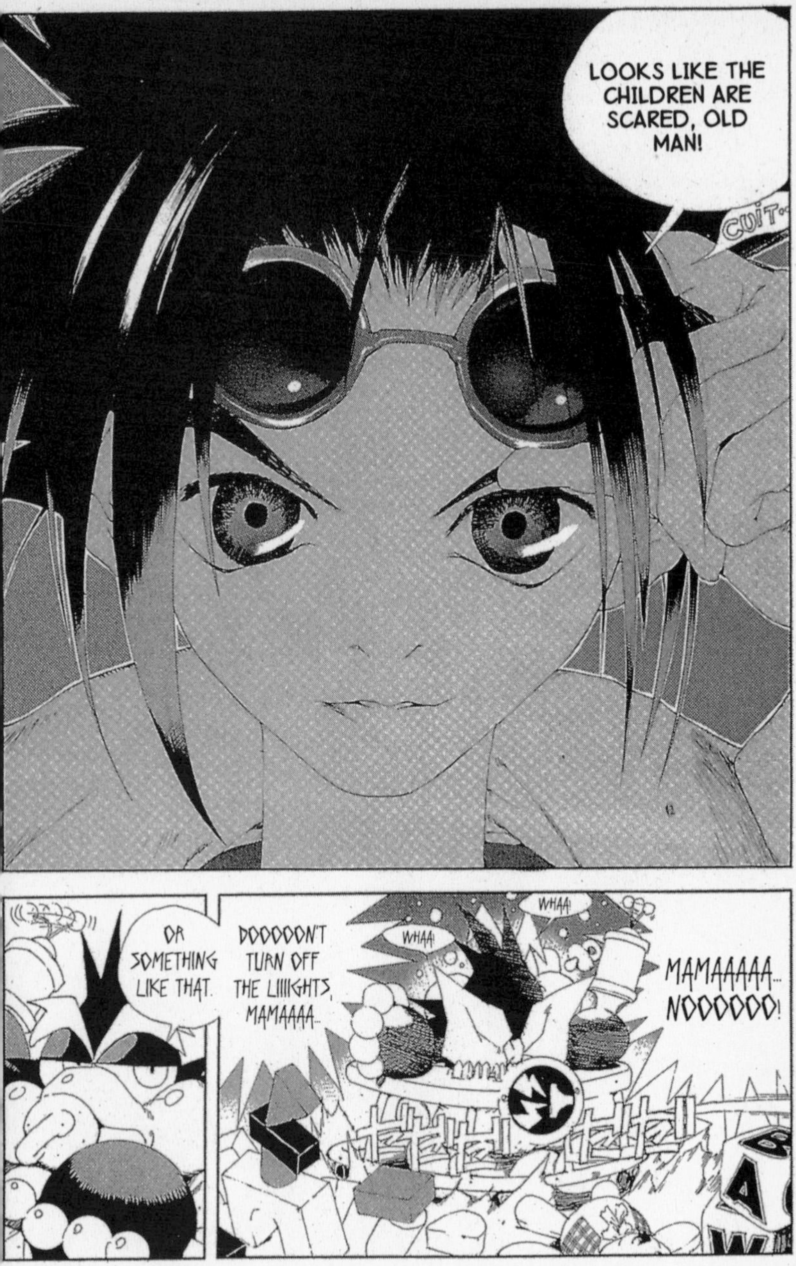
LOOKS LIKE THE CHILDREN ARE SCARED, OLD MAN!
CUIT..
WHAA!
MAMAAAAA... NOOOOOO!
WHAA!
DOOOOON'T TURN OFF THE LIIIIGHTS, MAMAAAA...
OR SOMETHING LIKE THAT.

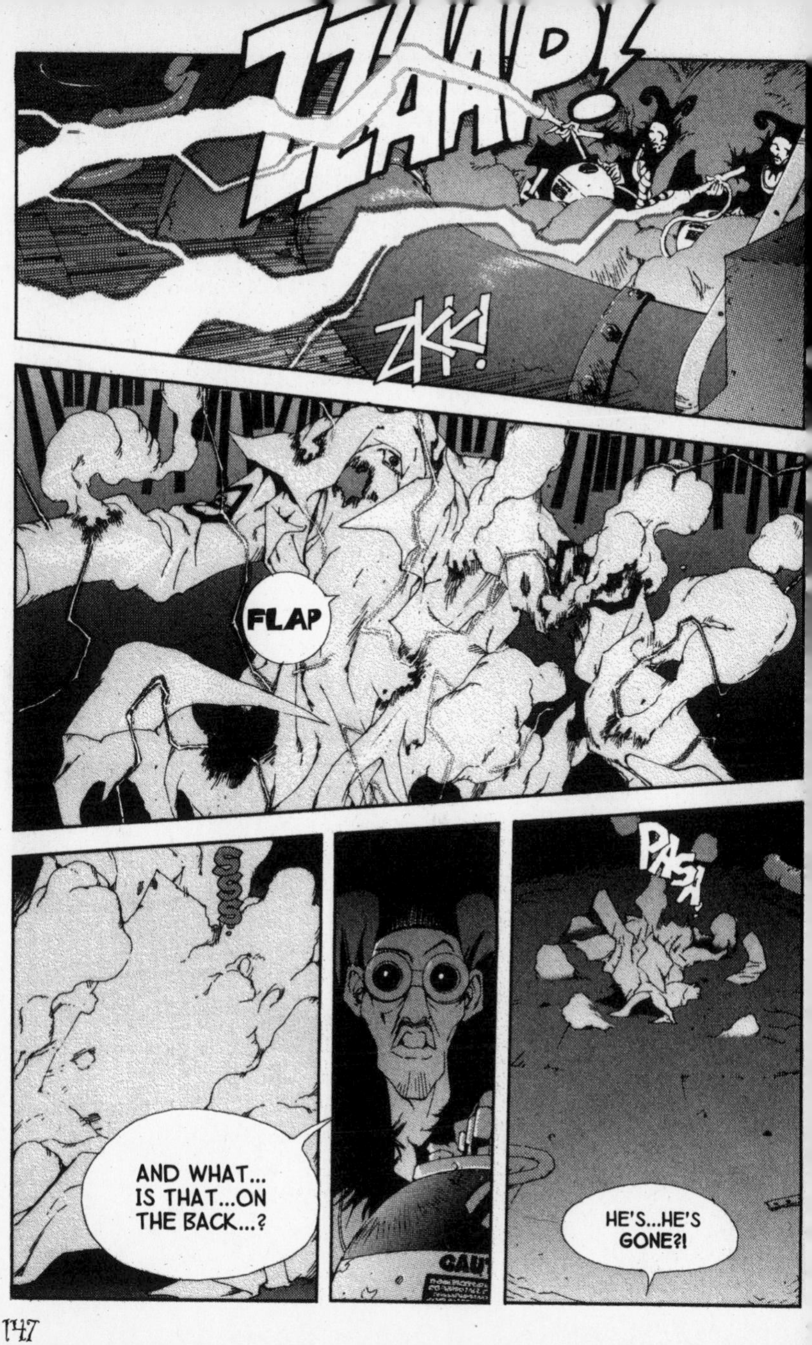
ZZAP!
ZKK!
FLAP
PASH!
HE'S...HE'S GONE?!
SSSS
AND WHAT... IS THAT...ON THE BACK...?

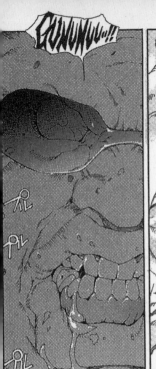

Mister Ruler of
Navel, Sir,
I'm going to take
clouds with
no place to go
from a sky where
there is no refuge.
--The King of Bandits

GET ARAK HERE RIGHT NOW!

ARAK...!

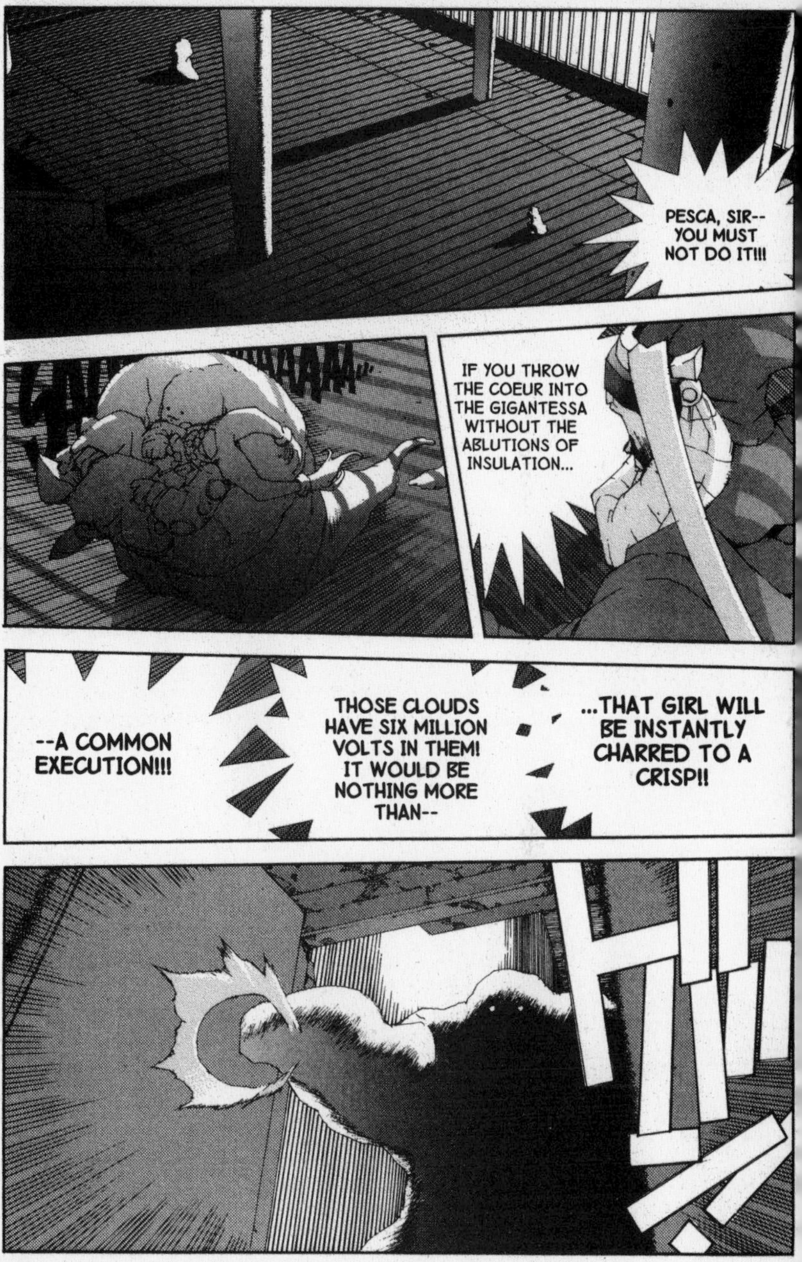
PESCA, SIR-- YOU MUST NOT DO IT!!!
IF YOU THROW THE COEUR INTO THE GIGANTESSA WITHOUT THE ABLUTIONS OF INSULATION...
...THAT GIRL WILL BE INSTANTLY CHARRED TO A CRISP!!
THOSE CLOUDS HAVE SIX MILLION VOLTS IN THEM! IT WOULD BE NOTHING MORE THAN--
--A COMMON EXECUTION!!!

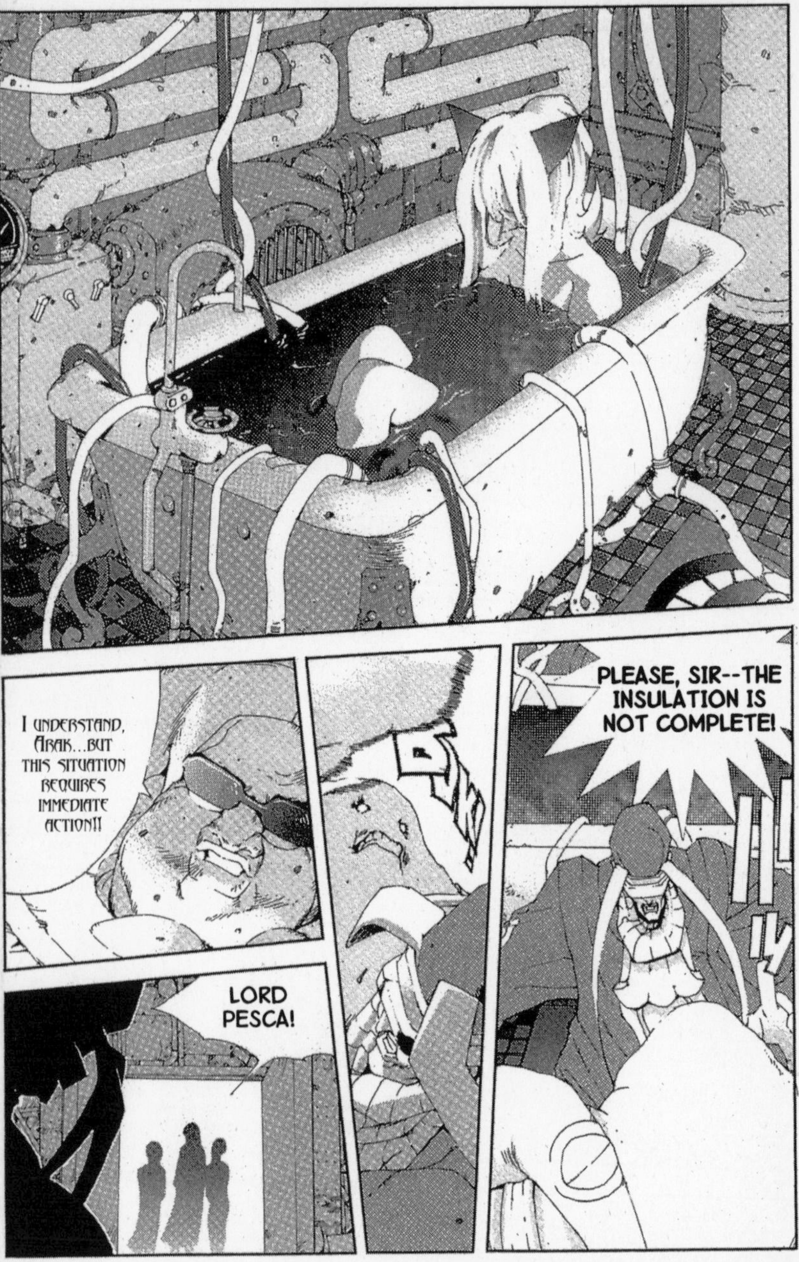

PLEASE, SIR--THE INSULATION IS NOT COMPLETE!
I UNDERSTAND, ARAK...BUT THIS SITUATION REQUIRES IMMEDIATE ACTION!!
LORD PESCA!

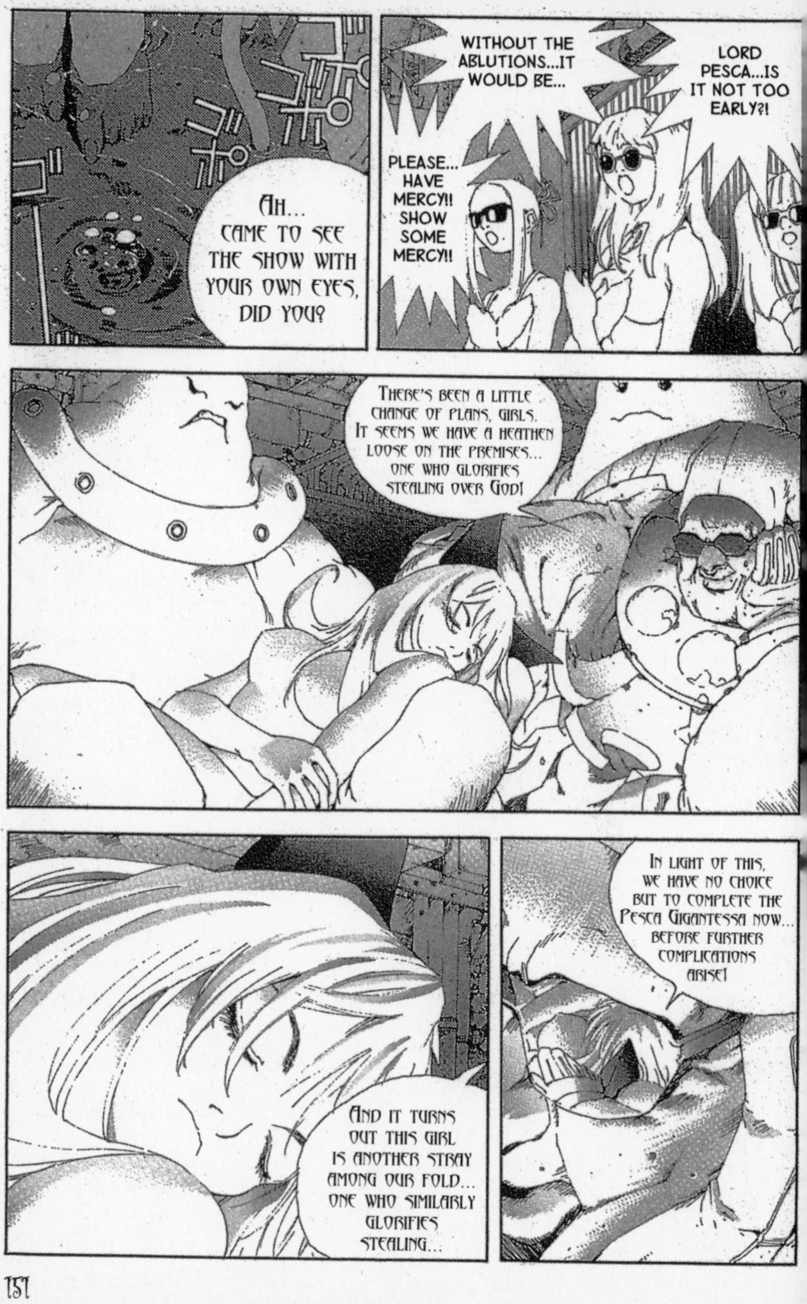
LORD PESCA...IS IT NOT TOO EARLY?!
WITHOUT THE ABLUTIONS...IT WOULD BE...
PLEASE... HAVE MERCY!! SHOW SOME MERCY!!
AH... CAME TO SEE THE SHOW WITH YOUR OWN EYES, DID YOU?
THERE'S BEEN A LITTLE CHANGE OF PLANS, GIRLS. IT SEEMS WE HAVE A HEATHEN LOOSE ON THE PREMISES... ONE WHO GLORIFIES STEALING OVER GOD!
IN LIGHT OF THIS, WE HAVE NO CHOICE BUT TO COMPLETE THE PESCA GIGANTESSA NOW... BEFORE FURTHER COMPLICATIONS ARISE!
AND IT TURNS OUT THIS GIRL IS ANOTHER STRAY AMONG OUR FOLD... ONE WHO SIMILARLY GLORIFIES STEALING...

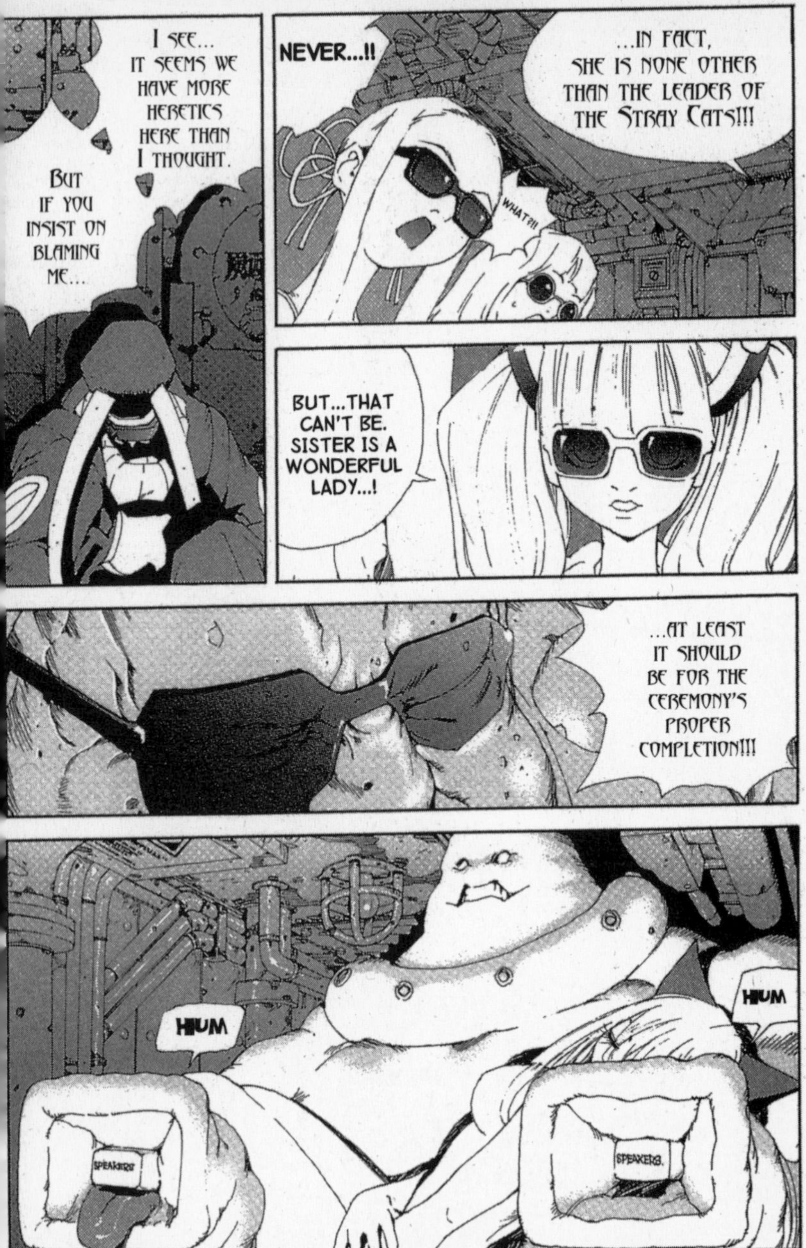
...IN FACT, SHE IS NONE OTHER THAN THE LEADER OF THE STRAY CATS!!!
NEVER...!!
WHAT?!!
BUT...THAT CAN'T BE. SISTER IS A WONDERFUL LADY...!
I SEE... IT SEEMS WE HAVE MORE HERETICS HERE THAN I THOUGHT.
BUT IF YOU INSIST ON BLAMING ME...
...AT LEAST IT SHOULD BE FOR THE CEREMONY'S PROPER COMPLETION!!!
HIUM
SPEAKERS.
HIUM
SPEAKERS

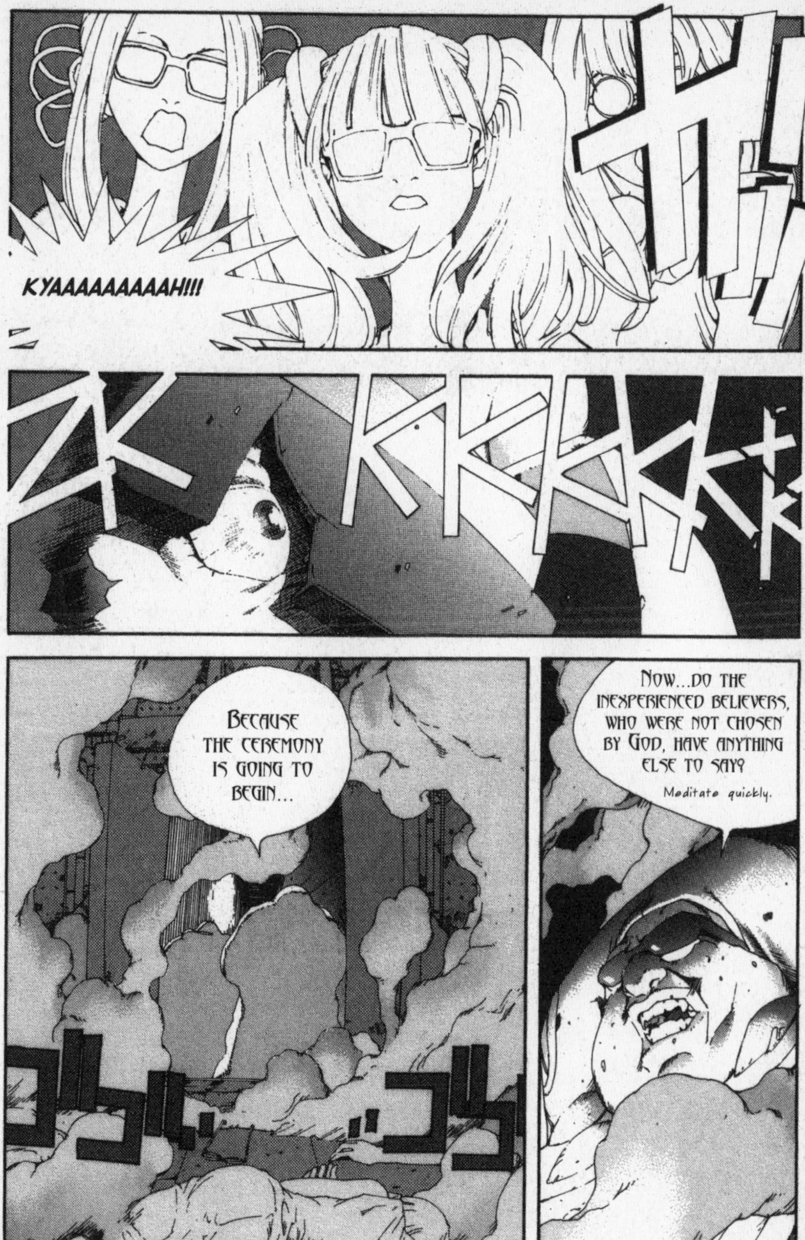
KYAAAAAAAAAAH!!!
Now...do the inexperienced believers, who were not chosen by God, have anything else to say?
Meditate quickly.
Because the ceremony is going to begin...

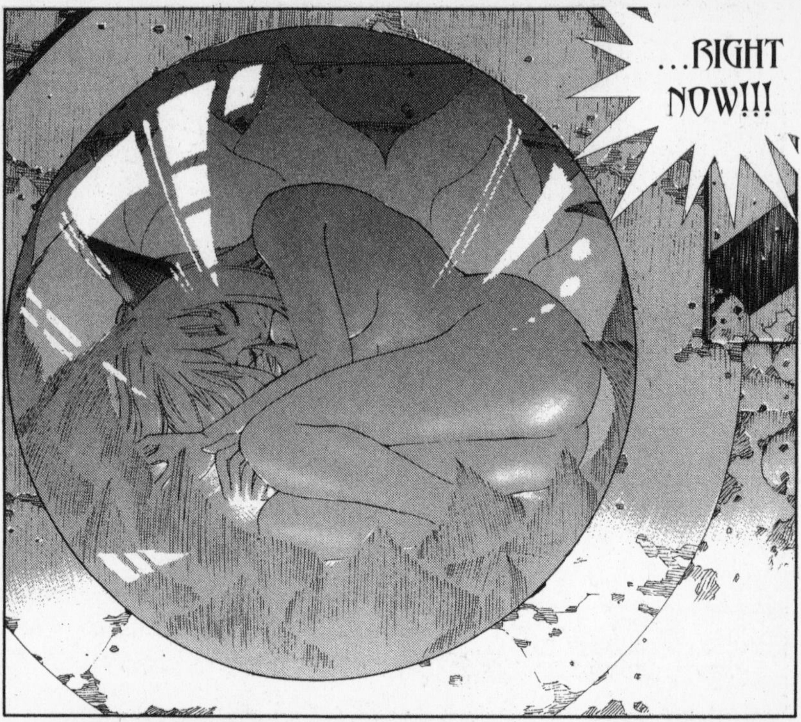
...RIGHT NOW!!!

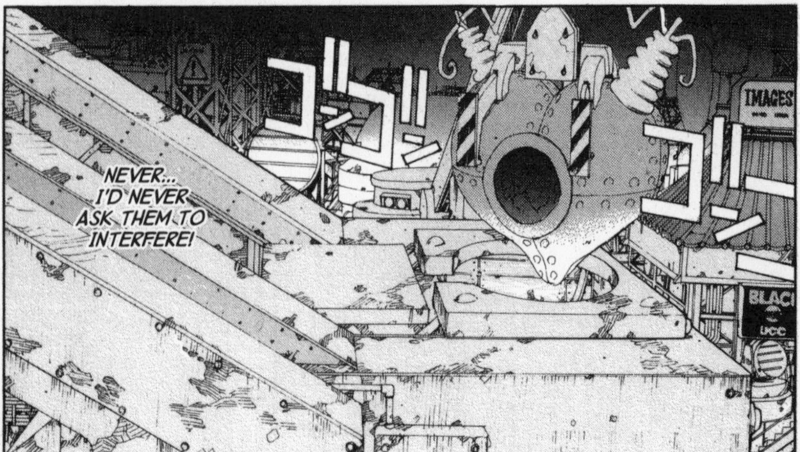
NEVER... I'D NEVER ASK THEM TO INTERFERE!
IMAGES
UCC

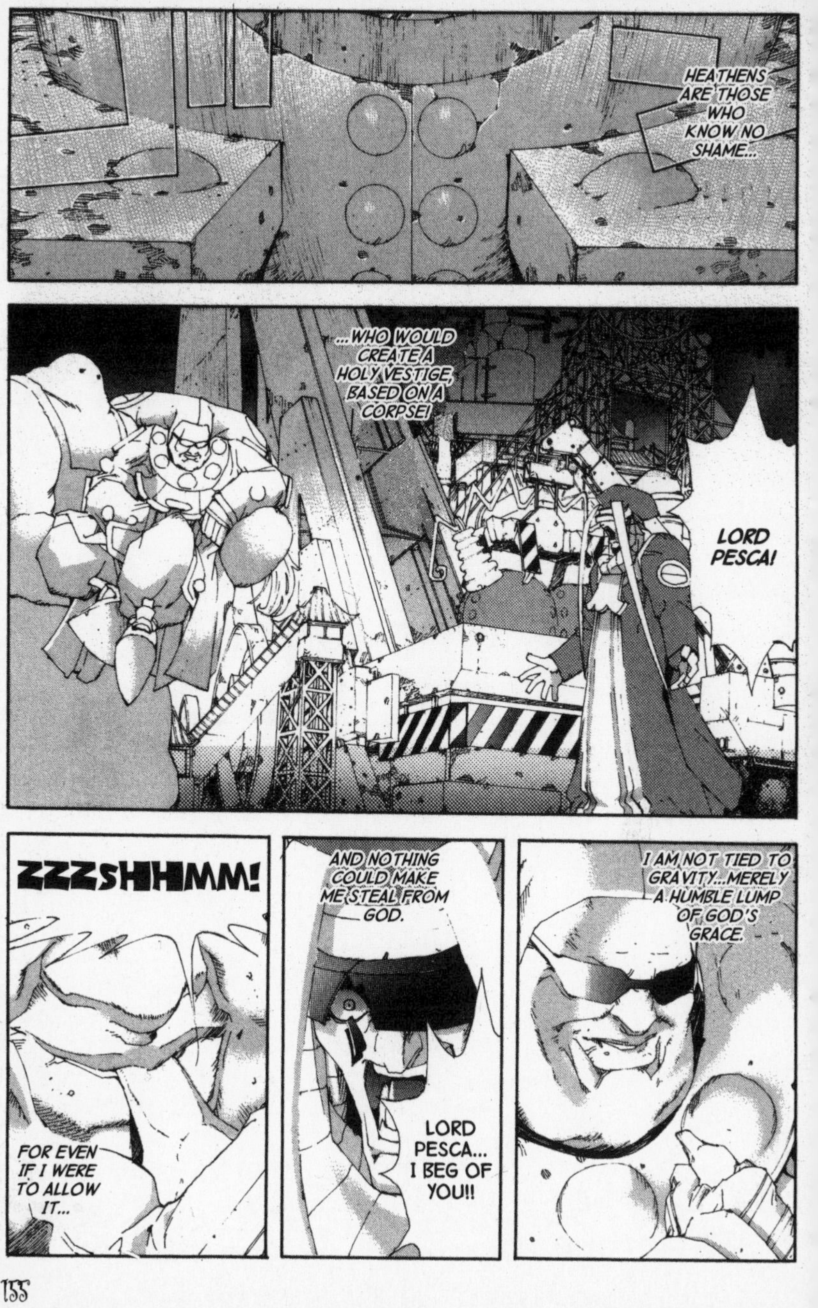
HEATHENS ARE THOSE WHO KNOW NO SHAME...
...WHO WOULD CREATE A HOLY VESTIGE, BASED ON A CORPSE!
LORD PESCA!
I AM NOT TIED TO GRAVITY...MERELY A HUMBLE LUMP OF GOD'S GRACE.
AND NOTHING COULD MAKE ME STEAL FROM GOD.
LORD PESCA... I BEG OF YOU!!
ZZZSHHMMM!
FOR EVEN IF I WERE TO ALLOW IT...

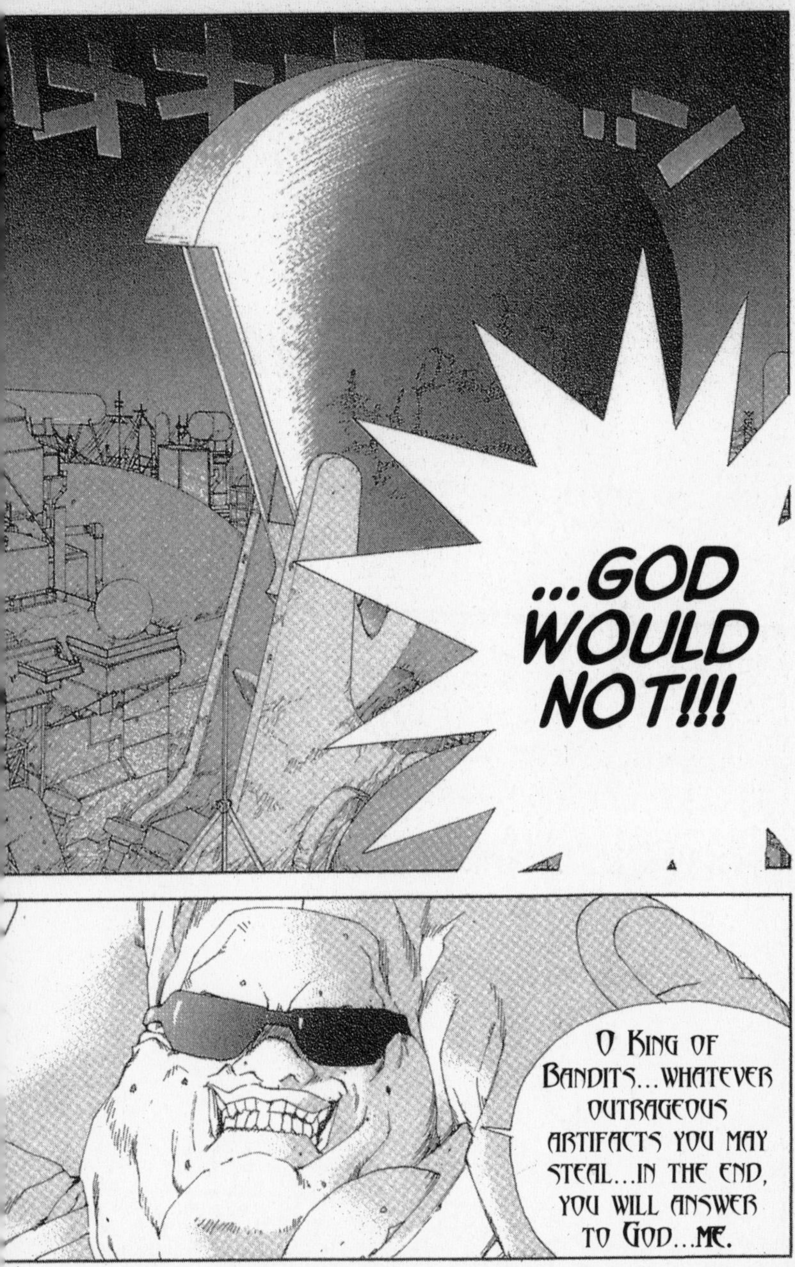
...GOD WOULD NOT!!!
O KING OF BANDITS...WHATEVER OUTRAGEOUS ARTIFACTS YOU MAY STEAL...IN THE END, YOU WILL ANSWER TO GOD...ME.

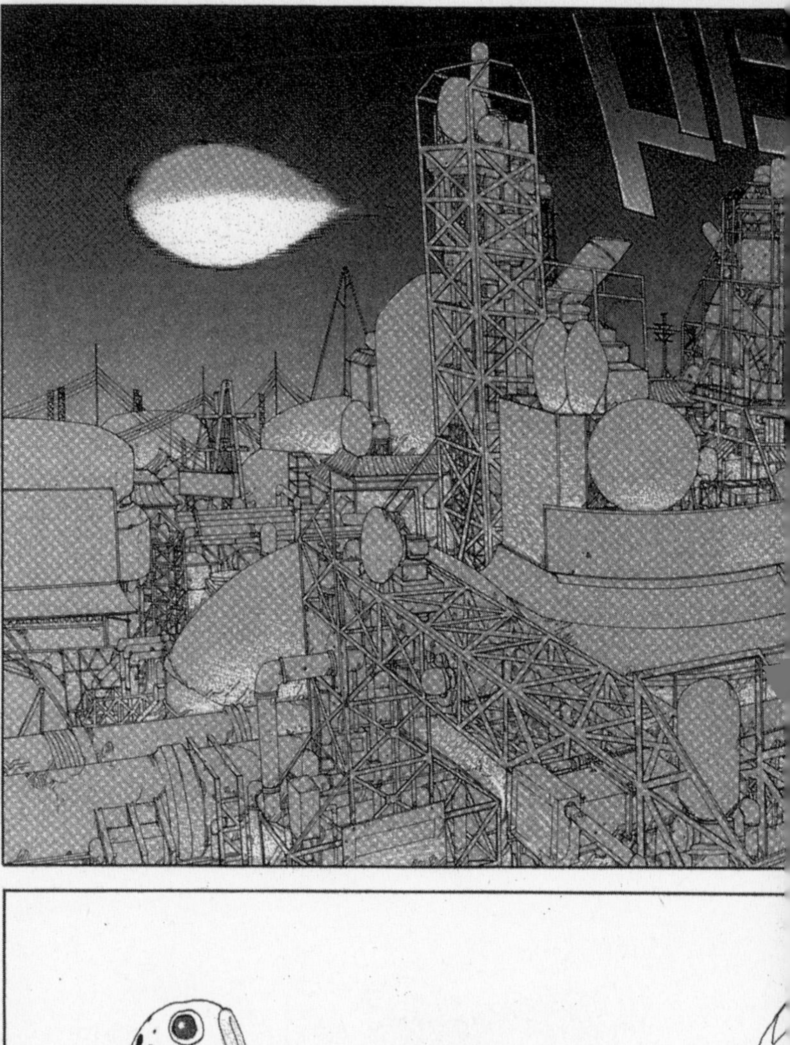
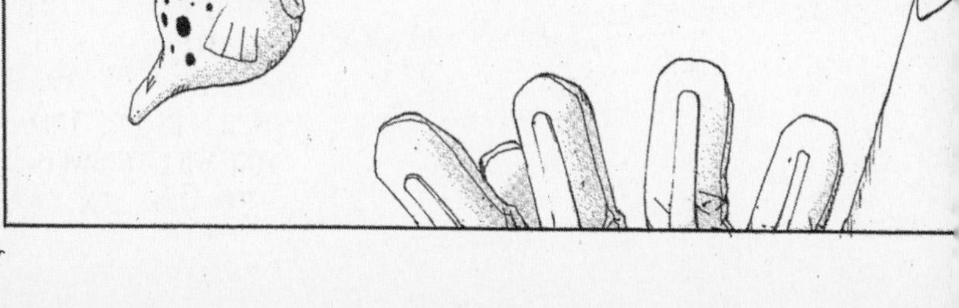

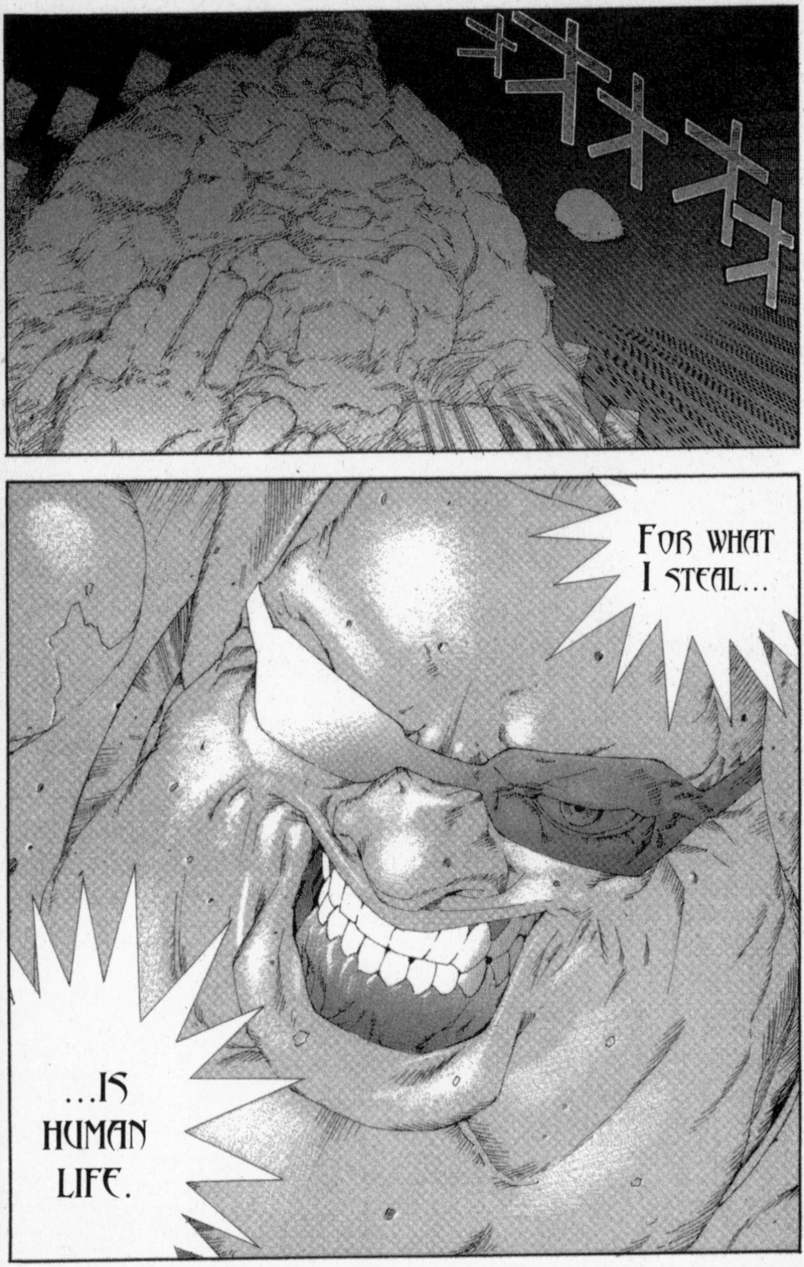
FOR WHAT I STEAL...
...IS HUMAN LIFE.

swing low, sweet chariot

comin' for to carry me home

I looked over Jordan and what

did I see

comin' for to carry me home

a band of angels comin' after me

comin' for to carry me home

oh, if you get there before I do

comin' for to carry me home

tell all my friends I'm comin' too

comin' for to carry me home

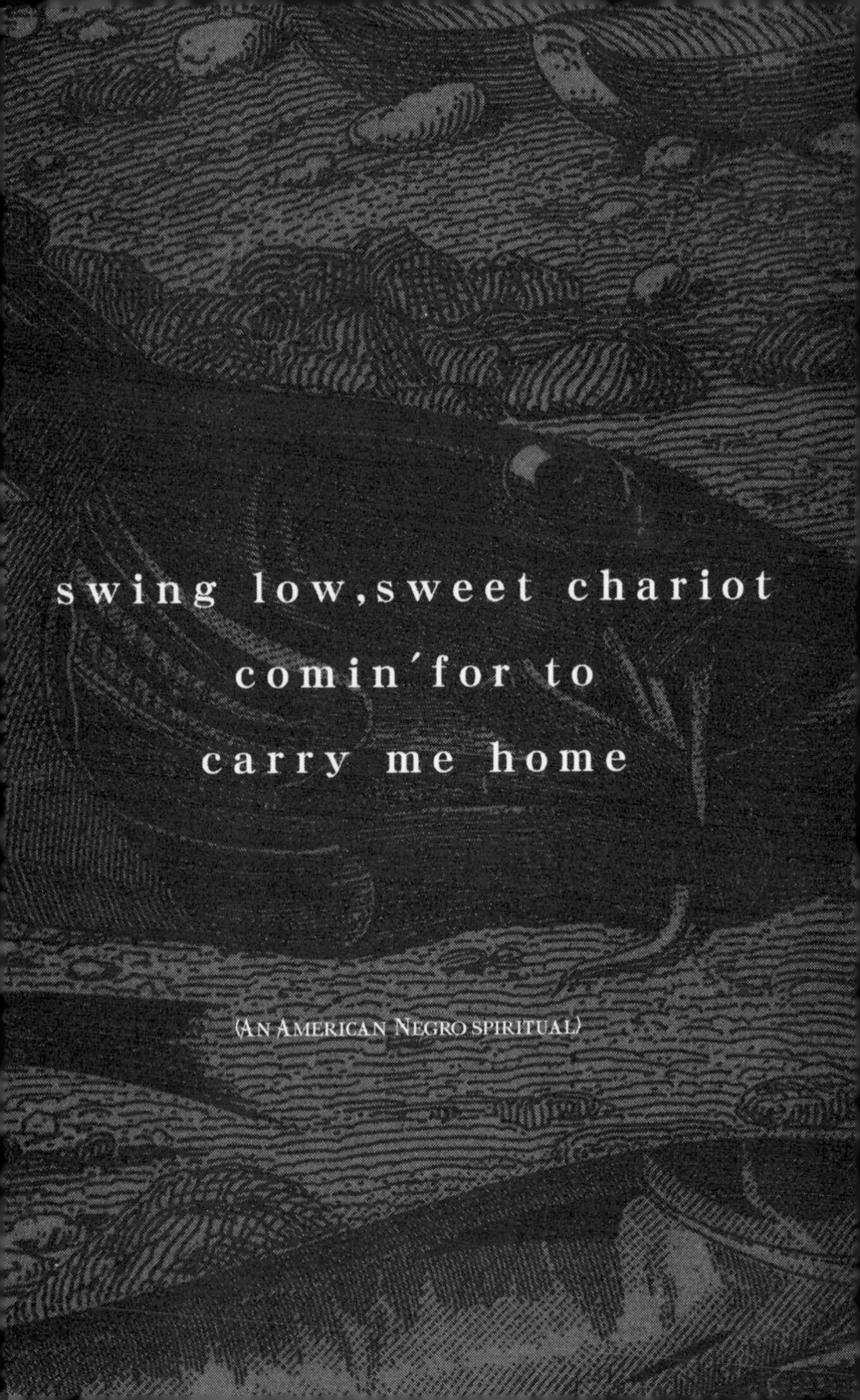

swing low, sweet chariot
comin' for to
carry me home

(An American Negro spiritual)

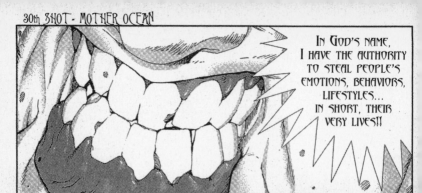

IN GOD'S NAME,
I HAVE THE AUTHORITY
TO STEAL PEOPLE'S
EMOTIONS, BEHAVIORS,
LIFESTYLES...
IN SHORT, THEIR
VERY LIVES!!

CAN YOU
DO THAT?
EH, KING OF
BANDITS?!!

A BIT MUCH
FOR A KID LIKE
YOU, WOULDN'T
YOU SAY?!

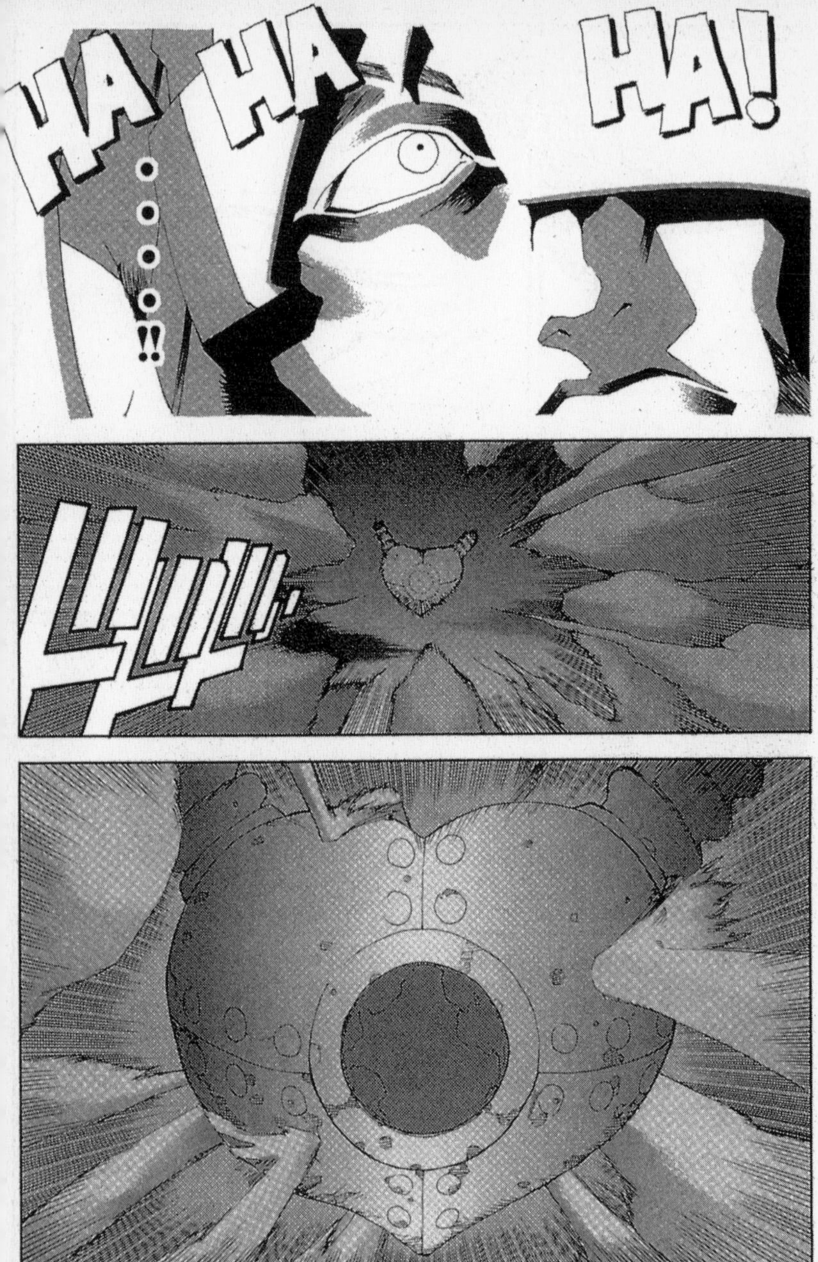
HA HA! HA!
....!!

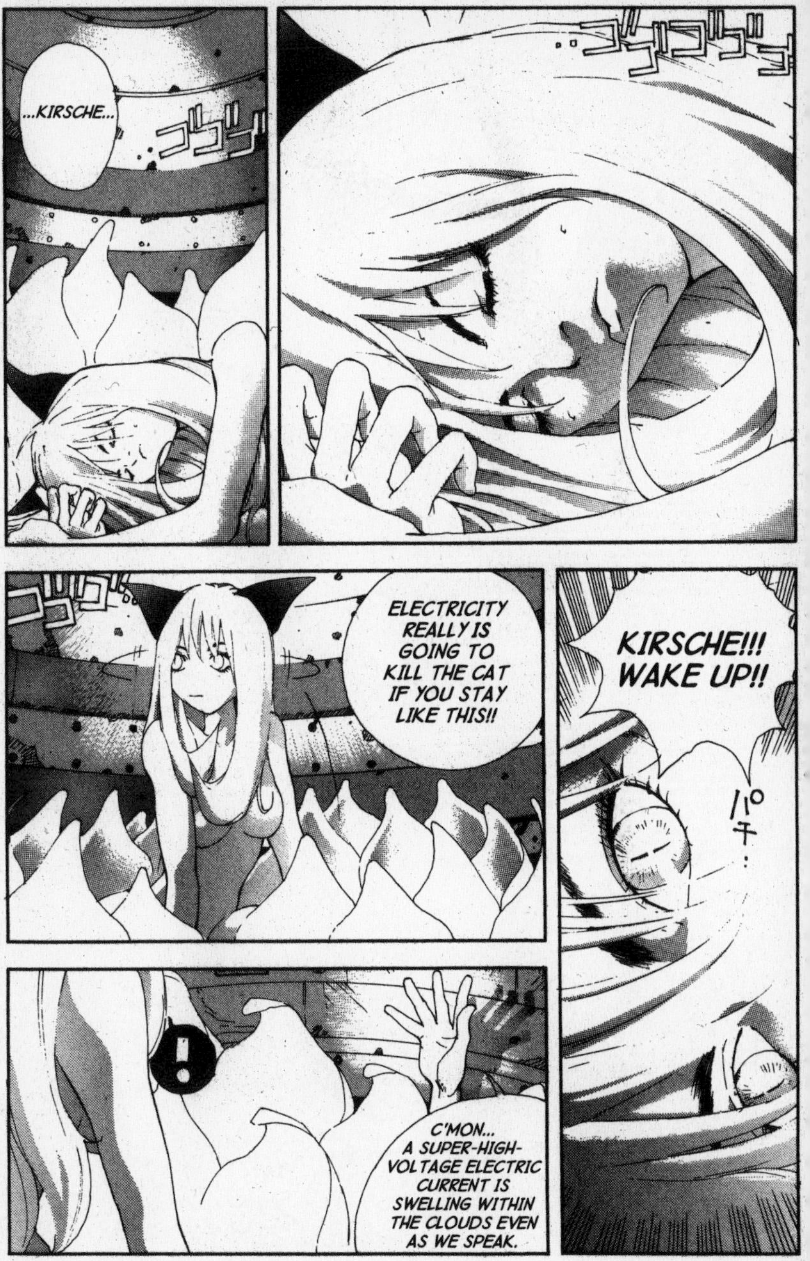

ゴゴゴゴ
...KIRSCHE...
ゴゴゴ
KIRSCHE!!! WAKE UP!!
パチ
ゴゴゴ
ELECTRICITY REALLY IS GOING TO KILL THE CAT IF YOU STAY LIKE THIS!!
!
C'MON... A SUPER-HIGH-VOLTAGE ELECTRIC CURRENT IS SWELLING WITHIN THE CLOUDS EVEN AS WE SPEAK.

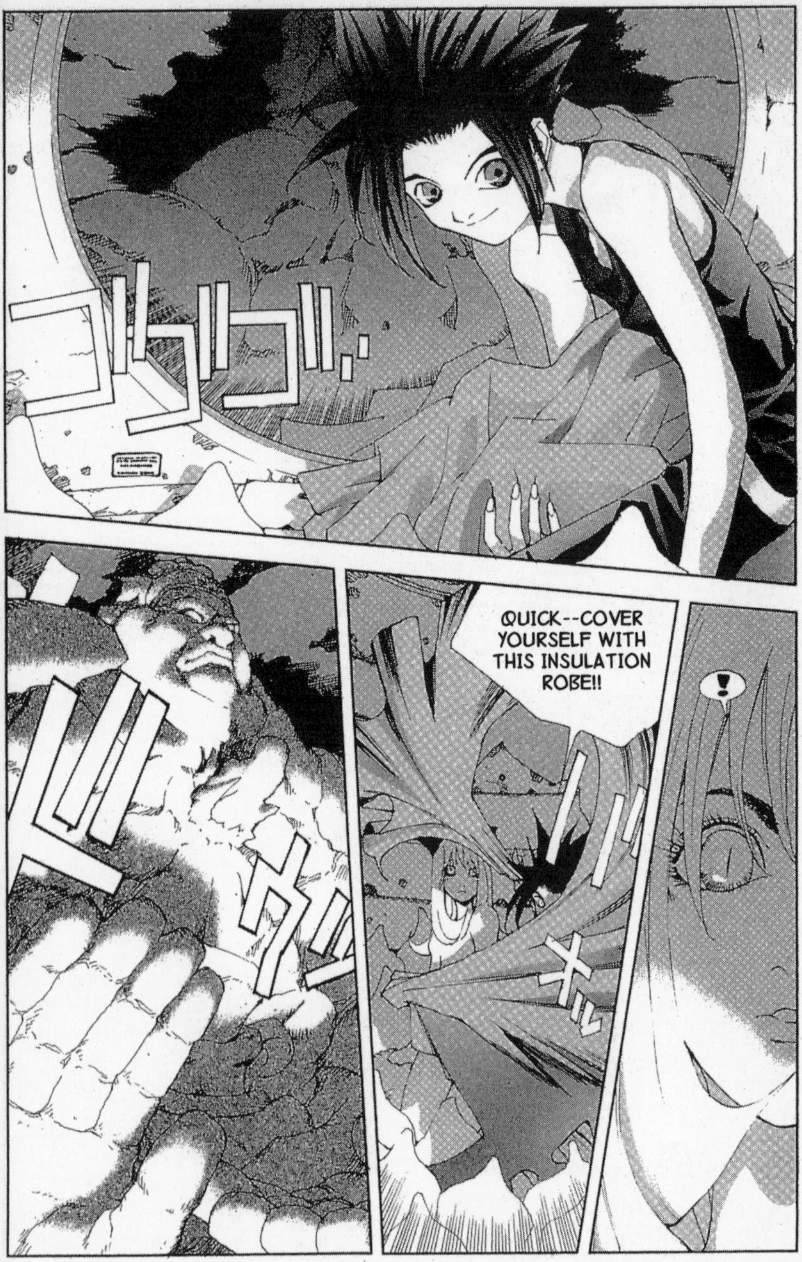
QUICK--COVER YOURSELF WITH THIS INSULATION ROBE!!
!

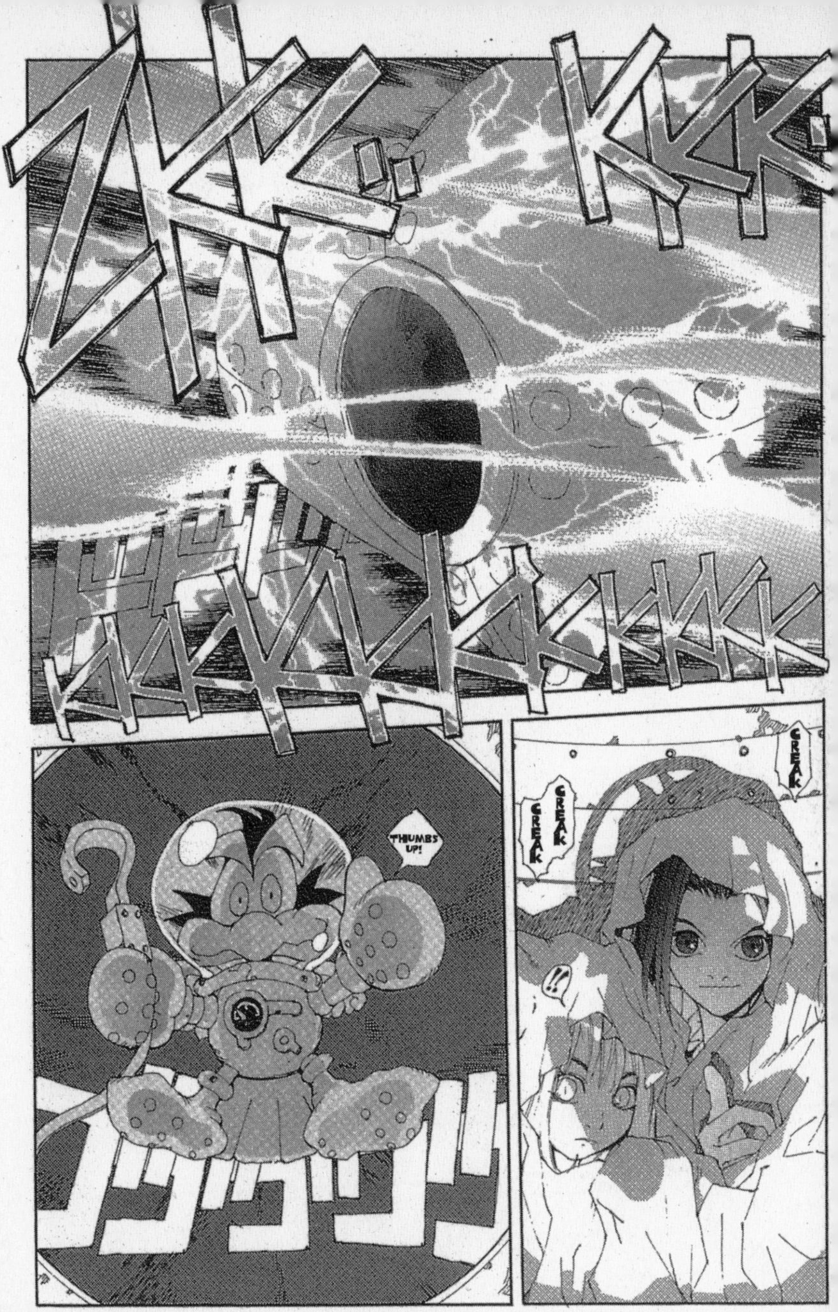
CREAK
CREAK
CREAK
!!
THUMBS UP!

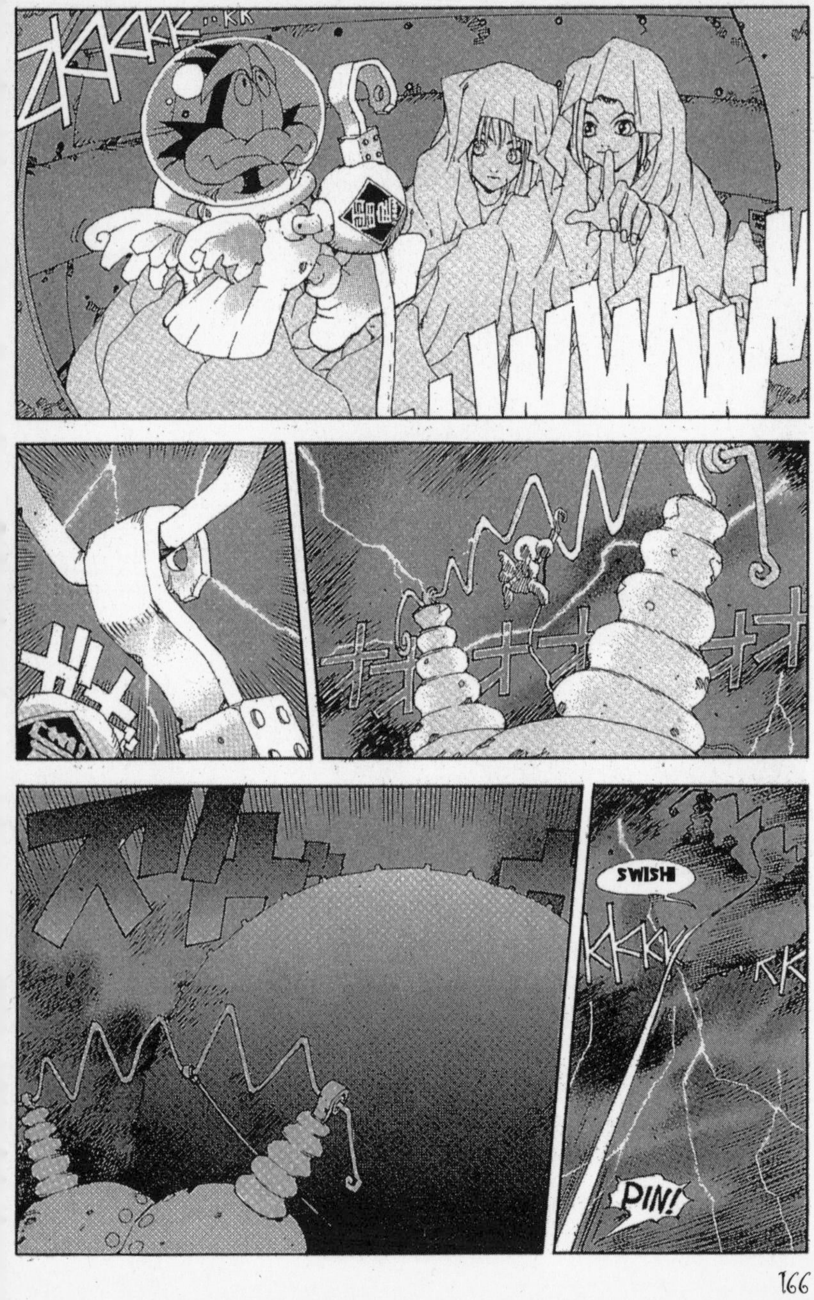
ZKAKAK..KR
SWISH
PIN!

HUFF
HUFF
HUFF
HUFF

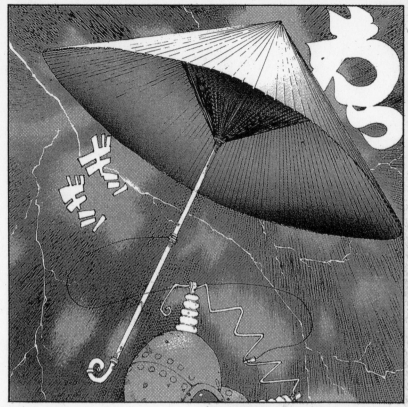

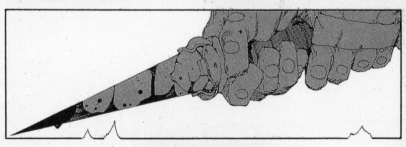

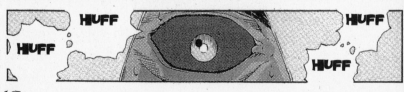

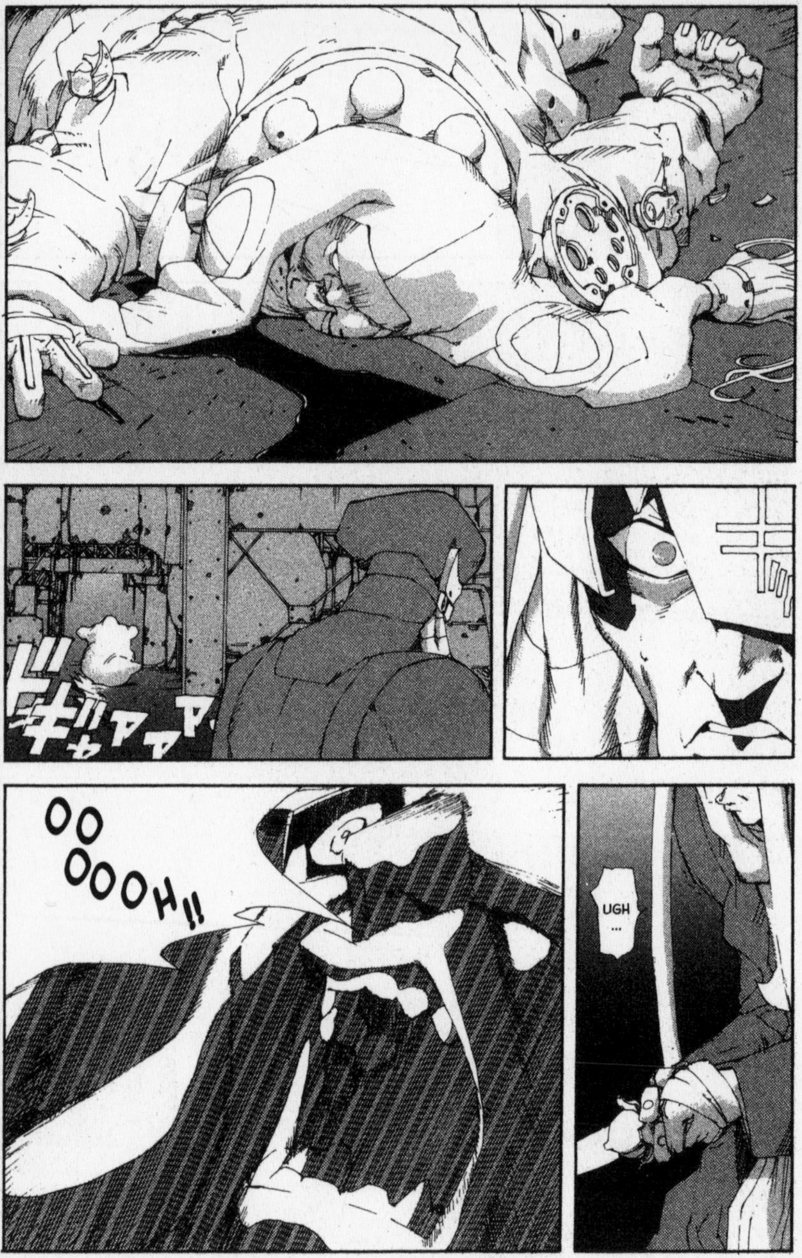
UGH ...
OOOOOH!!

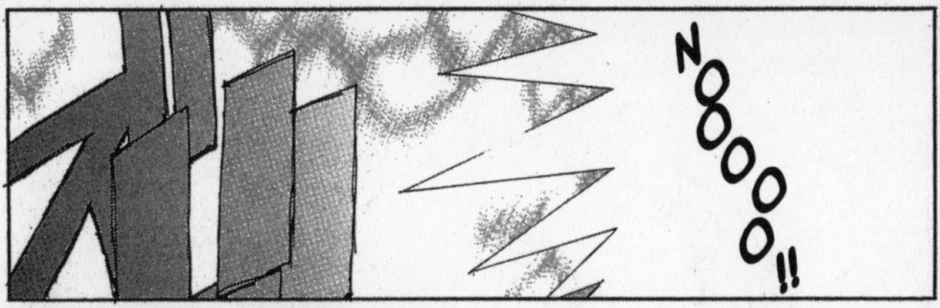
NOOOOO!!
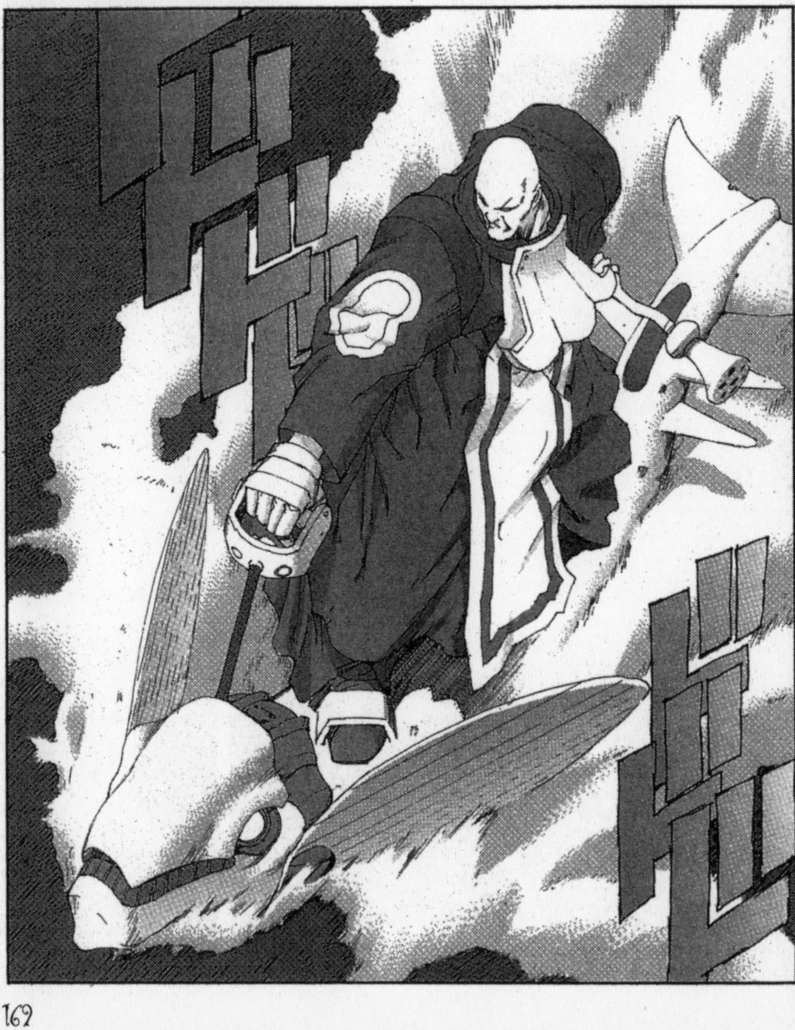

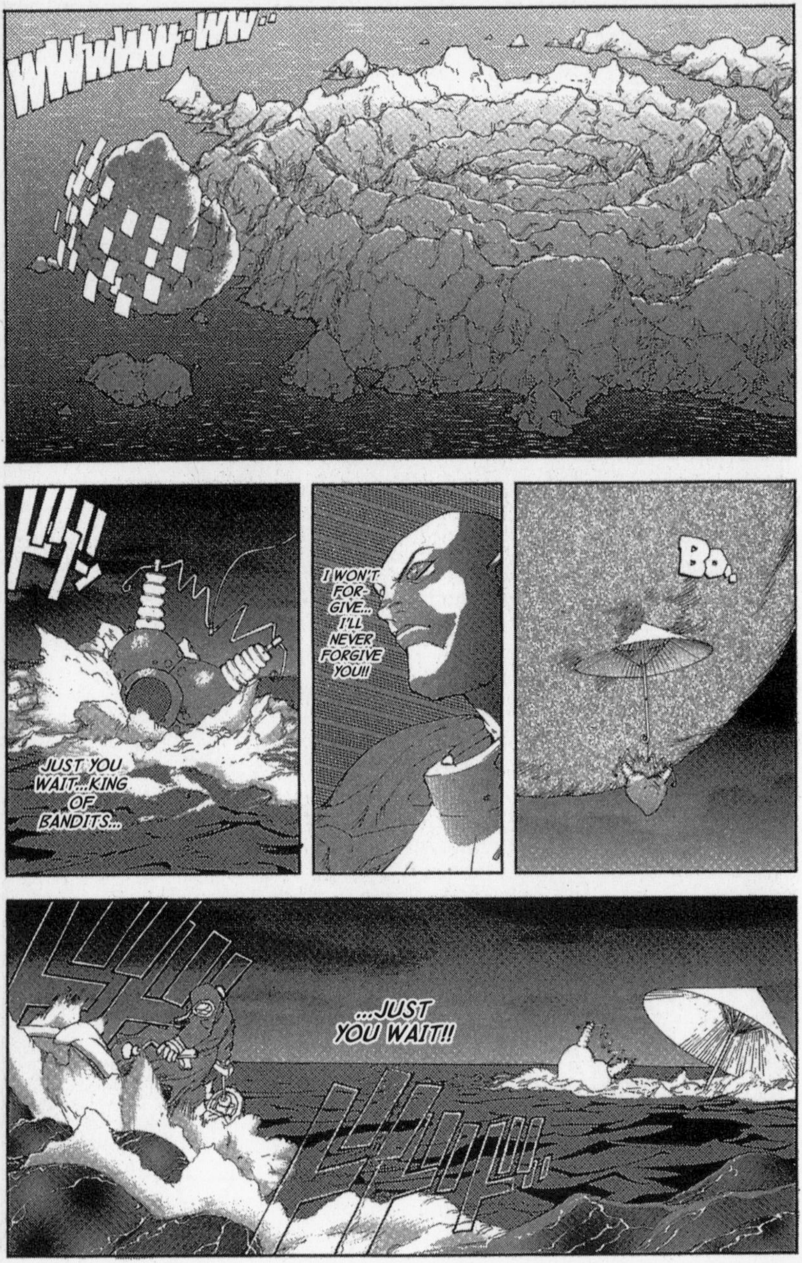

WWWWWW·WW..
Bo..
I WON'T FOR-GIVE... I'LL NEVER FORGIVE YOU!!
JUST YOU WAIT...KING OF BANDITS...
...JUST YOU WAIT!!

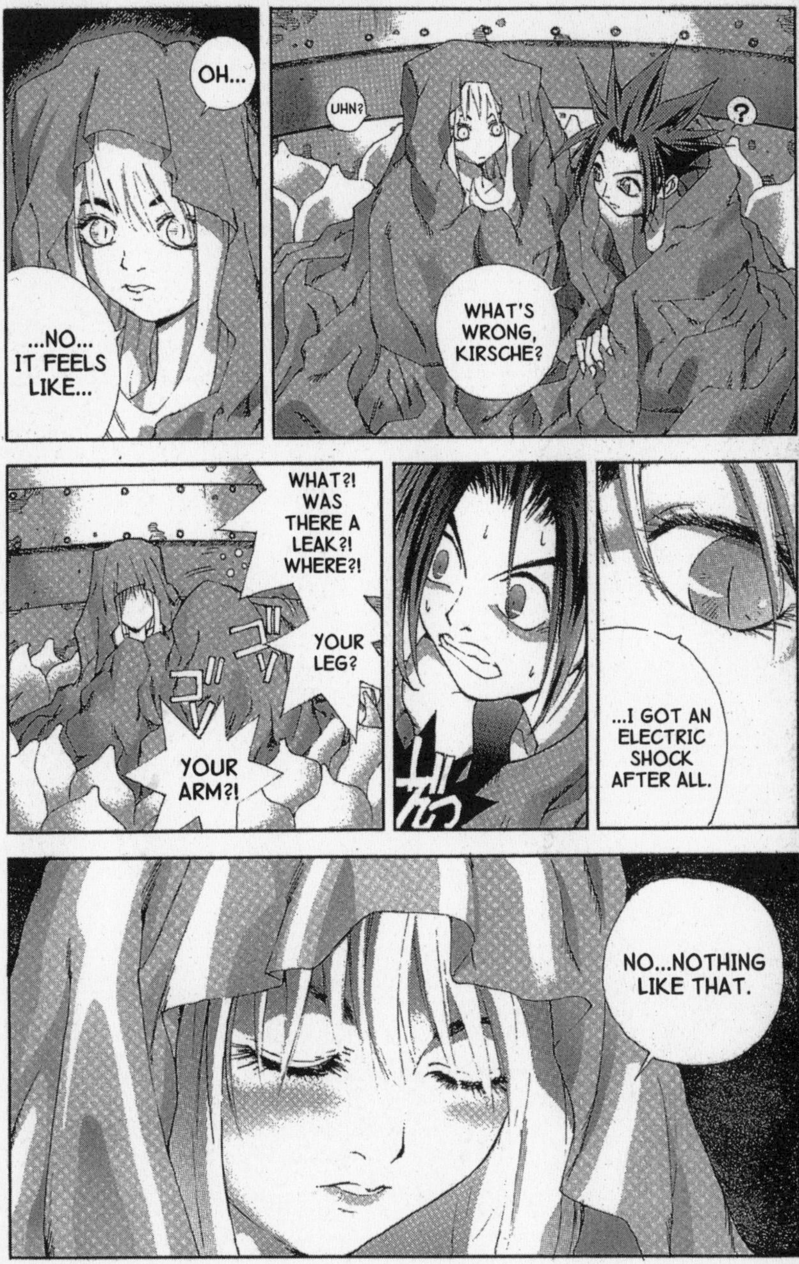
?
UHN?
WHAT'S WRONG, KIRSCHE?
OH...
...NO... IT FEELS LIKE...
...I GOT AN ELECTRIC SHOCK AFTER ALL.
WHAT?! WAS THERE A LEAK?! WHERE?!
YOUR LEG?
YOUR ARM?!
NO...NOTHING LIKE THAT.

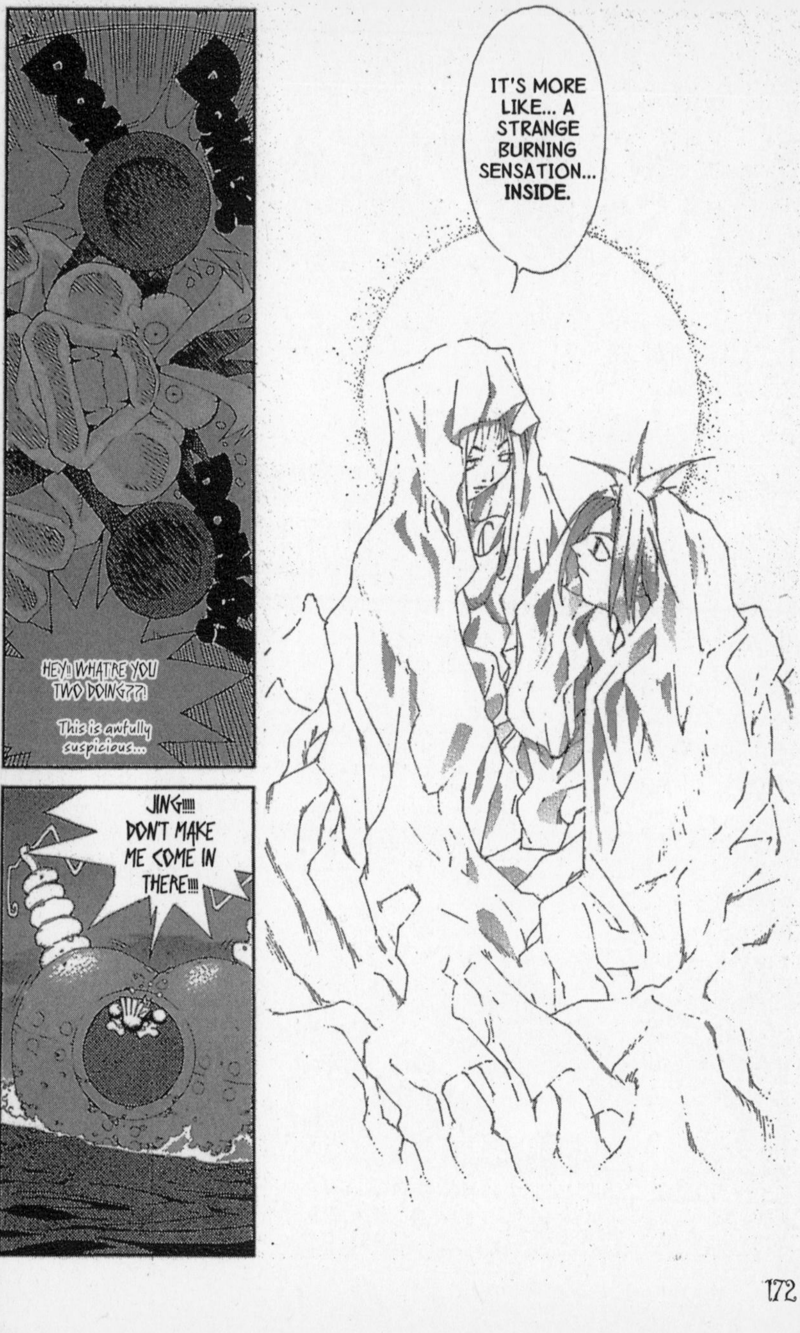
IT'S MORE LIKE... A STRANGE BURNING SENSATION... INSIDE.
HEY!! WHAT'RE YOU TWO DOING??!
This is awfully suspicious...
JING!!!!! DON'T MAKE ME COME IN THERE!!!!

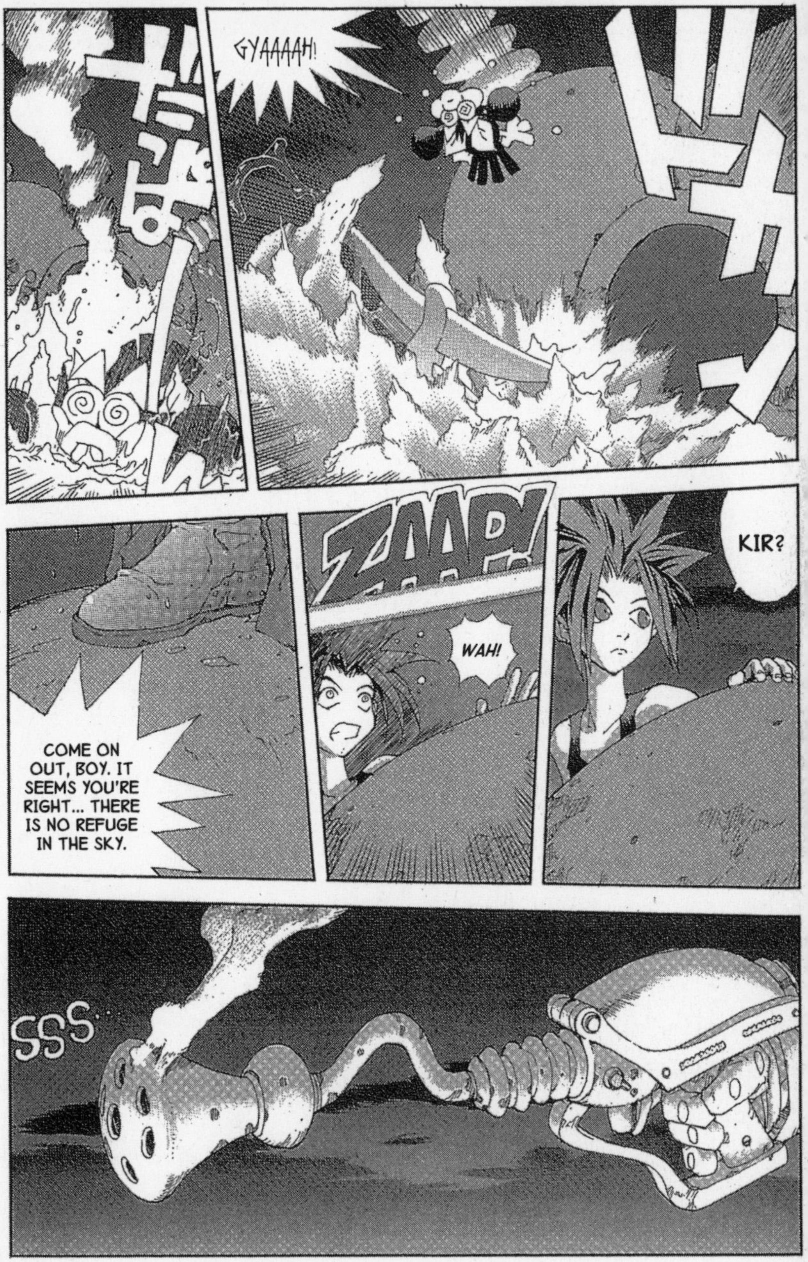
GYAAAAH!
KIR?
ZAAP!
WAH!
COME ON OUT, BOY. IT SEEMS YOU'RE RIGHT... THERE IS NO REFUGE IN THE SKY.
SSS

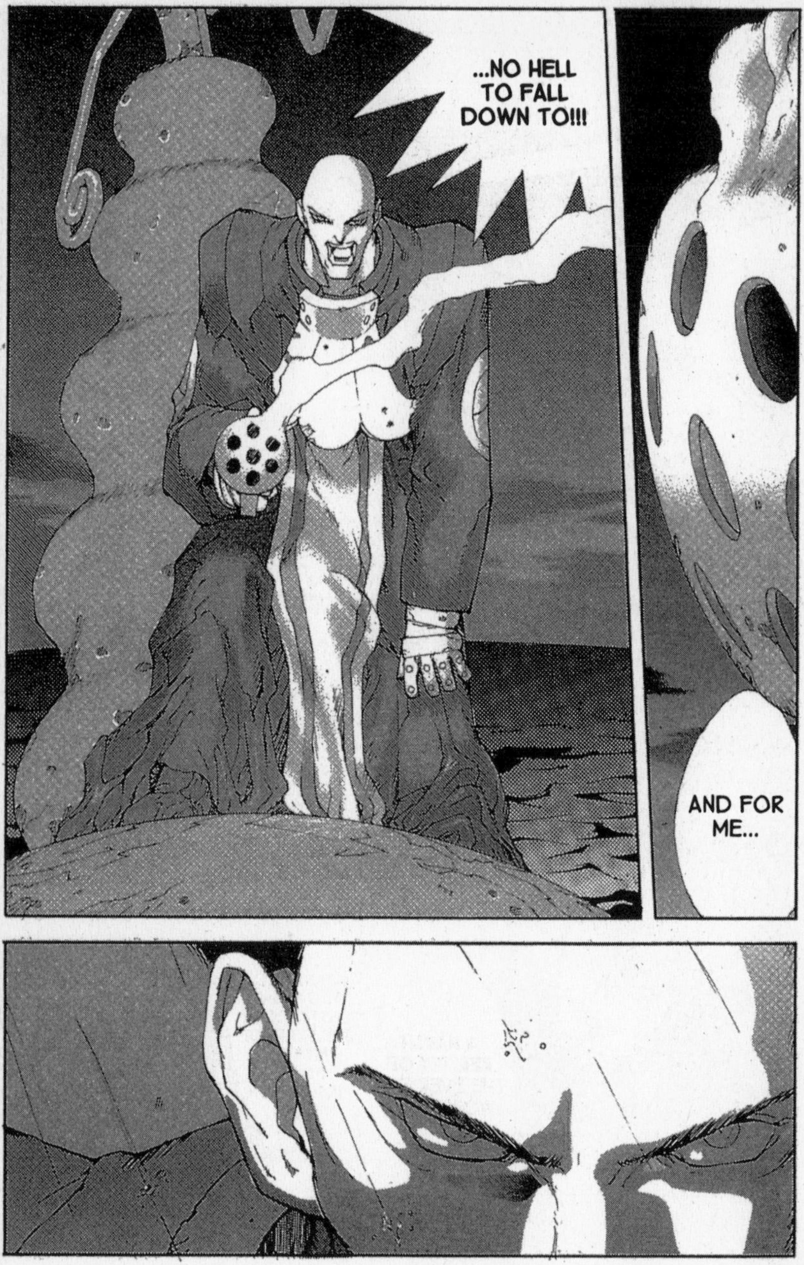
AND FOR ME...
...NO HELL TO FALL DOWN TO!!!

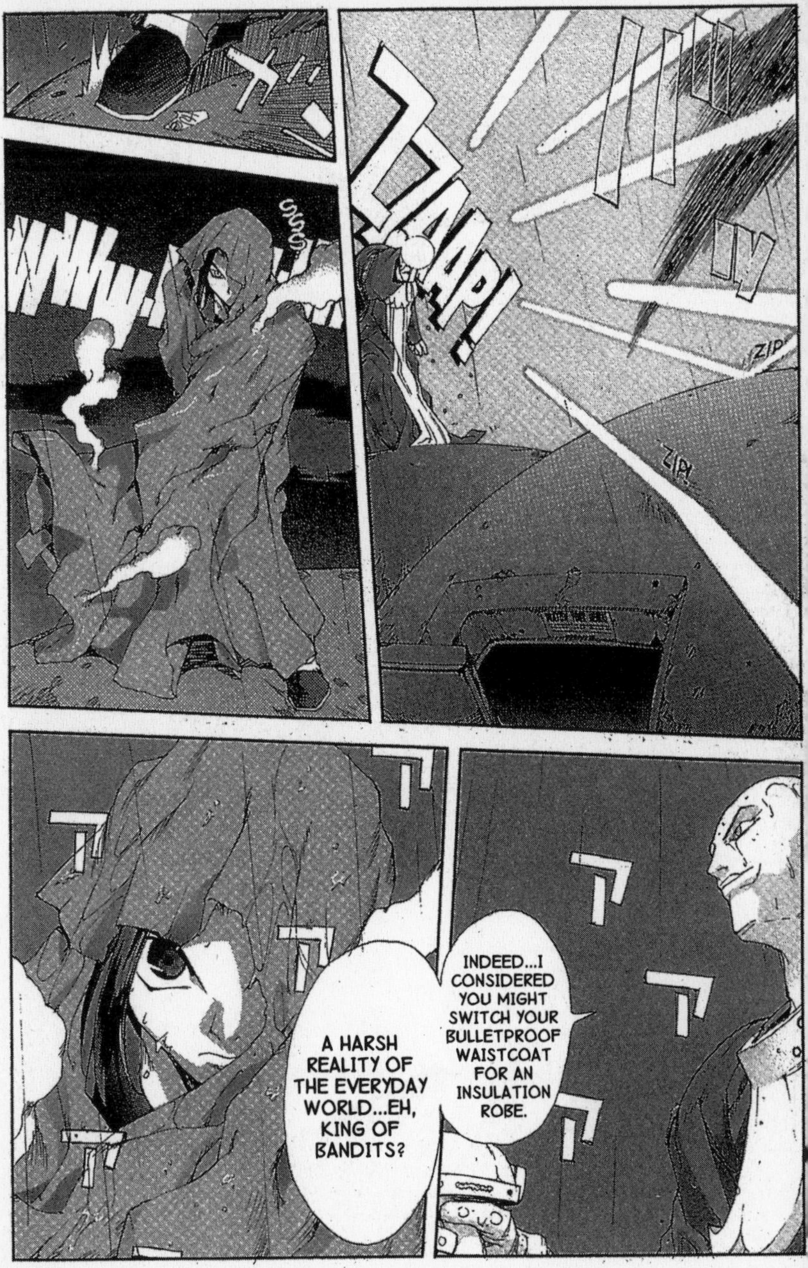
ZZAAP!!
ZIP!
ZIP!
INDEED...I CONSIDERED YOU MIGHT SWITCH YOUR BULLETPROOF WAISTCOAT FOR AN INSULATION ROBE.
A HARSH REALITY OF THE EVERYDAY WORLD...EH, KING OF BANDITS?

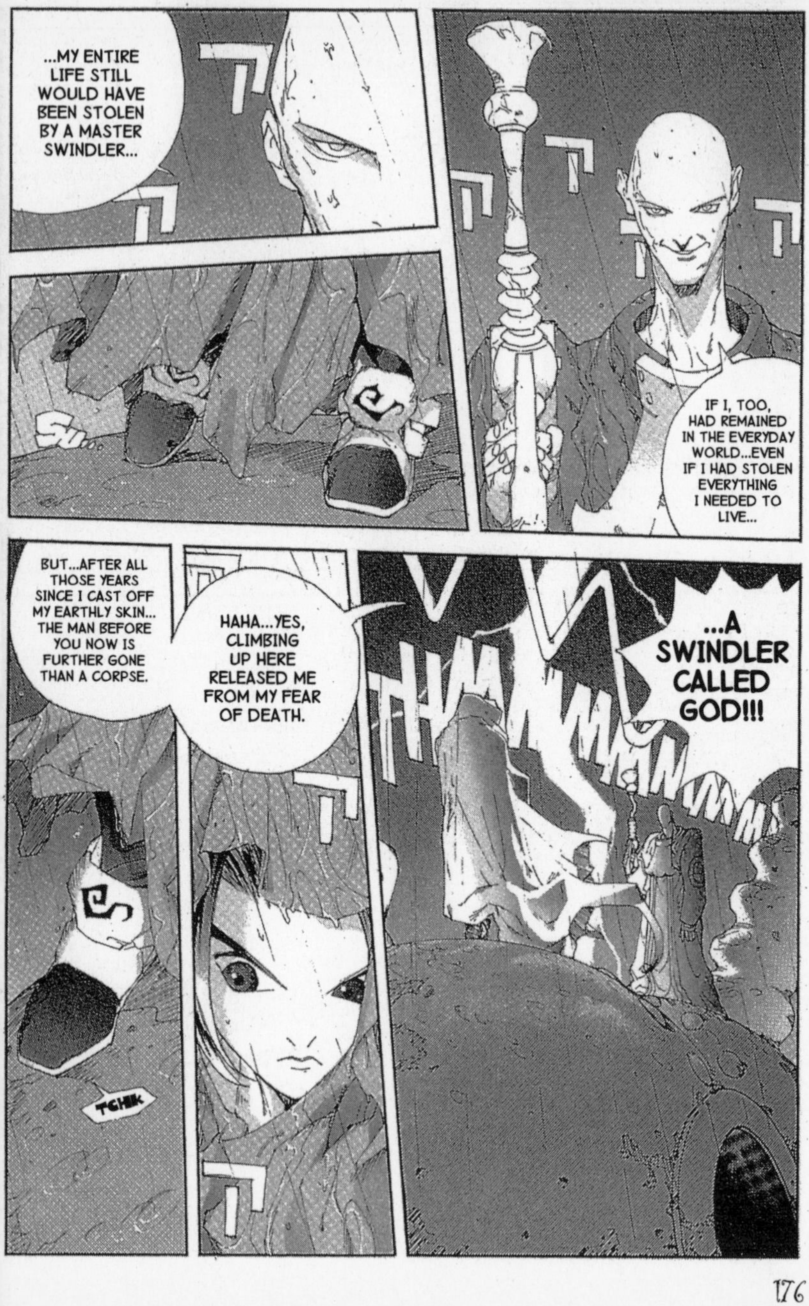
IF I, TOO, HAD REMAINED IN THE EVERYDAY WORLD...EVEN IF I HAD STOLEN EVERYTHING I NEEDED TO LIVE...
...MY ENTIRE LIFE STILL WOULD HAVE BEEN STOLEN BY A MASTER SWINDLER...
SU..
THMMMMMNNNMMMS
...A SWINDLER CALLED GOD!!!
HAHA...YES, CLIMBING UP HERE RELEASED ME FROM MY FEAR OF DEATH.
BUT...AFTER ALL THOSE YEARS SINCE I CAST OFF MY EARTHLY SKIN... THE MAN BEFORE YOU NOW IS FURTHER GONE THAN A CORPSE.
TCHIK

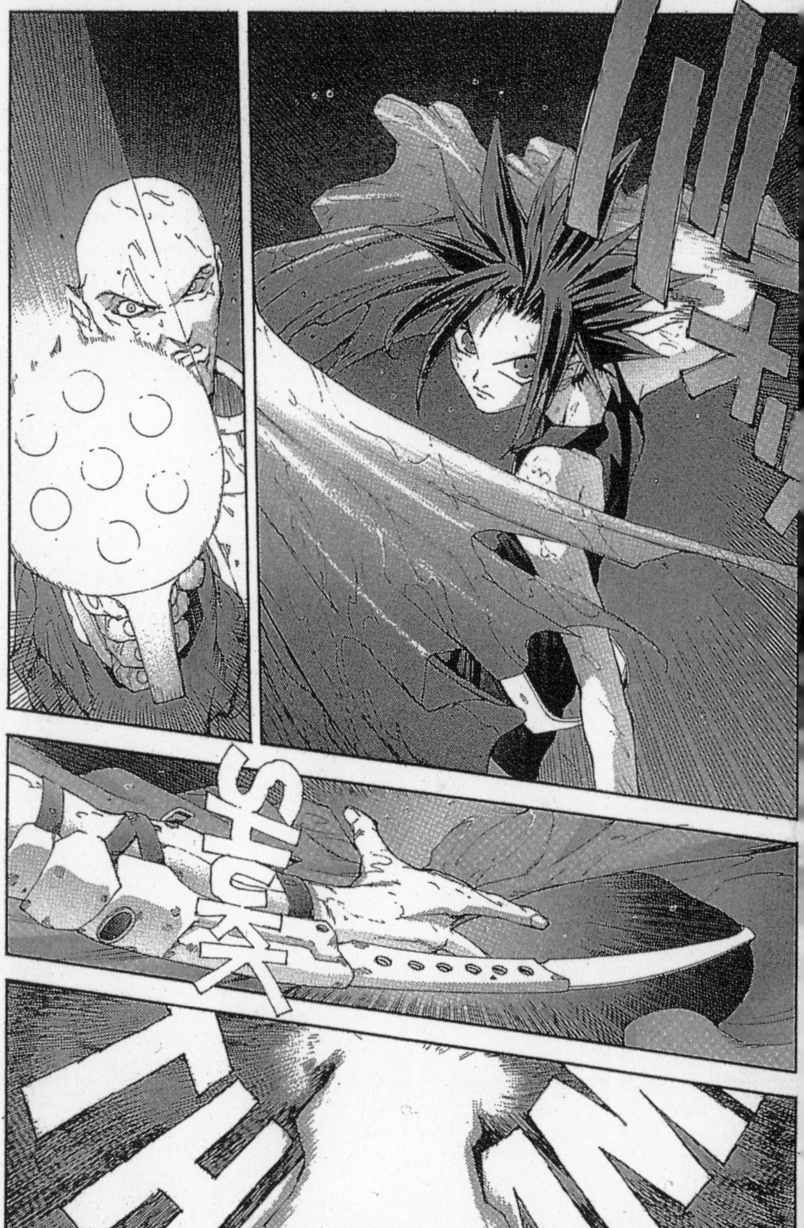
SHUK

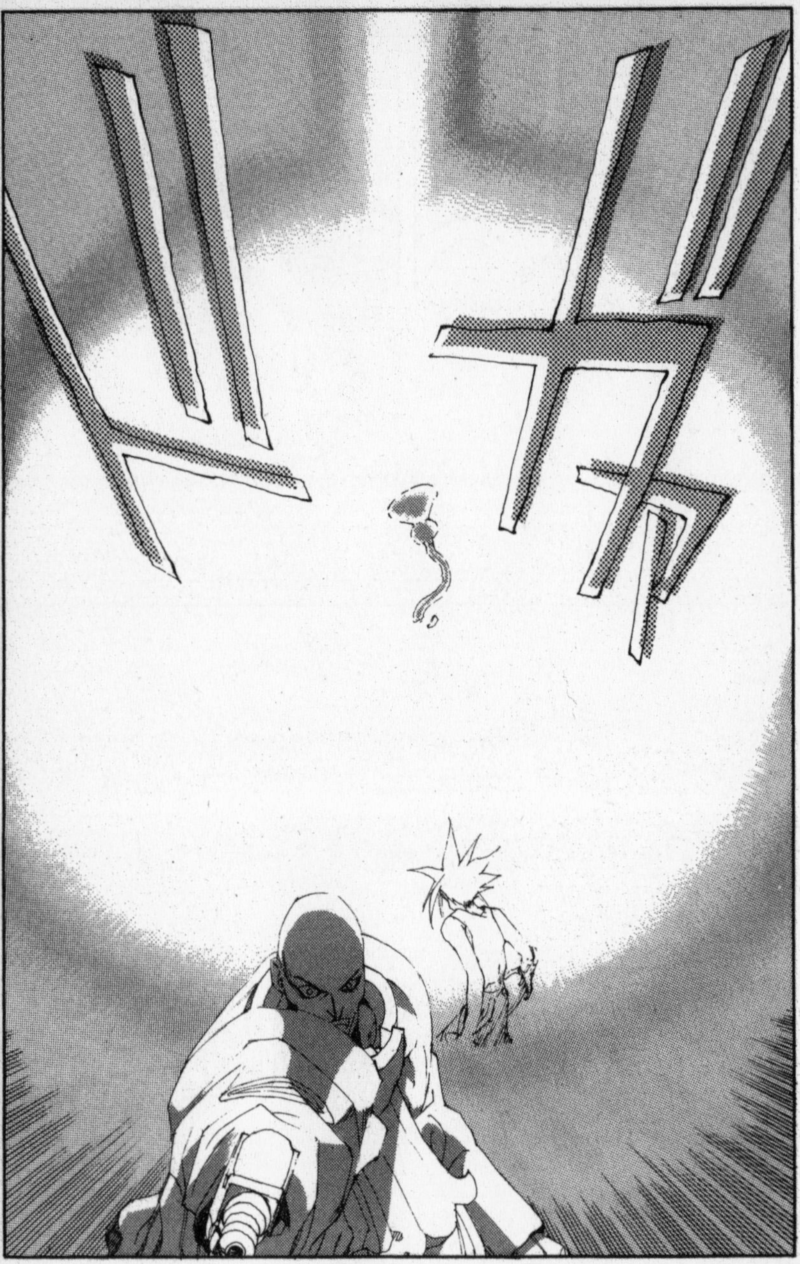

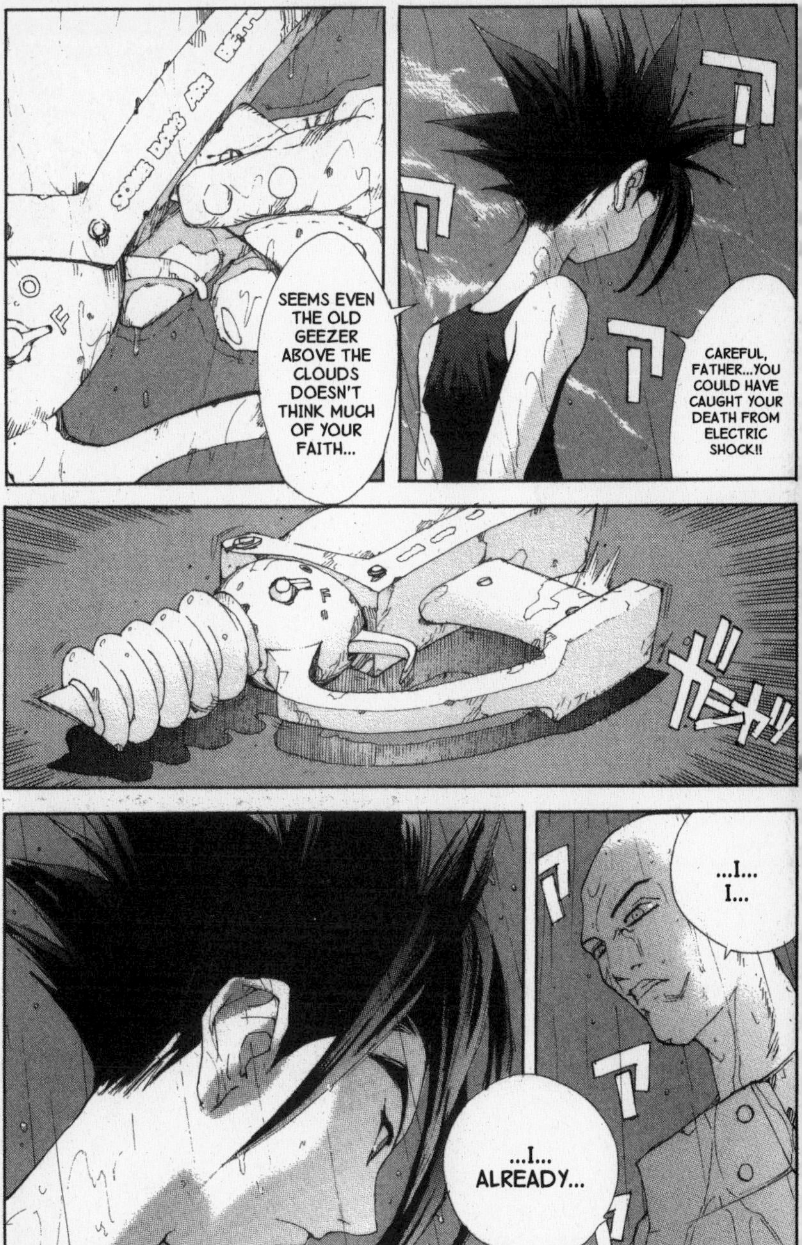
CAREFUL, FATHER...YOU COULD HAVE CAUGHT YOUR DEATH FROM ELECTRIC SHOCK!!
SEEMS EVEN THE OLD GEEZER ABOVE THE CLOUDS DOESN'T THINK MUCH OF YOUR FAITH...
...I... I...
...I... ALREADY...

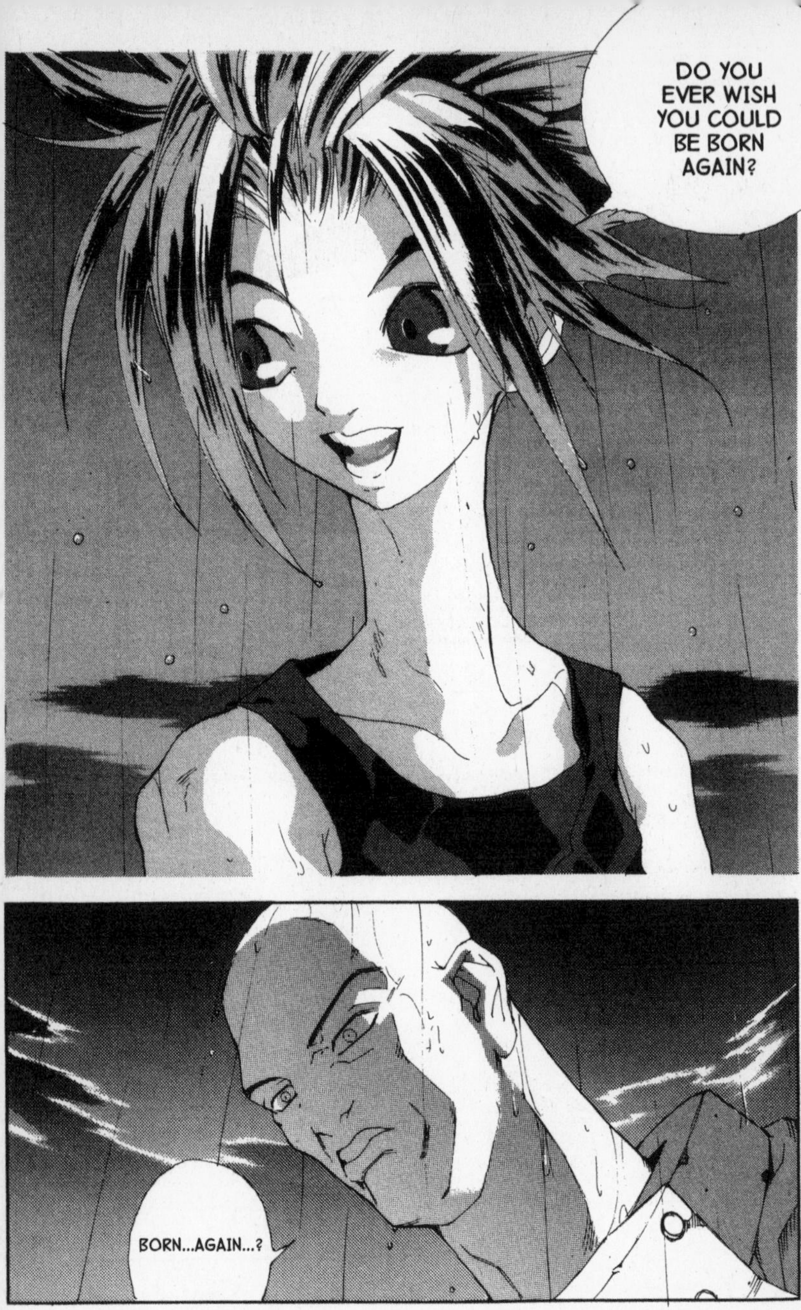
DO YOU EVER WISH YOU COULD BE BORN AGAIN?
BORN...AGAIN...?

SLIP
UWAH!
UHN...KIRSCHE, WATCH OVER... JING...FOR ME...
AAAA
AFTER ALL... THIS SEA IS EVERYONE'S BIRTHPLACE... EVERYONE'S MOTHER... RIGHT?

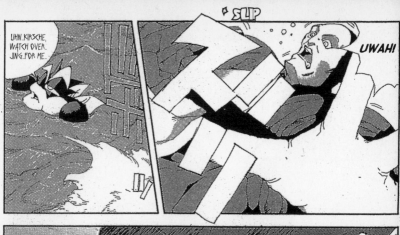

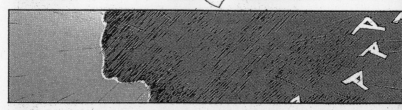

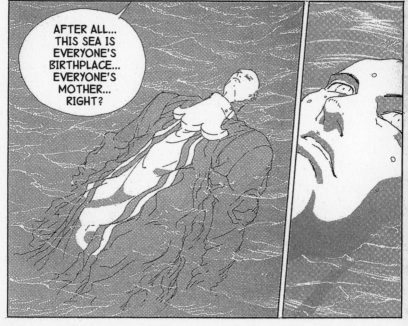

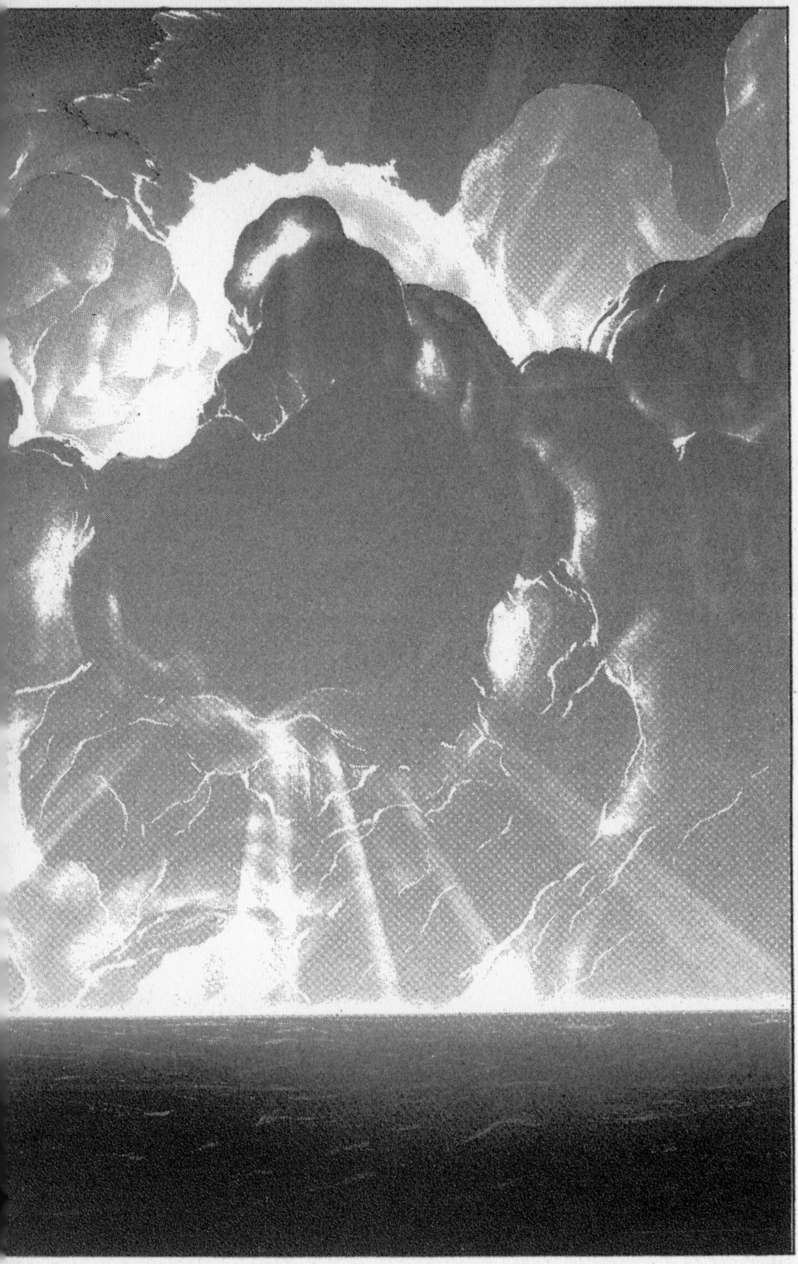

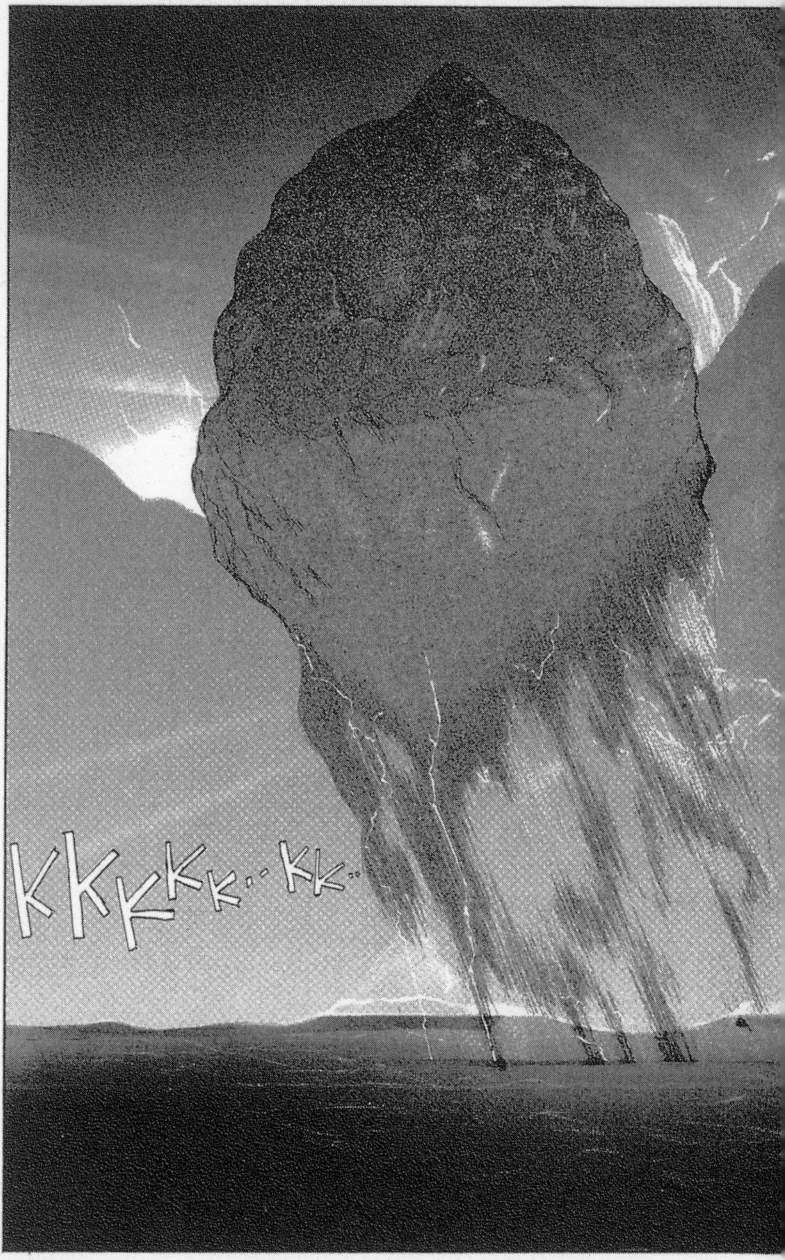
KKKKK..KK..

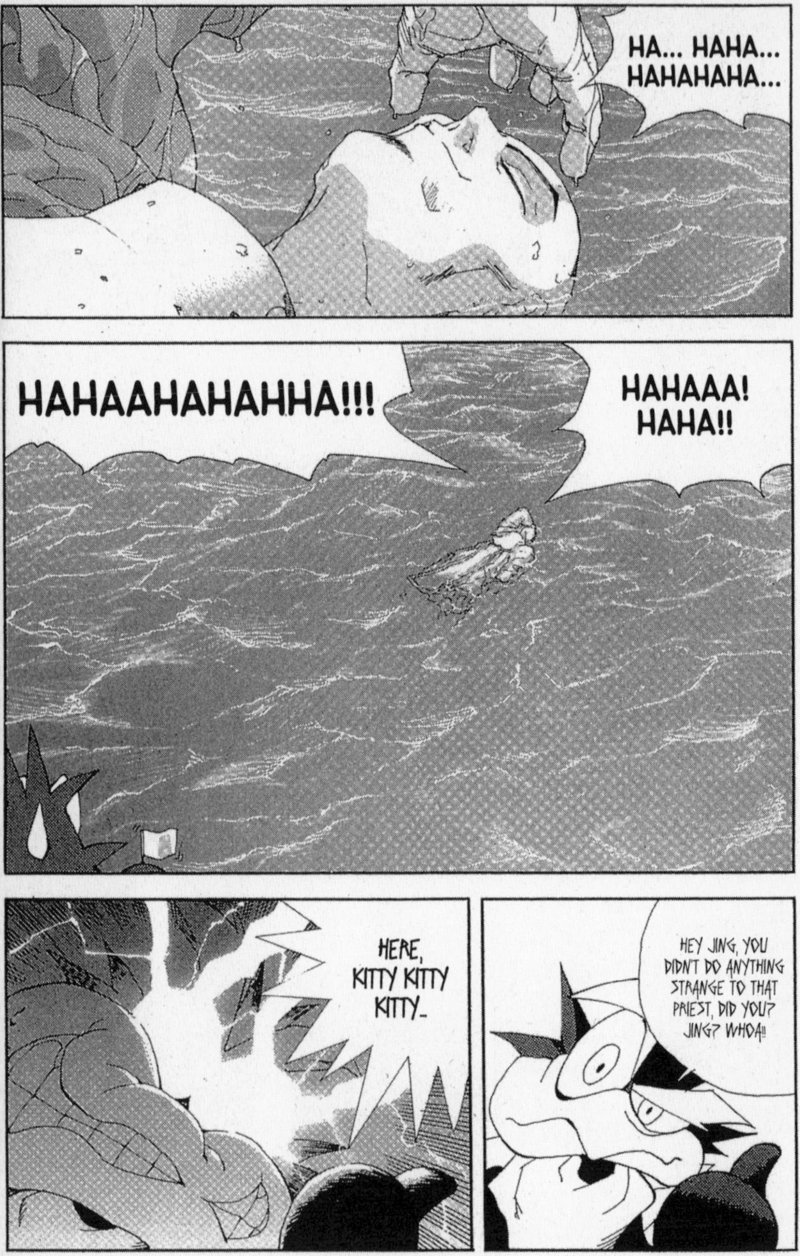
HA... HAHA... HAHAHAHA...
HAHAAA! HAHA!!
HAHAAHAHAHHA!!!
HEY JING, YOU DIDN'T DO ANYTHING STRANGE TO THAT PRIEST, DID YOU? JING? WHOA!!
HERE, KITTY KITTY KITTY..

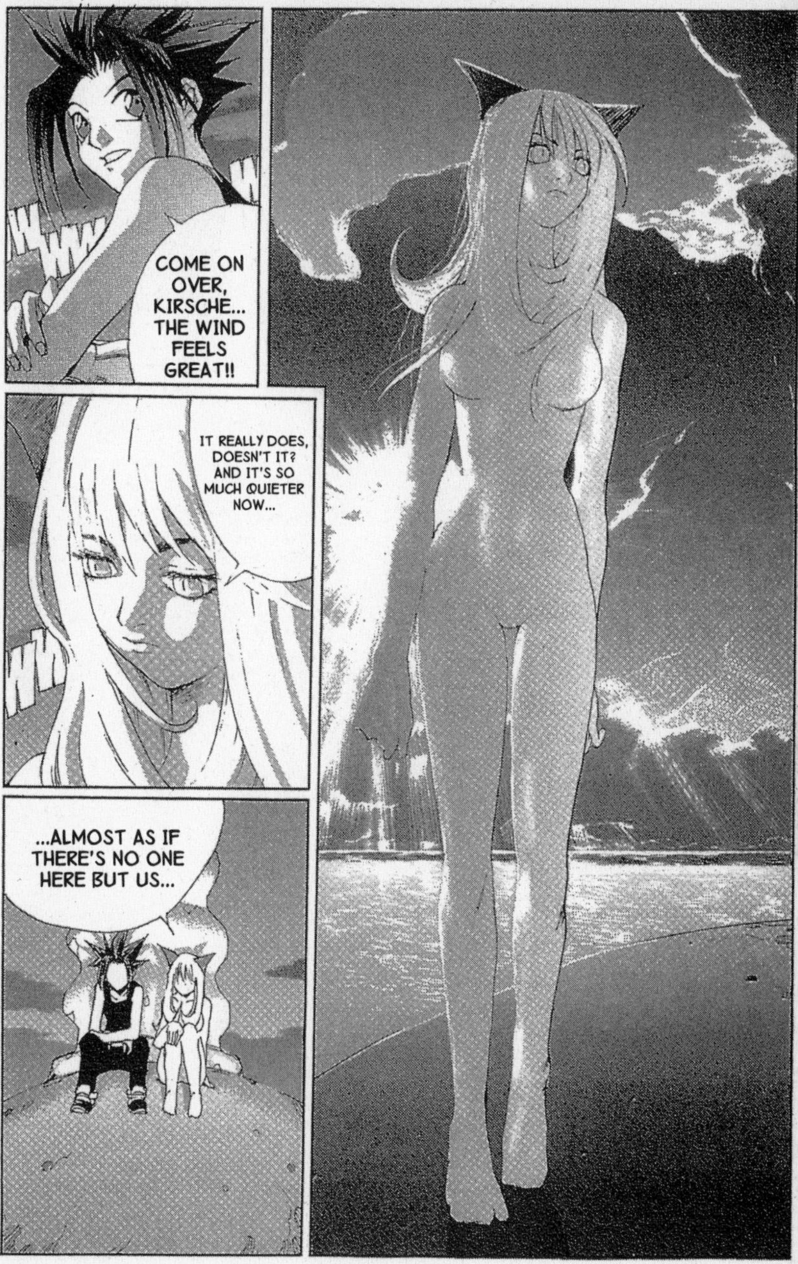
COME ON OVER, KIRSCHE... THE WIND FEELS GREAT!!
IT REALLY DOES, DOESN'T IT? AND IT'S SO MUCH QUIETER NOW...
...ALMOST AS IF THERE'S NO ONE HERE BUT US...

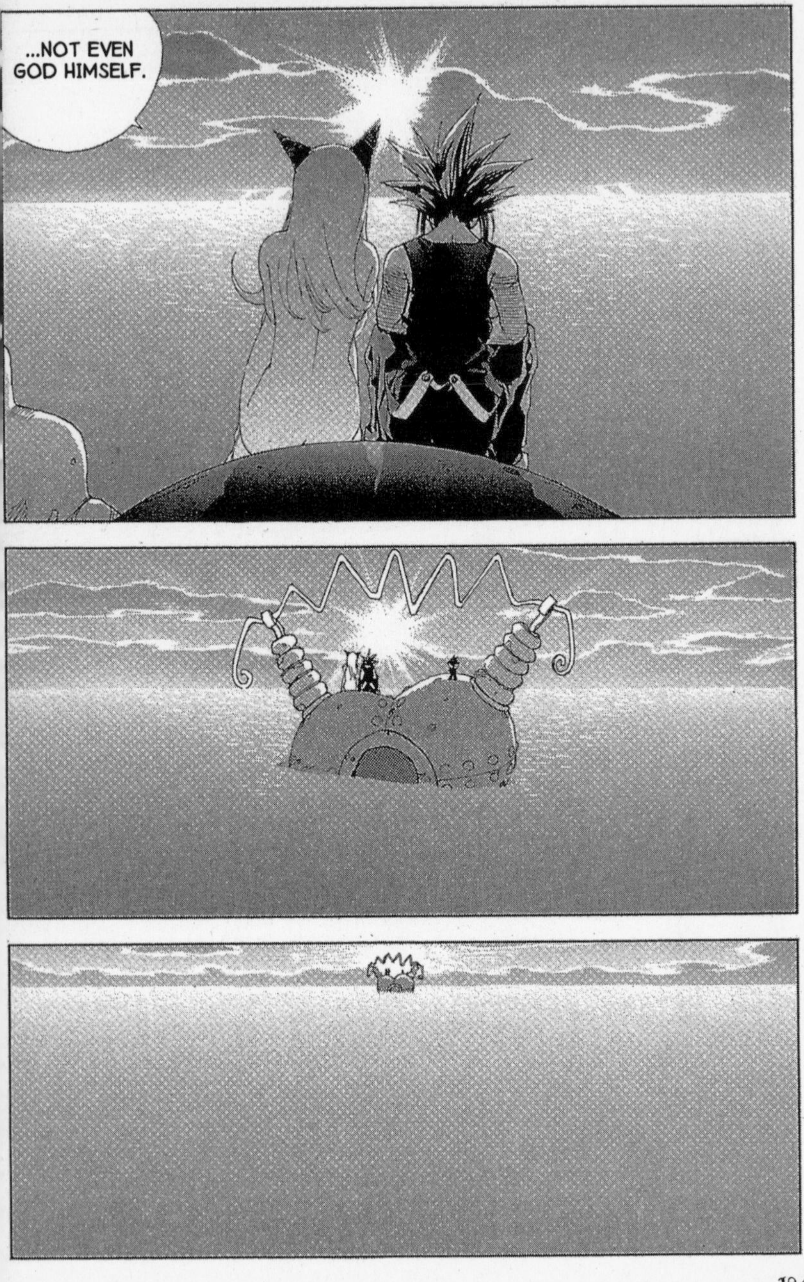
...NOT EVEN GOD HIMSELF.

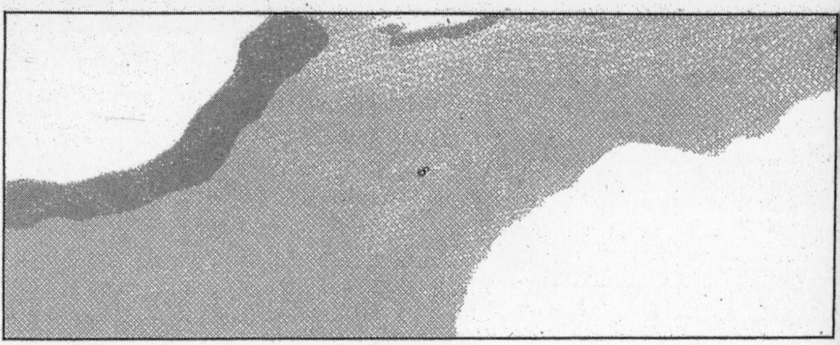

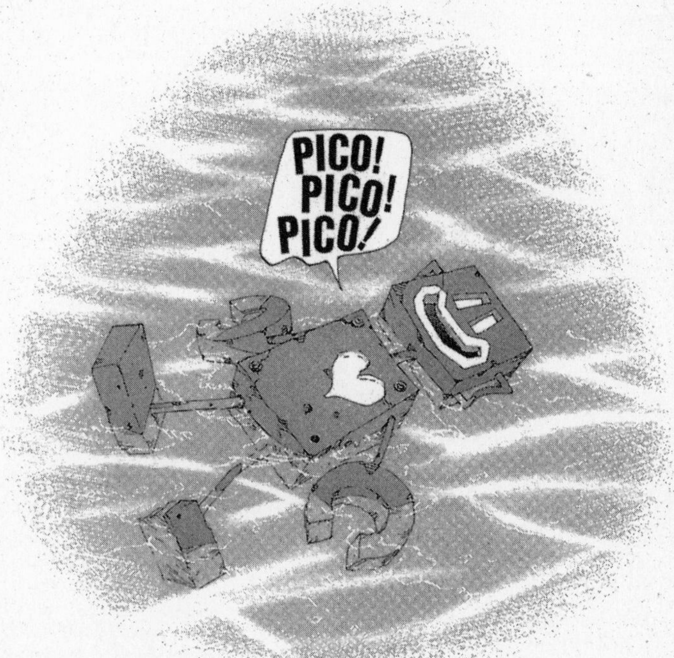
PICO! PICO! PICO!

Jing will return in Volume 7

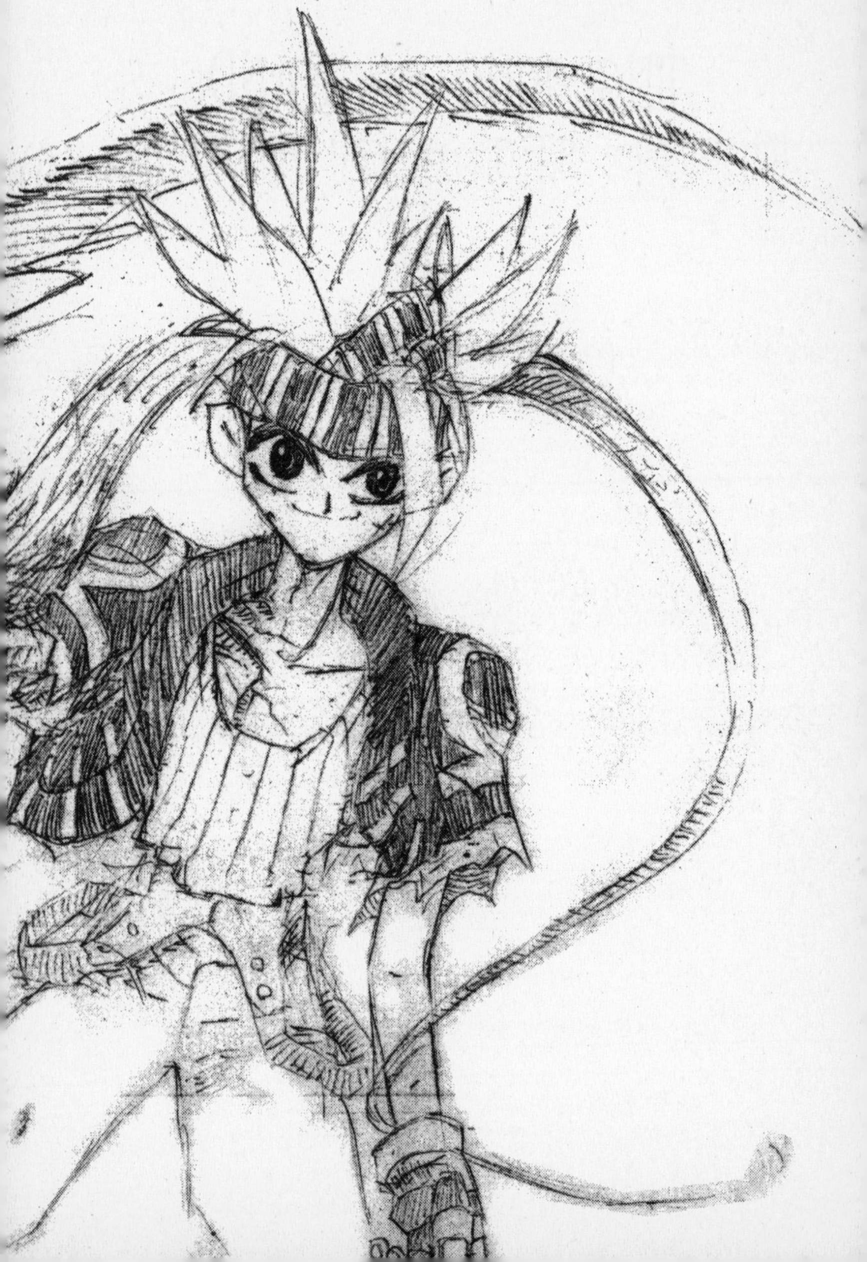

JING: KING OF BANDITS INITIAL SET-UP COLLECTION (5)

jing & kir

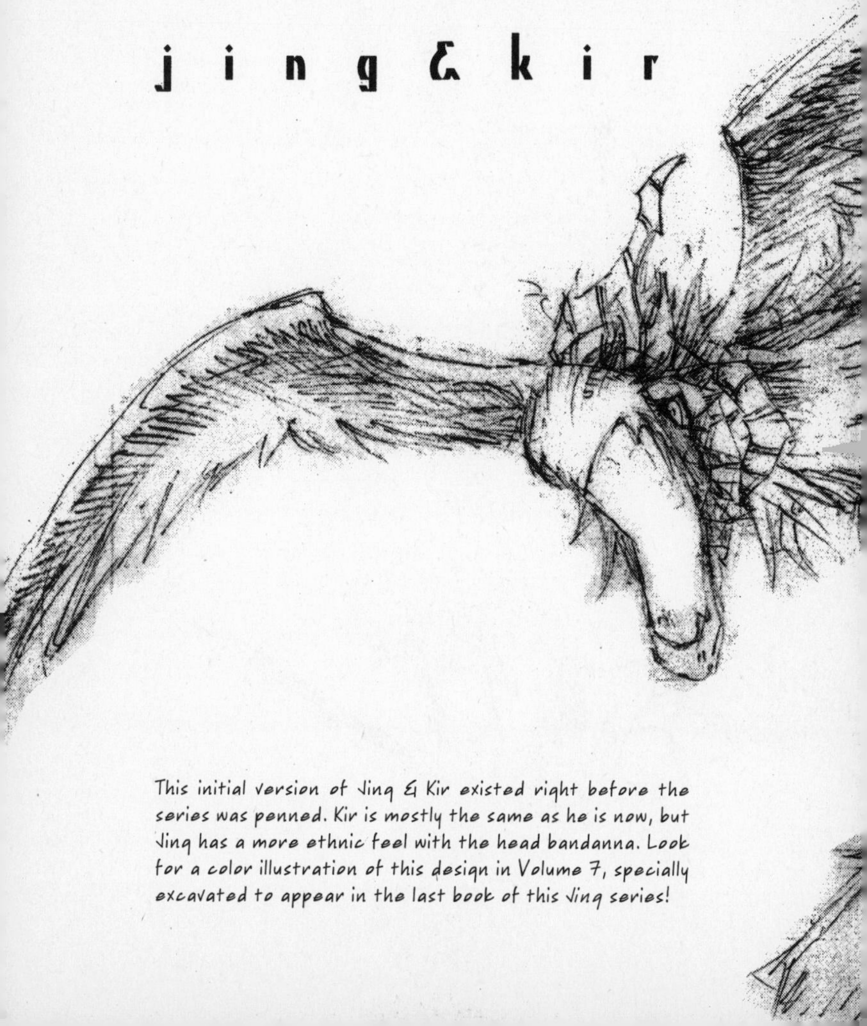

This initial version of Jing & Kir existed right before the series was penned. Kir is mostly the same as he is now, but Jing has a more ethnic feel with the head bandanna. Look for a color illustration of this design in Volume 7, specially excavated to appear in the last book of this Jing series!

jing a

Another rendering of the previous page's Jing and Kir. Kir playing off the dumb straight man is downright laughable. That extra-large rucksack in Jing's left hand is filled with various stolen goods and treasures, no doubt.

YER STEPPIN' ON MY FOOT!

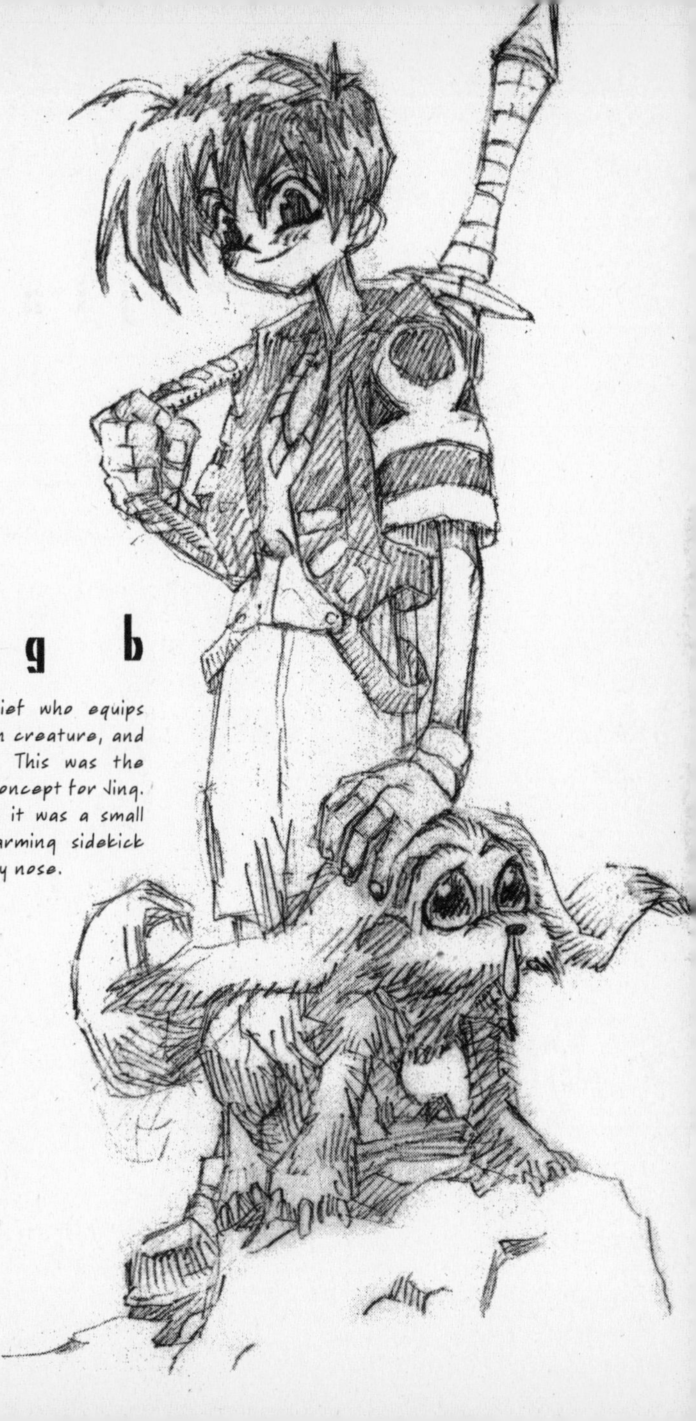

j i n g b

"A boy thief who equips himself with creature, and weapons..." This was the very first concept for Jing. Drawn with it was a small dog...a charming sidekick with a runny nose.

Meanwhile, here is a bird-type partner. In other words, an incarnation that came close to Kir. By himself, Jing just looks like a treasure hunter...an explorer rather than a thief. Also, his facial expression looks almost gentle when compared with the current version.

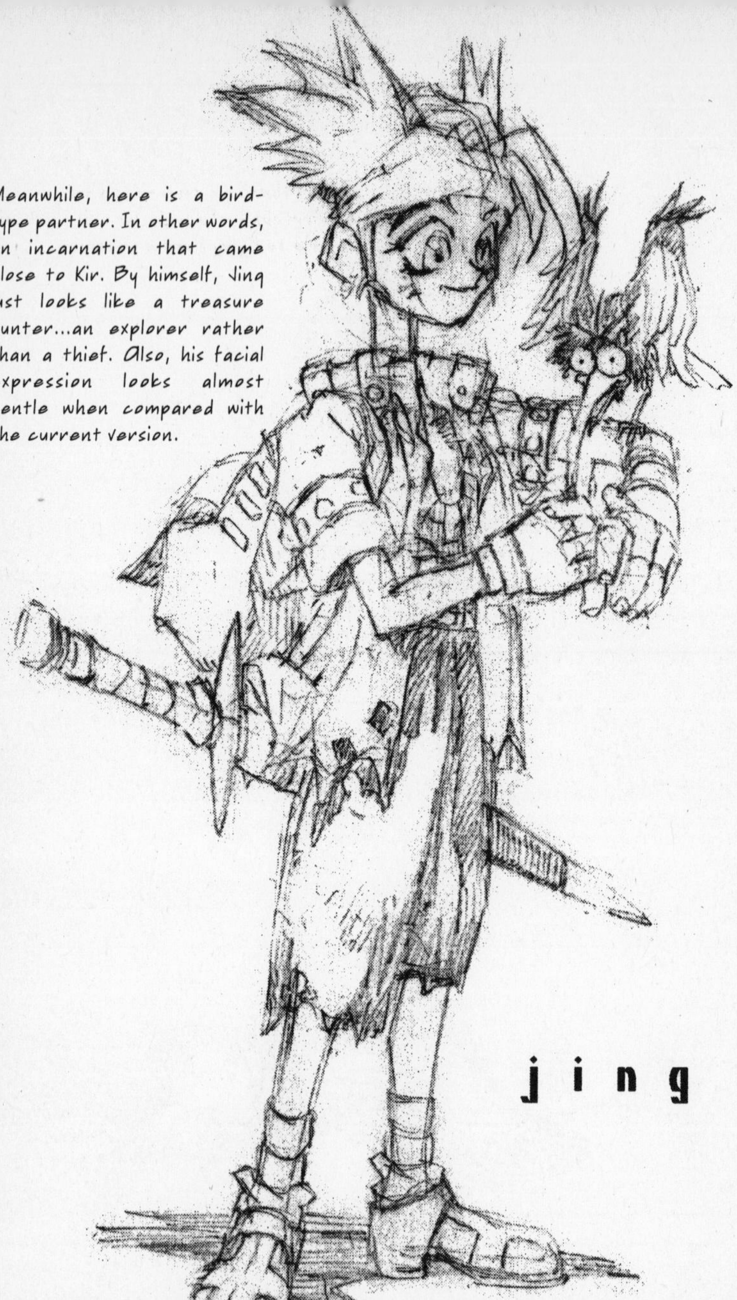

jing c

jing d

This super-duper partner was quite unexpected!! How short is Jing's hair in this picture?! His clothes also have an impish style to them, with the short pants and rolled-up sleeves. And the ears of Jing's partner--on whom he rides comfortably--are long. Do you think he'd be able to fly by flapping them?

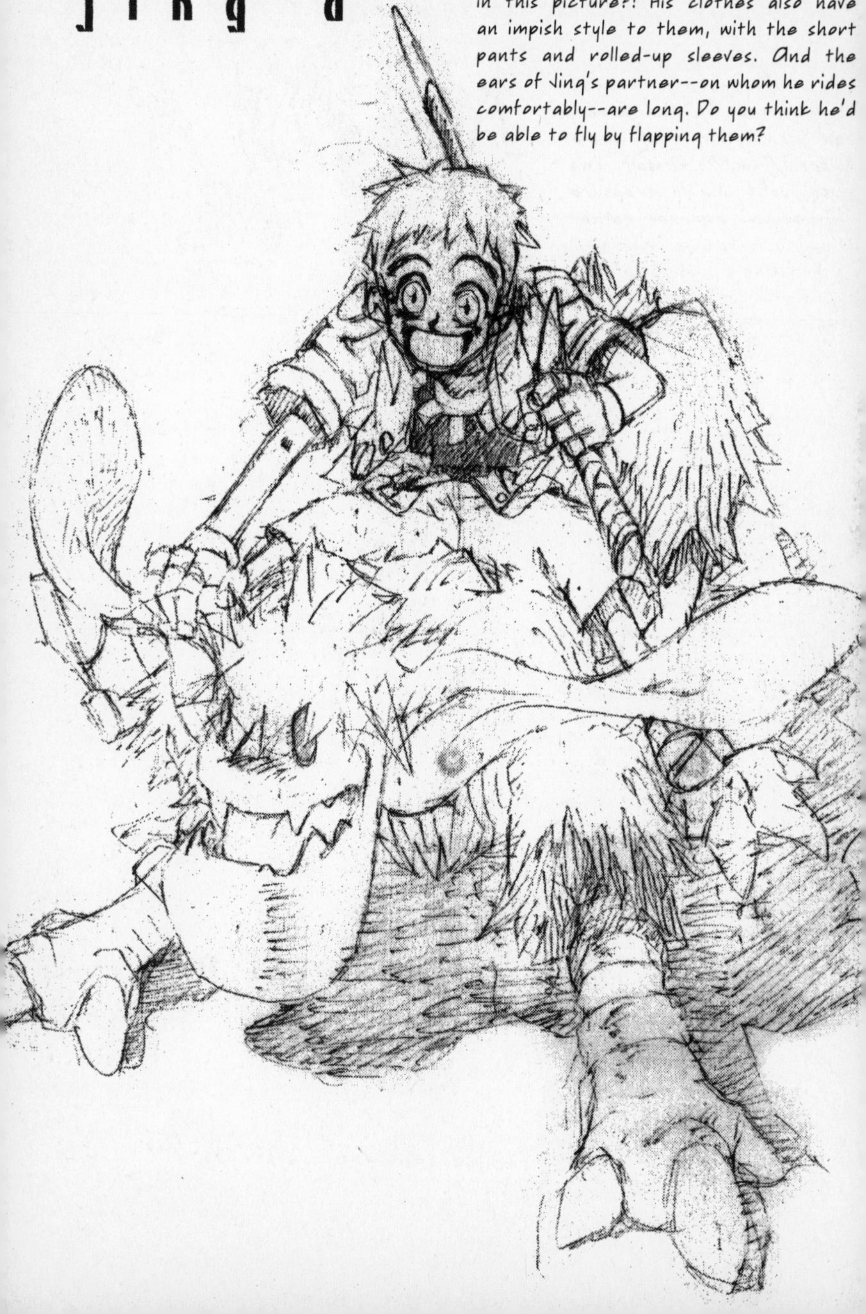

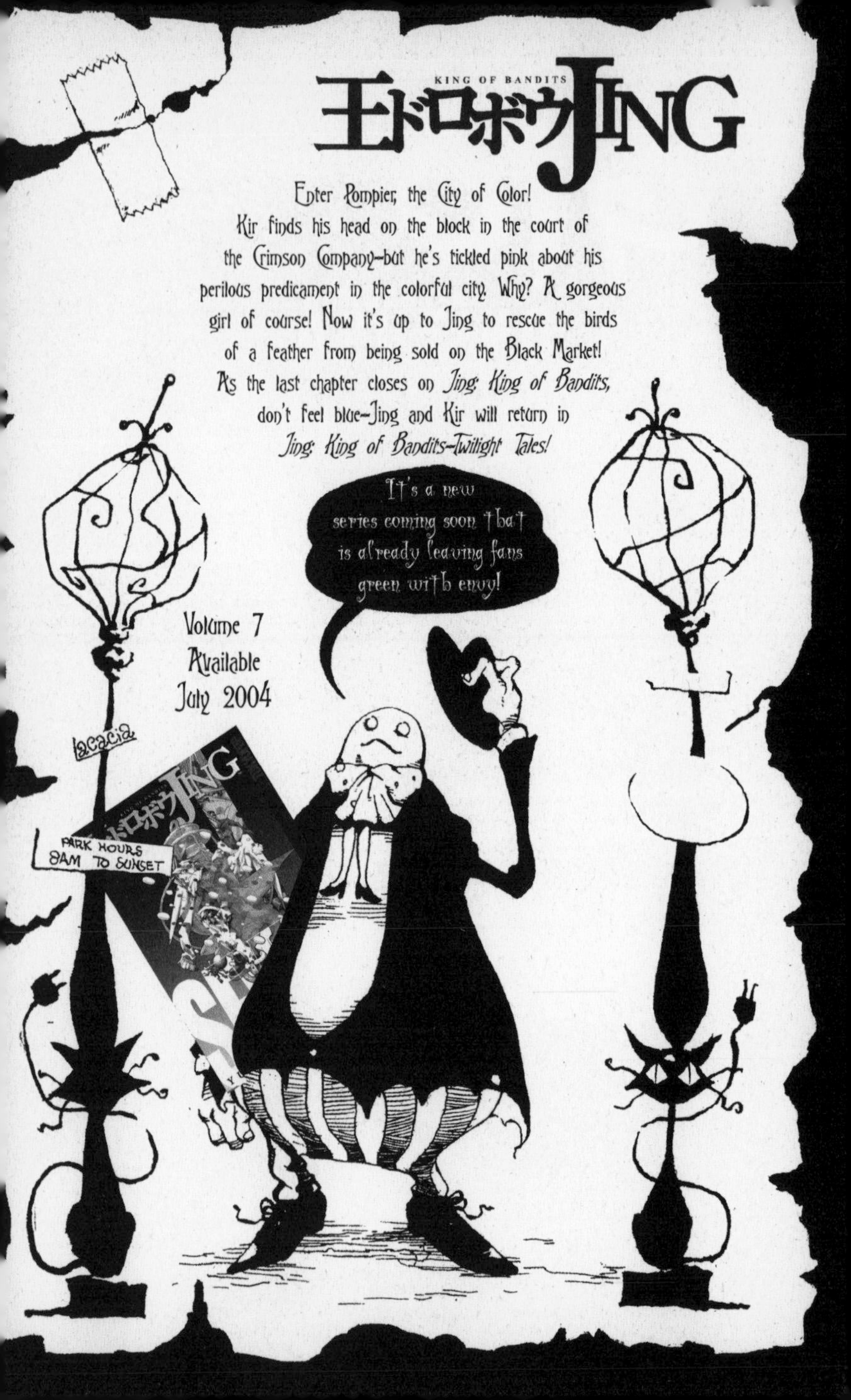
KING OF BANDITS
王ドロボウJING
Enter Pompier, the City of Color!
Kir finds his head on the block in the court of the Crimson Company—but he's tickled pink about his perilous predicament in the colorful city. Why? A gorgeous girl of course! Now it's up to Jing to rescue the birds of a feather from being sold on the Black Market!
As the last chapter closes on *Jing: King of Bandits,* don't feel blue—Jing and Kir will return in *Jing: King of Bandits—Twilight Tales!*
It's a new series coming soon that is already leaving fans green with envy!
Volume 7
Available
July 2004
acacia
PARK HOURS
8AM TO SUNSET

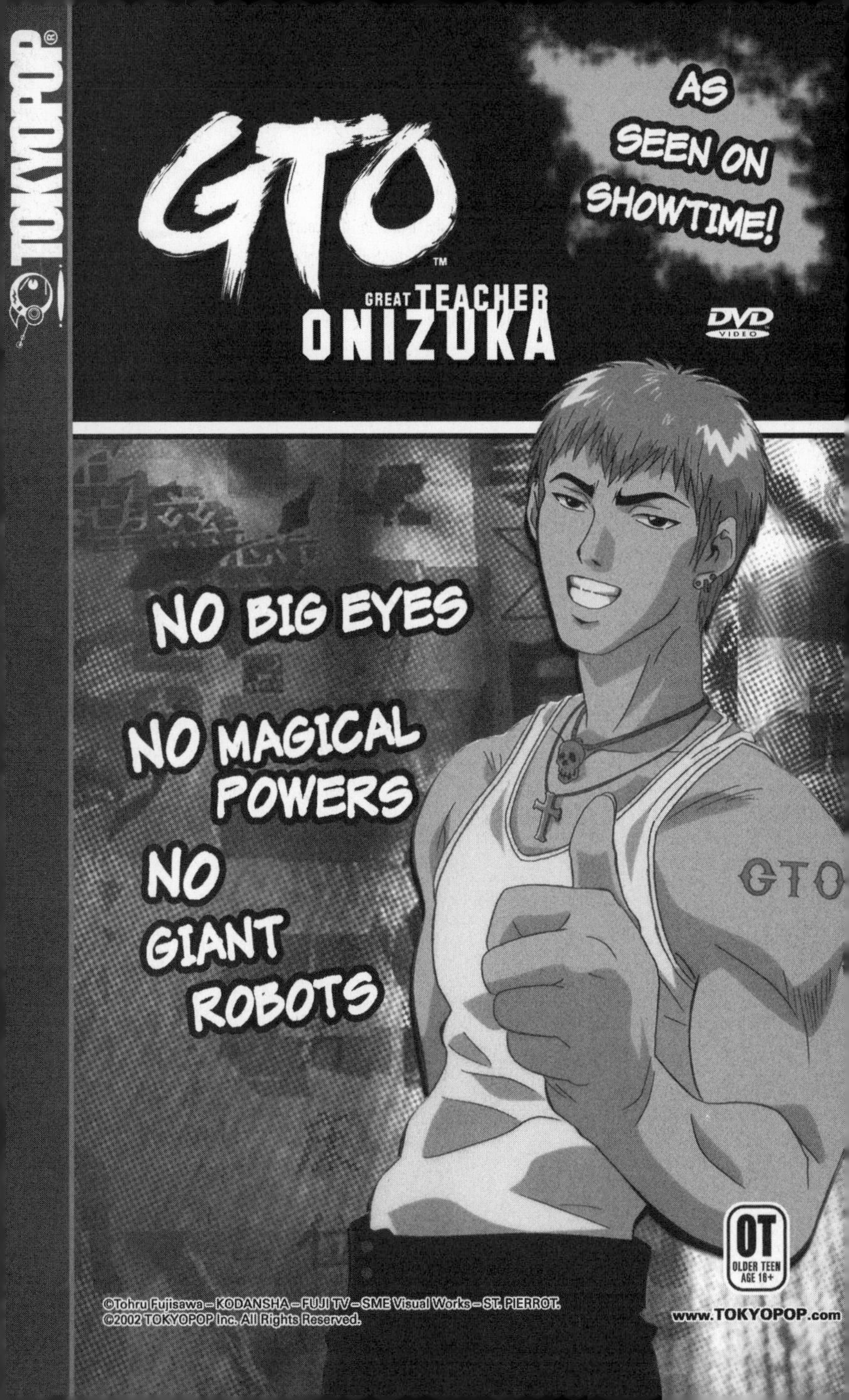
TOKYOPOP
GTO™
GREAT TEACHER ONIZUKA
AS SEEN ON SHOWTIME!
DVD VIDEO
NO BIG EYES
NO MAGICAL POWERS
NO GIANT ROBOTS
GTO
OT OLDER TEEN AGE 16+
©Tohru Fujisawa – KODANSHA – FUJI TV – SME Visual Works – ST. PIERROT.
©2002 TOKYOPOP Inc. All Rights Reserved.
www.TOKYOPOP.com

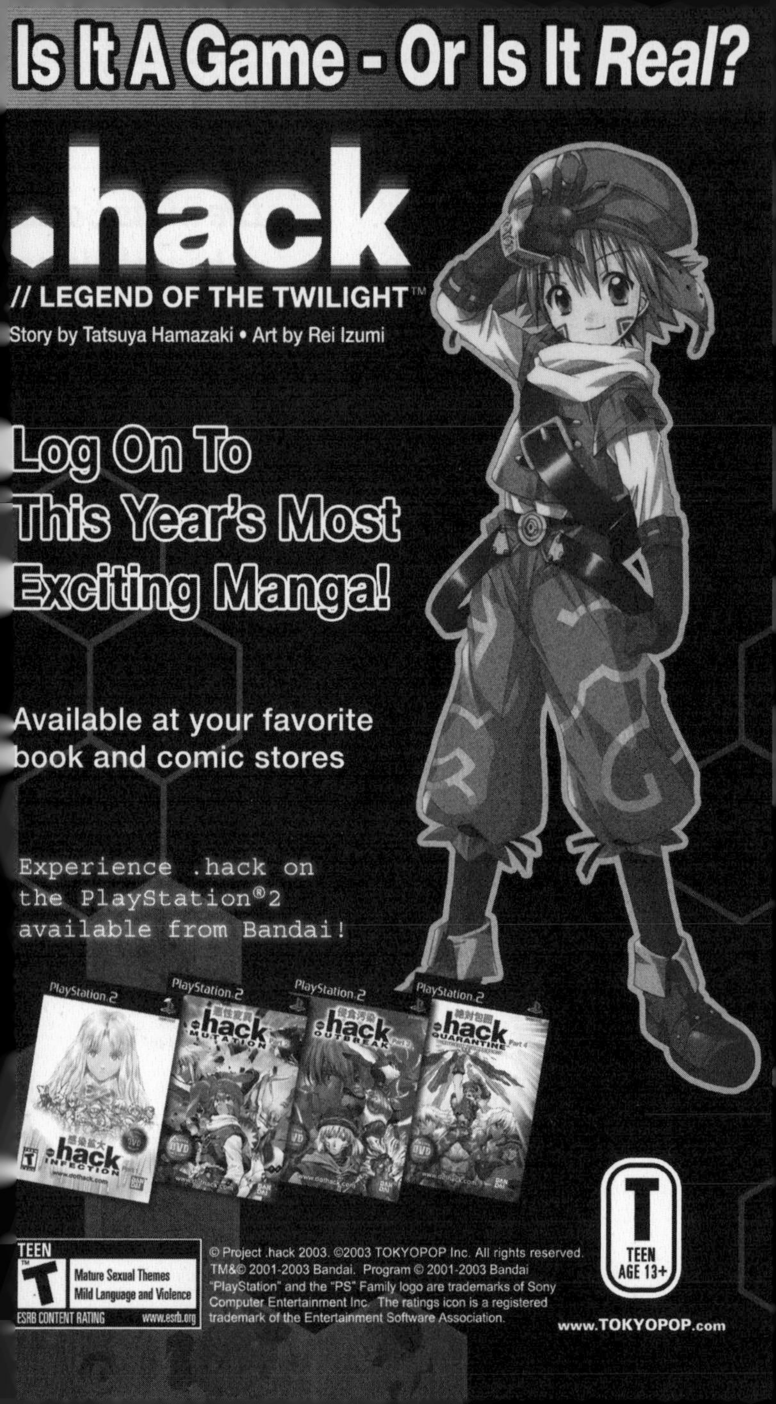
Is It A Game - Or Is It Real?
.hack
// LEGEND OF THE TWILIGHT™
Story by Tatsuya Hamazaki • Art by Rei Izumi
Log On To
This Year's Most
Exciting Manga!
Available at your favorite
book and comic stores
Experience .hack on
the PlayStation®2
available from Bandai!
PlayStation 2
.hack INFECTION
PlayStation 2
.hack MUTATION
PlayStation 2
.hack OUTBREAK
PlayStation 2
.hack QUARANTINE Part 4
TEEN
T
Mature Sexual Themes
Mild Language and Violence
ESRB CONTENT RATING www.esrb.org
© Project .hack 2003. ©2003 TOKYOPOP Inc. All rights reserved.
TM&© 2001-2003 Bandai. Program © 2001-2003 Bandai
"PlayStation" and the "PS" Family logo are trademarks of Sony
Computer Entertainment Inc. The ratings icon is a registered
trademark of the Entertainment Software Association.
T
TEEN
AGE 13+
www.TOKYOPOP.com

Fruits Basket

Life in the Sohma household can be a real zoo

TEEN
AGE 13+

©2003 Natsuki Takaya

ALSO AVAILABLE FROM  TOKYOPOP®

PLANETES
PRIEST
PRINCESS AI
PSYCHIC ACADEMY
RAGNAROK
RAVE MASTER
REALITY CHECK
REBIRTH
REBOUND
REMOTE
RISING STARS OF MANGA
SABER MARIONETTE J
SAILOR MOON
SAINT TAIL
SAIYUKI
SAMURAI DEEPER KYO
SAMURAI GIRL REAL BOUT HIGH SCHOOL
SCRYED
SEIKAI TRILOGY, THE
SGT. FROG
SHAOLIN SISTERS
SHIRAHIME-SYO: SNOW GODDESS TALES
SHUTTERBOX
SKULL MAN, THE
SMUGGLER
SNOW DROP
SORCERER HUNTERS
STONE
SUIKODEN III
SUKI
THREADS OF TIME
TOKYO BABYLON
TOKYO MEW MEW
TOKYO TRIBES
TRAMPS LIKE US
UNDER THE GLASS MOON
VAMPIRE GAME
VISION OF ESCAFLOWNE, THE
WARRIORS OF TAO
WILD ACT
WISH
WORLD OF HARTZ
X-DAY
ZODIAC P.I.

MANGA NOVELS

CLAMP SCHOOL PARANORMAL INVESTIGATORS
KARMA CLUB
SAILOR MOON
SLAYERS

ART BOOKS

ART OF CARDCAPTOR SAKURA
ART OF MAGIC KNIGHT RAYEARTH, THE
PEACH: MIWA UEDA ILLUSTRATIONS

ANIME GUIDES

COWBOY BEBOP
GUNDAM TECHNICAL MANUALS
SAILOR MOON SCOUT GUIDES

TOKYOPOP KIDS

STRAY SHEEP

CINE-MANGA™

ALADDIN
ASTRO BOY
CARDCAPTORS
CONFESSIONS OF A TEENAGE DRAMA QUEEN
DUEL MASTERS
FAIRLY ODDPARENTS, THE
FAMILY GUY
FINDING NEMO
G.I. JOE SPY TROOPS
JACKIE CHAN ADVENTURES
JIMMY NEUTRON: BOY GENIUS, THE ADVENTURES OF
KIM POSSIBLE
LILO & STITCH
LIZZIE MCGUIRE
LIZZIE MCGUIRE MOVIE, THE
MALCOLM IN THE MIDDLE
POWER RANGERS: NINJA STORM
SHREK 2
SPONGEBOB SQUAREPANTS
SPY KIDS 2
SPY KIDS 3-D: GAME OVER
TEENAGE MUTANT NINJA TURTLES
THAT'S SO RAVEN
TRANSFORMERS: ARMADA
TRANSFORMERS: ENERGON

For more information visit www.TOKYOPOP.com

ALSO AVAILABLE FROM TOKYOPOP®

MANGA

.HACK//LEGEND OF THE TWILIGHT
@LARGE
ABENOBASHI: MAGICAL SHOPPING ARCADE
A.I. LOVE YOU
AI YORI AOSHI
ANGELIC LAYER
ARM OF KANNON
BABY BIRTH
BATTLE ROYALE
BATTLE VIXENS
BRAIN POWERED
BRIGADOON
B'TX
CANDIDATE FOR GODDESS, THE
CARDCAPTOR SAKURA
CARDCAPTOR SAKURA - MASTER OF THE CLOW
CHOBITS
CHRONICLES OF THE CURSED SWORD
CLAMP SCHOOL DETECTIVES
CLOVER
COMIC PARTY
CONFIDENTIAL CONFESSIONS
CORRECTOR YUI
COWBOY BEBOP
COWBOY BEBOP: SHOOTING STAR
CRAZY LOVE STORY
CRESCENT MOON
CULDCEPT
CYBORG 009
D•N•ANGEL
DEMON DIARY
DEMON ORORON, THE
DEUS VITAE
DIGIMON
DIGIMON TAMERS
DIGIMON ZERO TWO
DOLL
DRAGON HUNTER
DRAGON KNIGHTS
DRAGON VOICE
DREAM SAGA
DUKLYON: CLAMP SCHOOL DEFENDERS
EERIE QUEERIE!
END, THE
ERICA SAKURAZAWA: COLLECTED WORKS
ET CETERA
ETERNITY
EVIL'S RETURN
FAERIES' LANDING
FAKE
FLCL
FORBIDDEN DANCE
FRUITS BASKET
G GUNDAM
GATEKEEPERS

GETBACKERS
GIRL GOT GAME
GRAVITATION
GTO
GUNDAM BLUE DESTINY
GUNDAM SEED ASTRAY
GUNDAM WING
GUNDAM WING: BATTLEFIELD OF PACIFISTS
GUNDAM WING: ENDLESS WALTZ
GUNDAM WING: THE LAST OUTPOST (G-UNIT)
GUYS' GUIDE TO GIRLS
HANDS OFF!
HAPPY MANIA
HARLEM BEAT
I.N.V.U.
IMMORTAL RAIN
INITIAL D
INSTANT TEEN: JUST ADD NUTS
ISLAND
JING: KING OF BANDITS
JING: KING OF BANDITS - TWILIGHT TALES
JULINE
KARE KANO
KILL ME, KISS ME
KINDAICHI CASE FILES, THE
KING OF HELL
KODOCHA: SANA'S STAGE
LAMENT OF THE LAMB
LEGAL DRUG
LEGEND OF CHUN HYANG, THE
LES BIJOUX
LOVE HINA
LUPIN III
LUPIN III: WORLD'S MOST WANTED
MAGIC KNIGHT RAYEARTH I
MAGIC KNIGHT RAYEARTH II
MAHOROMATIC: AUTOMATIC MAIDEN
MAN OF MANY FACES
MARMALADE BOY
MARS
MARS: HORSE WITH NO NAME
METROID
MINK
MIRACLE GIRLS
MIYUKI-CHAN IN WONDERLAND
MODEL
ONE
ONE I LOVE, THE
PARADISE KISS
PARASYTE
PASSION FRUIT
PEACH GIRL
PEACH GIRL: CHANGE OF HEART
PET SHOP OF HORRORS
PITA-TEN
PLANET LADDER

03.03.04T

STOP!

This is the back of the book.
You wouldn't want to spoil a great ending!

This book is printed "manga-style," in the authentic Japanese right-to-left format. Since none of the artwork has been flipped or altered, readers get to experience the story just as the creator intended. You've been asking for it, so TOKYOPOP® delivered: authentic, hot-off-the-press, and far more fun!

DIRECTIONS

If this is your first time reading manga-style, here's a quick guide to help you understand how it works.

It's easy... just start in the top right panel and follow the numbers. Have fun, and look for more 100% authentic manga from TOKYOPOP®!